On concepts and measures
of multifactor productivity
in Canada, 1961–1980

On concepts and measures of multifactor productivity in Canada, 1961–1980

ALEXANDRA CAS

Commission of the European Communities, Brussels

THOMAS K. RYMES

Carleton University, Ottawa

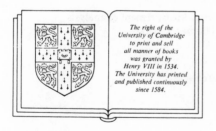

The right of the
University of Cambridge
to print and sell
all manner of books
was granted by
Henry VIII in 1534.
The University has printed
and published continuously
since 1584.

CAMBRIDGE UNIVERSITY PRESS

Cambridge
New York   Port Chester   Melbourne   Sydney

Published by the Press Syndicate of the University of Cambridge
The Pitt Building, Trumpington Street, Cambridge CB2 1RP
40 West 20th Street, New York, NY 10011, USA
10 Stamford Road, Oakleigh, Melbourne 3166, Australia

© Cambridge University Press 1991

First published 1991

Printed in the United States of America

Library of Congress Cataloging-in-Publication Data
Cas, Alexandra.
On concepts and measures of multifactor productivity in Canada,
1961–1980 / Alexandra Cas and Thomas K. Rymes.
p. cm.
Includes bibliographical references.
ISBN 0-521-36536-8
1. Industrial productivity – Canada.   2. Input–output analysis –
Canada.   I. Rymes, Thomas K.   II. Title.
HC120.I52C37   1991
338.4′5′0971 – dc20   90–1955
                                                             CIP

British Library Cataloguing in Publication Data
Cas, Alexandra
On concepts and measures of multifactor productivity in
Canada, 1961–1980.
1. Industries. Productivity. Measurement & analysis
I. Series   II. Rymes, Thomas K. *1932–*
338.060287

ISBN 0-521-36536-8 hardback

Contents

vii

Tables

Acknowledgements

Earlier drafts of this study were written while Rymes was on sabbatical with support from the Social Sciences and Humanities Research Council of Canada at Australian National University and by Alexandra Cas when she was with Statistics Canada. The penultimate draft, "On the feasibility of measuring multifactor productivity in Canada", winter 1985, was circulated by Statistics Canada for comment and served as one focal point of the Conference on the Measurement of Multifactor Productivity, sponsored by the Centre of Quantitative Social Analysis at Carleton University in October 1987.

The authors thank everyone who has commented on this study. Statistics Canada, in particular, should be congratulated for making this study possible. It is absolutely clear, however, that Statistics Canada is in no way responsible for the study, its theoretical arguments, nor its empirical results.

Support for the Conference on the Measurement of Multifactor Productivity from the Social Sciences and Humanities Research Council of Canada and the Canadian Labor Market and Productivity Centre is gratefully acknowledged.

Different versions of the research have been presented at meetings of the Canadian Economics Association, to seminars, and in lectures at Australian National University, Australian Bureau of Statistics, Economic Council, Carleton and McMaster universities, and Statistics Canada. It was also presented, thanks to Kishori Lal, to the Braden Meeting on Problems of Computation of Input–Output Tables, 19–25 May 1985.[1]

Along the way, many people have earned our thanks. We salute Richard Cornes, Michael Carter, and Fred Gruen at the Australian National University; Keith Blackburn of the Australian Bureau of Statistics, Basil McCormick, Kishori Lal, Yusuf Sidiqui, Terry Gigantes, Michael Wolfson, Claude Simard, and René Durand of Statistics Canada; W. Erwin Diewert of the University of British Columbia; Harry Postner of the

---

[1] See T. K. Rymes, "The Measurement of Multifactor Productivity in an Input–Output Framework: New Canadian Estimates", eds. A. Franz and N. Rainer, *Problems of Compilation of Input–Output Tables* (Wien: Orac-Verlag, 1986).

Economic Council of Canada; James Johnson of McMaster University; Edward Denison, Senior Fellow of the Brookings Institution; Edward Dean, Bureau of Labour Statistics, the U.S. Department of Labor; and many scholars at the International Colloquium on Structural Change and New Technology held at Manchester University in September 1985 and at the Conference on the Measurement of Multifactor Productivity at Carleton University in October 1987.

Finally, great and lasting indebtedness must be expressed to Professor Ian Steedman, who has extensively analyzed the theory behind this study, in particular when he invited Rymes to the Manchester Colloquium, when he was a participant at the Conference on the Measurement of Multifactor Productivity, and when he was a visiting professor in the Department of Economics in the fall 1987 term at Carleton University.

To all who at these seminars, lectures, and conferences offered criticisms, we extend our thanks.

Special thanks must be extended to Gwen McBride, who typed beautifully a difficult manuscript.

Despite their best efforts, we no doubt continue to err and the errors are ours.

Professor Rymes is largely responsible for Part I while Ms Cas is the writer of Part II.

Lectori salutem.

Introduction

The study of economic growth focusses primarily on capital accumulation and advances in productivity. These fundamental forces determine how much the real incomes of people increase over time, and an understanding of such increases is the basic motivation behind the study of economic growth.[1] What determines the rates of advance in productivity recorded in modern economies remains the subject of debate. This debate extends also to how advances in productivity should be measured.

Single-factor productivity measures – when labour is the factor – are commonplace. Despite the difficulties associated with the measurement of output, labour input, and the construction of index numbers, measures of changes in output per unit of labour are now published on a regular basis by many statistical agencies[2] and help in our understanding of the processes of economic growth.

More general measures of productivity advance have also long been available from private and academic researchers. They may be called measures of multifactor productivity. They measure the increases in efficiency with which an economy uses *all* (measurable) economic inputs, not just labour. This study shows that general measures of productivity advance – when, in particular, theoretically appropriate measures of "capital" and its contribution to growth have been formulated – are feasible for Canada and other nations. Our new measures of multifactor productivity advance may be called the Harrod–Robinson–Read measures.[3] Another set

[1] *Differences* in productivity across nations are also of interest in the study of international differences in real incomes.

[2] See, e.g., Statistics Canada, *Aggregate Productivity Measures, 1985–1986* (Ottawa: Supply and Services, June 1988).

[3] The measures developed and advocated in this study are called Harrod–Robinson–Read measures because they were theoretically conceived by the late Sir Roy Harrod and the late Joan Robinson and were made operational by the insights of Professor Larry Read. See R. Harrod, *Towards a Dynamic Economics* (London: Macmillan, 1948); J. Robinson, *The Accumulation of Capital* (London: Macmillan, 3rd ed. 1969) and *Essays in the Theory of Economic Growth* (London: Macmillan, 1962); and L. M. Read, "The Measurement of Total Factor Productivity" (Ottawa: Dominion Bureau of Statistics, mimeo, 1961) and "The Measurement of Total Factor Productivity Appropriate to Wage–Price Guidelines", *Canadian Journal of Economics,* I, May 1968, 349–58. The connection

of multifactor measures, which may be called the traditional, Hicksian, or neo-classical, are also provided. Such traditional measures, now common, are founded on a basic difference in the treatment of capital as an input. They are presented both for those who prefer the traditional treatment of capital and for comparison with the new Harrod–Robinson–Read measures.[4]

The fundamental difference between the new and traditional measures of multifactor productivity is that the new measures rigorously take into account the increases in efficiency with which produced inputs of all kinds (e.g., intermediate inputs like steel in automobile production and capital goods like computers in the provision of banking services) are themselves produced. The consequence of this simple difference in the treatment of produced or producible inputs for measures of multifactor productivity is the main subject matter of this study.

Economists classify the sources of output growth into growth in the quantity of measurable inputs and increases in their efficiency, or multifactor productivity, or advances in knowledge. One set of the measurable inputs is capital in all its forms, and in traditional measures all the growth in such capital inputs is treated as a separate source of output growth. If, however, some of the growth of the capital inputs is due to improvements in the efficiency with which such inputs are produced, then the new measures will transfer that part from measurable inputs to, where it would seem logically to belong, part of multifactor productivity or advances in knowledge. The new measures will, then, show that advances in productivity or knowledge are more important sources of growth than the traditional measures.[5]

between Read's work and the Harrod–Robinson theory is set out in T. K. Rymes, "Professor Read and the Measurement of Total Factor Productivity", *Canadian Journal of Economics,* I, May 1968, 359–67. The basic theory behind the new measures is set out in T. K. Rymes, *On Concepts of Capital and Technical Change* (Cambridge: Cambridge University Press, 1971).

[4] Aggregate and sectoral measures of multifactor productivity, of the traditional type, are being published by the U.S. Government. See "Multifactor productivity: A new BLS measure", Bureau of Labor Statistics *Monthly Labour Review,* 106, December 1983, 3–15 and U.S. Department of Labor, *Trends in Multifactor Productivity, 1948–81* (Washington, D.C., BLS Bulletin 2178, September 1983). After copy-editing of this volume had been completed, Statistics Canada published traditional measures of multifactor productivity and some experimental measures which are halfway towards the new measures advocated in this study. See Statistics Canada, *Aggregate Productivity Measures 1988* (Ottawa: Ministry of Supply and Services, June 1990). The traditional measures are called Hicksian and neoclassical because their theoretical base was provided by Sir John Hicks in *The Theory of Wages* (London: Macmillan, second edition 1963) and Robert Solow in his classic "Technological change and the aggregate production function", *The Review of Economics and Statistics,* XXXIX, August 1957, 312–20.

[5] The theoretical question of distinguishing between capital accumulation and technological progress ranges all the way from the validity of attempts to separate "shifts in the

The new measures also take into account the technological interdependence of the production structure of economies. The Canadian input–output tables capture such interdependence and provide therefore the ideal data base upon which to develop the new measures. Researchers in countries where similar input–output accounts are available could also develop the new measures of multifactor productivity advanced in this study.

Productivity is the relationship between changes in outputs and changes in inputs. The National Accounts, whether at an aggregate economy or at detailed industrial and sectoral levels, are also concerned with the measurement of outputs and inputs. Multifactor productivity measures have been for some time part of new major developments in National Accounting. Past years have witnessed in Canada, for example, the emergence of national and sectoral accounts, measures of industry outputs in "real" or constant price terms, financial transactions accounts, input–output accounts, and recently, national and sectoral balance sheets. An important new development – measures of multifactor productivity – in National Accounting is also then what is presented in our study. The question is: What are the most illuminating and theoretically meaningful ways to present changes in real or constant price outputs and inputs that shed light on questions raised about the growth and development of modern economies? Productivity measures should help us understand such matters as movements in relative prices, increases in real wages, and the contribution of various industries or sectors to overall economic advance. Our measures of multifactor productivity for Canada will be of interest, not only to students of theories of economic growth, capital, and technical change but also to builders of systems of national accounts.[6]

To illustrate in an introductory way the differences in measured advances in multifactor productivity that result from the alternative treatments of capital, annual rates of growth and indexes of new and traditional measures of multifactoral productivity are provided in Tables I-1 and I-2. (A comparison with official Statistics Canada labour productivity measures and those of this study is also provided.) The new measures of multifactor productivity run substantially ahead of the traditional measures – in the early period before the major downturn in productivity advance in the 1970s – whereas both run below output per person-hour

production function" from "movements along the function" to practical problems of index numbers connected with distinguishing between increases in the stock of capital and advances in knowledge when the capital goods are said to be improving in their quality or their *net* capacity to contribute to production.

[6] Hicks argues that the System of National Accounts or Social Accounting is the tool for the study of economic anatomy, so essential for the testing of economic theory. See J. R. Hicks, *The Social Framework: An Introduction to Economics* (Oxford: Clarendon Press, 4th ed. 1971).

Table I-1. *Annual rates of growth, new and traditional measures of multifactor productivity, private Canadian economy, 1961–80 (and partial labour productivity measures)*

	Multifactor		Partial labour productivity	
	New (1)	Traditional (2)	(3)	(4)
1961–2	6.86	5.10	3.6	4.7
1962–3	2.77	2.20	3.4	4.2
1963–4	3.29	2.41	3.9	4.3
1964–5	2.29	1.76	2.8	4.0
1965–6	2.00	1.63	3.6	4.7
1966–7	−0.29	−0.62	0.9	1.6
1967–8	4.24	3.16	5.7	6.9
1968–9	2.25	1.65	3.5	4.2
1969–70	−0.16	−0.18	1.5	3.0
1970–1	1.83	1.46	4.8	5.2
1971–2	2.48	1.99	3.4	4.0
1972–3	3.62	2.72	3.5	3.7
1973–4	−1.55	−1.36	−0.9	0.6
1974–5	−1.71	−1.85	−1.1	0.1
1975–6	2.92	2.55	4.5	4.9
1976–7	−0.13	−0.07	1.0	2.4
1977–8	−0.30	−0.07	0.6	0.4
1978–9	0.87	0.72	1.4	−0.1
1979–80	0.26	0.22	−0.4	−0.1

Sources: Columns 1–3, this study; column 4, Statistics Canada, *Aggregate Productivity Measures* (various issues).

labour productivity measures. The changing efficiency with which the Canadian economy used its labour input was apparently greater than that with which its nonlabour inputs were employed – even prior to the major downturn in productivity advance in the 1970s. For the decade of the 1960s our new measures show that the rate of advance of the knowledge with which inputs are combined to produce output increased by 28.5 percent whereas the traditional measures show this to be 20.3 percent, a 40 percent difference. Over that decade, the *average* annual rate of advances in knowledge for the new measures was 31 percent higher than for the old. These are substantial differences in sources of economic growth. Although great care must be taken in interpreting the numbers provided in

Table I-2. *Indexes of new and traditional measures of multifactor productivity, private Canadian economy, 1961–80 (and partial labour productivity indexes), 1971 = 100.0*

	Multifactor		Partial labour productivity	
	New (1)	Traditional (2)	(3)	(4)
1961	77.8	83.1	71.3	65.8
1962	83.3	87.4	74.0	68.9
1963	85.7	89.4	76.6	71.8
1964	88.5	91.5	79.6	74.9
1965	90.6	93.2	81.8	77.9
1966	92.4	94.7	84.8	81.6
1967	92.2	94.1	85.6	82.9
1968	96.2	97.1	90.7	88.6
1969	98.3	98.7	93.9	92.3
1970	98.2	98.6	95.3	95.1
1971	100.0	100.0	100.0	100.0
1972	102.5	102.1	103.5	104.0
1973	106.3	104.8	107.2	107.8
1974	104.7	103.4	106.2	108.4
1975	102.9	101.5	105.0	108.5
1976	105.9	104.1	109.9	113.8
1977	105.8	104.0	111.0	116.5
1978	105.5	104.0	111.8	117.0
1979	106.4	104.7	114.4	118.1
1980	106.7	104.5	112.9	118.0

Sources: Columns 1–3, this study; column 4, Statistics Canada, *Aggregate Productivity Measures* (various issues).

this study,[7] the differences between the two multifactor productivity estimates (and the published labour productivity measures) are interesting and invite new questions about our understanding of the behaviour of the Canadian economy in the two decades 1961–80.

The structure of our study is as follows:

We make a general theoretical statement, set out the accounting framework to be followed, in both static and dynamic terms, discuss major

---

[7] Unavailability of input–output data, incorporating revisions arising out of changes in industrial classifications, at the time this study was written prevented us from producing our experimental estimates beyond 1980.

strengths and problems found with the traditional and new multifactor productivity measures, present the traditional and new empirical estimates, and comment on the empirical problems involved in preparing these measures of multifactor productivity in Canada.

The specific purpose of this study is to compare the traditional and new measures, to advocate the new measures, and to show how they may be prepared. Common data problems abound and are discussed, but we shall comment primarily on the empirical difficulties in estimating the new measures, for these are not so well known.

Part I is the theoretical framework. Part II presents the measures of multifactor productivity for Canada for 1961–80.

We turn now to the theoretical framework.

CHAPTER 1

Theoretical framework

A   Introduction

All economic measures and empirical constructs must have a theoretical base. The productivity measures advanced in this study can be said to rest primarily, though not entirely, on the Cambridge theory of capital.[1]

In recent years a controversy occurred over whether any aggregate measure of "capital" would be, in comparisons of economies, helpful in "explaining" why levels of consumption per head, "real" wage rates, or real net rates of return to capital differed across such economies. The conclusion was that such aggregate constant-price measures of capital would not, except under the most restrictive assumptions, be found.[2] The problem was *not* whether an aggregate measure could or could not be constructed. Many such measures can be and are put together. The question was whether knowledge of the constant-price aggregate stock of capital would, for the comparison of economies, permit one to "predict" certain variables. For instance, in a comparison of economies where, other things

---

[1] See T. K. Rymes, *On Concepts of Capital and Technical Change* (Cambridge: Cambridge University Press, 1971) and "The Measurement of Capital and Total Factor Productivity in the Context of the Cambridge Theory of Capital", *Review of Income and Wealth,* XVIII, March 1972, 79–108.

[2] The Cambridge capital controversy is reviewed in G. Harcourt, *Some Cambridge Controversies in the Theory of Capital* (Cambridge: Cambridge University Press, 1972); M. Blaug, *The Cambridge Revolution: Success or Failure* (London: Institute for Economic Affairs, 1974); A. K. Sen, "On Some Debates in Capital Theory", *Economica,* XLI, February 1974, 328–35; L. L. Pasinetti, *Structural Change and Economic Growth* (Cambridge: Cambridge University Press, 1981); E. Burmeister, "Cambridge Controversies in Capital Theory", *Capital Theory and Dynamics* (Cambridge: Cambridge University Press, 1980), ch. 4; M. Brown, "The Measurement of Capital Aggregates: A Postswitching Problem", ed. D. Usher, *The Measurement of Capital* (Chicago: University of Chicago Press for the NBER, 1980); C. Dougherty, *Interest and Profit* (London: Methuen, 1980); F. Hahn, "The Neo-Ricardians", *Cambridge Journal of Economics,* VI, December 1982, 353–74, reprinted in his *Equilibrium and Macroeconomics* (Oxford: Blackwell, 1984); R. M. Solow, "Modern Capital Theory", eds. E. Cary Brown and R. M. Solow, *Paul Samuelson and Modern Economic Theory* (New York: McGraw-Hill, 1983); and articles by T. Hatta, H. D. Kurz, L. L. Pasinetti, and R. Scazzieri, in *The New Palgrave: A Dictionary of Economics,* I (London: Macmillan, 1987).

7

being equal, the stock of capital in one was greater than in the other, would this lead one to predict a lower rate of return to capital in the former compared to the latter? In general, it is now recognized, following the controversy, no such "predictions" are necessarily entailed.

The problem was neither a measurement nor an aggregation problem but a conceptual one – what was meant by capital as a factor of production?[3]

At a theoretical level, the economist need not aggregate,[4] and so the question of whether capital measurement is useful would appear to be merely an empirical aggregation problem. At the practical level, of course, aggregation must be pursued – a system of price and quantity measures to record every specific value in the economic universe, even if conceivable, would be as useful as a map drawn on a one-to-one scale.[5]

The Cambridge capital controversy was, by and large, carried out in the context of the comparison of economies not experiencing productivity advance or technical progress. Under such assumptions, the fact that each intermediate input such as steel used in automobile production, each commodity stock such as the inventory of men's shirts in a retail store, each building and machine such as the offices, computers, and assembly lines in the production of computers, each machine service such as the services of tank cars and jet aircraft rented to air lines, that is, each and every manifestation of capital input, is capable of being reproduced more efficiently by the economic system may be ignored. When productivity advance or technical progress is occurring, however, an entirely different concept of capital must emerge based on the essential fact that capital inputs are produced inputs.

Improvements in productivity will be associated with more capital goods and capital services of all kinds being produced without any person, firm, or government in the economic system necessarily working harder or longer hours or saving higher fractions of income or foregoing more present consumption. Because capital inputs are produced means of production, increases in efficiency due to advances in knowledge or increasing returns to scale will bring about increases in the output, input, and stocks of such capital inputs even when primary input flows remain constant, that is, if all the preferences and behaviour of all the individuals and institutions

---

[3] "The real dispute is not about the *measurement* of capital but about the *meaning* of capital". J. Robinson, *Collected Economic Papers,* III (Oxford: Blackwell, 1975), Introduction 1974: "Comments and Explanations", vi (emphasis in original).

[4] See C. Bliss, *Capital Theory and the Distribution of Income* (Amsterdam: North-Holland, 1975).

[5] A different and difficult theoretical problem is not whether aggregation over economic quantities and prices is possible or will yield consistent results but rather why it is that we observe aggregations constructed in all private and public sectors of the economy – why firms, e.g., construct and publish profit and loss statements and balance sheets, why fiat money is used, and so forth.

that compose the economy remain unchanged. The question that then arises is: What is (are) the primary input(s) that is (are) behind the produced means of production? This is the question that is at the heart of the Cambridge capital controversy and has nothing whatever to do with the question of the need or the feasibility of consistent aggregation.

As this study demonstrates, measures of multifactor productivity can be prepared that take into account the essential character of capital inputs that they are produced inputs. Traditional measures that fail to take account of this characteristic of capital inputs are also presented and examined. It will be shown that the latter (i) are at best a partial equilibrium measure of the former, which are more general in nature, and (ii) in an economy characterised by substantial technical change in the context of technological interdependence exhibited by countries such as Canada, can not only be seriously misleading and unilluminating about the process of capital accumulation and economic growth but also lead, as was shown in the Introduction, to an understatement of the importance of productivity advance in any accounting for economic growth.[6]

In a world in which capital goods are intermediate or produced inputs and not primary or exogenous to production inputs, one must distinguish between the services of the capital goods and the services of capital, such as waiting in the Marshallian sense of the postponement of consumption.[7]

---

[6] See T. K. Rymes "More on the Measurement of Total Factor Productivity", *Review of Income and Wealth,* XXXIX, September 1983, 297–316; C. K. Hulten, "On the 'Importance' of Productivity Change", *American Economic Review,* LXIX, March 1979, 126–36; D. Usher, *The Measurement of Economic Growth* (New York: Columbia University Press, 1980); W. Peterson, "Total Factor Productivity in the U.K.: A Disaggregated Analysis", eds. K. D. Patterson and K. Schott, *The Measurement of Capital: Theory and Practice* (London: Macmillan, 1979); H. H. Postner and L. Wesa, *Canadian Productivity Growth: An Alternative (Input–Output) Analysis* (Ottawa: Economic Council of Canada, 1983); and I. Steedman, "On the Measurement and Aggregation of Productivity Increase", *Metroeconomica,* XXXV, October 1983, 223–33 and "On the Impossibility of Hicks-Neutral Technical Change", *Economic Journal,* XCV, September 1985, 746–58.

[7] As Arrow and Starrett say: "As the multiplicity of current and ancient debates has revealed, capital in the abstract sense is not an identifiable commodity like labour, land or specific capital goods, it is rather the willingness to wait". K. J. Arrow and D. A. Starrett, "Cost- and Demand-Theoretical Approaches to the Theory of Price Determination", eds. J. R. Hicks and W. Weber, *Carl Menger and the Austrian School of Economics* (Oxford: Clarendon Press, 1973), 140.

For a discussion of the concept of waiting, see A. Marshall, *Principles of Economics* (London: Macmillan, Guillebaud ed. 1961), I, 233, 353, 523, 542. In II, Marshall, later echoed by Arrow and Starrett, says, "on the whole, it is perhaps best to say that there are three factors of production, land, labour, and the sacrifice involved in waiting" (643n.1).

The concept of waiting has been recently reviewed in L. B. Yeager, "Capital Paradoxes and the Concept of Waiting", ed. M. J. Rizzo, *Time, Uncertainty and Disequilibrium: Exposition of Austrian Themes* (Lexington, Mass.: D.C. Heath, 1979).

For a critique of the concept of waiting as a factor of production, see K. H. Hennings, "Waiting", *The New Palgrave,* IV (London: Macmillan, 1987), 846–48.

Where technical progress is ignored, set aside by assumption, or considered to be nil by that part of general equilibrium theory that denies the existence of "income effects" or costless shifts in constraints governing behaviour, the waiting that lies behind capital can also be ignored. Where technical progress occurs, the measure of capital that takes the changed effectiveness of waiting into account will differ from ones that ignore it. The associated measures of multifactor productivity or technical progress will also diverge.

In a technically progressive economy, the real incomes of suppliers of labour and owners of capital and land (individuals or households are generally simultaneously all three) will tend to increase. The productivity of labour is increasing, which is reflected in rising real wage rates. The productivity of the services of land is increasing, which permits owners of land to earn higher real rentals on the land. What about "capital"? *Some* of the greater amounts of physical capital, which owners are accumulating by postponing consumption, thus earning greater returns, arise from technical progress. Accumulation of capital may occur not only as a result of more postponed consumption but also because the same quantity of postponed consumption produces more capital goods when there is technical progress. The productivity of waiting, the efficiency of the willingness to postpone present consumption, is increasing, and the higher real incomes of owners of capital take the form of the accumulation of some of the income-earning capital. Our new measures of multifactor productivity attempt to measure the increasing efficiency of basic primary inputs such as labour and waiting.

The amount of consumption that has to be forgone to acquire a certain amount of capital formation is clearly reduced if the capital formation can be more efficiently undertaken, that is, if the industries producing capital goods are experiencing advances in productivity. Similarly, the amount of consumption that must not be undertaken to maintain the capital stock, that is, to ensure that the capital goods industries are producing replacements for capital goods wearing out, is also reduced if such productivity advance is occurring. The mere carrying of capital goods through time involves forgoing consumption, whether by individuals as individuals or by individuals acting collectively. If capital goods industries experience advances in productivity, then to maintain permanent consumption levels unchanged, stocks of capital goods could be maintained with, in fact, some increase in present consumption. The community may well decide not to increase relatively present consumption. The enhanced productivity of the capital goods industries permit capital stocks and permanent consumption streams to be higher. The flow of waiting could be unchanged and the permanent flow of consumption could be higher.

Individuals, supplying labour time, give up the immediate consumption of such time in exchange for the indirect consumption that the selling or nonimmediate consumption of such time avails them. Labour time sold is the measure of the labour input in productivity measures. Individuals, by forgoing present consumption and accumulating capital directly or indirectly through the bond and stock exchanges, are exchanging present for permanent consumption. The accumulation of capital is the embodiment of the waiting individuals have done. With technical progress, a given flow of waiting (or the forgoing of a given flow of present consumption) may be embodied in an increasing accumulation of capital that reflects the ever-increasing efficiency of waiting and results in higher levels of permanent consumption.

The measured efficiency of waiting and working (the advances in productivity of the factors of working or labour, waiting or capital) is what this study attempts to measure. If there are no advances in productivity in capital goods industries, then any increased waiting that does occur and may show up in increased capital represents an increase not in multifactor productivity but in factors of production since the greater stock results from the increased waiting.

If advances in productivity were restricted to activities that produced only consumption goods, then the new and traditional measures of multifactor productivity would be the same. The measures of capital as factors of production would be the same since, by assumption, there would be no need to account for advances in productivity by which produced inputs of production are being made.

Modern economies are characterized, however, by a vast number of produced means of production. In all of the industries in which such capital inputs are produced, advances in productivity take place. In any measure of productivity improvement, such advances in efficiency through improvement in technology in the production of capital goods must be taken into account.

Increases in output will in general be said to be accounted for by changes in working (a growing labour force or a constant one working longer or shorter hours), changes in waiting (larger or smaller rates of saving appearing as higher or lower rates of capital accumulation), *and improvements in the economic efficiency of working and waiting*. It is those improvements that this study attempts to measure.

There is always unfinished theoretical business. To the late Sir Roy Harrod, the Keynesian short-run amendment to Marshallian analysis was of absolutely vital importance, but it was an amendment.[8] In his growth

---

[8] See R. F. Harrod's review of the general theory in his 1937 *Econometrica* article "Keynes and Traditional Theory", reprinted in his *Economic Essays* (London: Macmillan, 2nd ed. 1972).

theory, Harrod maintained the conception of capital inputs as the result of waiting.[9] To the late Joan Robinson, the Keynesian revolution and the Cambridge capital controversy left the Marshallian conception of waiting in disarray, and she could be said to champion the cause of the neo-Ricardians who attach no significance to the meaning and measurement of capital as waiting. Throughout this study, this fundamental debate, whose full resolution awaits further theoretical development and advance, will be continually referenced. It appears foremost when changes in the utilization of capital capacity are considered. For not only will there be unemployment of labour, which in general does not show up in labour input or employment and hence productivity data, but also there will be unemployment of capital. When Keynesian problems of insufficient aggregate demand are experienced, the waiting or saving of owners of capital is largely spilled onto the sands, and this shows up as a decline in multifactor productivity measures. Traditional measures seek to adjust for the Keynesian underutilization of capital, neglecting the fact that the mere carrying of such capital through time, whether utilized or not to its expected capacity, involves nonconsumption or waiting and capital underutilization involves a reduction in the productivity of such waiting.

Nonetheless, a satisfactory integration of modern Cambridge capital theory with Keynesian monetary economics remains to be undertaken and achieved, particularly with respect to measures of the changing efficiency of the services of fiat money and the treatment of the banking industry.

Though the theoretical arguments of the late Sir Roy Harrod and Joan Robinson in relation to the problem of multifactor productivity measurement have been reviewed elsewhere,[10] the theory is better understood when set out more concretely within the context of Leontief–Sraffa–Pasinetti expressions of technology or modern input–output accounts. We first consider some very simple static input–output accounts. We then show how dynamic versions of the accounts can be used to prepare traditional measures of multifactor productivity. More importantly, we show they are most useful for our new measures of multifactor productivity advance.

Such accounts illustrate how the measures of multifactor productivity advanced in this study contribute as well an important new addition to the System of National Accounts. To such accounts we now turn.

B   The static accounting system

Multifactor productivity measurement requires information about the prices and quantities of all (measurable) inputs and outputs. To establish

---

[9] R. F. Harrod, "The Neutrality of Improvements", *Economic Journal,* LXXI, June 1961, 300–4, and *Money* (London: Macmillan, 1969), 202.
[10] Rymes, *On Concepts of Capital and Technical Change.*

the groundwork for our measurement procedures, we set out a simple set of input–output accounts for the Canadian economy, abstracting from government and foreign trade, assuming that competitive prices prevail and that each industry produces a single different good or service. (These restrictive assumptions can be and are relaxed.)

A simple static input–output system

A year's value of outputs and inputs for any industry may be expressed in the following identity: The value of gross output is identical to the value of intermediate inputs supplied by other industries *plus* the value of labour services used *plus* the value of the net rental services on all the various capital goods produced by other industries of the economy and used in the industry in question *plus* the value of all the capital used up during the year. In imprecise language, the identity might also be that the value of sales must be identically equal to the cost of sales including materials used, wages, net returns to capital, and depreciation.[11] In short, the value of gross outputs is identical to the value of gross inputs. The identity may be written symbolically for the jth industry as

$$P_j Q_j = P_i M_{ij} + W_h L_{hj} + R_{ij} P_i K_{ij} - p_i' P_i K_{ij} \tag{1-1}$$

The industry is said to produce a value of gross output, $P_j Q_j$, where Q_j is the annual quantity of output produced and P_j is its price (the average price over the year). The gross inputs are the value of intermediate inputs, $P_i M_{ij}$, where M_{ij} is the quantity of the commodity or service produced in the ith industry used in the jth industry and P_i is the price of such goods[12]; the value of the many kinds of labour services used in industry j, $W_h L_{hj}$, where L_{hj} is the quantity of the hth kind of labour service and W_h is the price (i.e., wage or salary rate) paid for that kind of labour; $R_{ij} P_i K_{ij}$ is the value of the *net* returns to all capital used in industry j; and $-p_i' P_i K_{ij}$ is the value of depreciation experienced by the capital employed or the value of capital used up in the jth industry. The intermediate inputs will be, for example, materials used; intermediate services purchased from other industries such as telephone and legal services; power used, such as the value of electricity purchased or value of purchased gas and oil used, so that energy inputs are included; as well as the services of research and development by the industry itself and purchased from

---

[11] The discussion of rents paid on inexhaustible natural agents of production and rent and depletion allowances for exhaustible natural agents is in Appendix I of this chapter.

[12] The expression $P_i M_{ij}$ is a scalar made up of a row vector of prices and a column vector of quantities. That is, $P_i M_{ij} = P_1 M_{1j} + P_2 M_{2j} + \cdots + P_n M_{nj}$, where n is the number of distinct industries in the economy (though not all industries need supply directly the jth industry with intermediate inputs). The value of *all* inputs, such as material inputs, labour, etc., will be represented then as the products of such row and column vectors.

other industries if not capitalized. Similarly, the flow of labour services will be those not only of production workers but also of lawyers, scientists working on in-house or own-account research and development, salesmen, executive officers, and so forth.

The net returns to capital and depreciation may be examined more closely. The value of depreciation[13] of the capital used up in the industry is sometimes taken to be the result of physical rates of decay that capital goods experience. More generally, however, economic depreciation[14] will appear as a decline in the price of a capital good as it ages. Thus, p_i' represents the rate of *decline* (abstracting from any changes over time in the prices of capital goods of exactly the same characteristics) in the price of a capital good of given characteristics produced in the ith industry and used in the jth industry at a certain rate of utilization *as it ages*. The term $p_i' P_i K_{ij}$ shows the rate of change in the price of the ith type capital good as it ages in industry j times the market value or net stock of the ith type of capital good used in the jth industry (the vector notation implies again that reference is being made to many kinds of capital goods of many different vintages produced or producible in many capital goods industries). Similarly, the term $R_{ij} P_i K_{ij}$ may be interpreted as the net rate of return earned on capital of the ith type in the jth industry times the market value or net stock of the ith type of capital good used in the jth industry.

Knowledge of an industry's inputs and outputs incorporates the fact that its intermediate inputs and capital goods may be the products of one, some, or all of the other industries. Indeed, the industry in question may be producing some of its own intermediate inputs (steel mills may use steel to produce steel) or may, through own-account construction, produce some of its own fixed capital (construction firms may build their own office buildings). Not all of the gross output of an industry flows as intermediate outputs to other industries (though for some industries that may be the case); some of it (for some industries all of it) is final output. Final output will be flowing into the final demands of households and final demands of industries as capital formation in the forms of additions to inventories and fixed capital.

The accounts for an industry can be assembled with those of others to produce a Leontief–Sraffa–Pasinetti set of accounts. In Table 1-1 a very

---

[13] The measurement problems associated with depreciation are more fully discussed in Rymes, *On Concepts of Capital and Technical Change* (see especially ch. 4), and in T. K. Rymes, "Comments", ed. D. Usher, *The Measurement of Capital* (Chicago: National Bureau of Economic Research, 1980).

[14] See C. R. Hulten and F. C. Wykoff, "The Measurement of Economic Depreciation", ed. C. R. Hulten, *Depreciation, Inflation and the Taxation of Income from Capital* (Washington, D.C.: The Urban Institute, 1981).

Table 1-1. *Simple static input–output accounts*

	Intermediate output				Final output					Gross output
	Industry 1	Industry 2	...	Industry n	House-holds C	Industry 1	Industry 2	...	Industry n	
Intermediate input by industry										
1	$P_1 M_{11}$	$P_1 M_{12}$	...	$P_1 M_{1n}$	$P_1 C_1$	$P_1 \Delta K_{11}$	$P_1 \Delta K_{12}$	...	$P_1 \Delta K_{1n}$	$P_1 Q_1$
2	$P_2 M_{21}$	$P_2 M_{22}$	...	$P_2 M_{2n}$	$P_2 C_2$	$P_2 \Delta K_{21}$	$P_2 \Delta K_{22}$	...	$P_2 \Delta K_{2n}$	$P_2 Q_2$
$\vdots$	...	...		...	...	...	...		...	...
n	$P_n M_{n1}$	$P_n M_{n2}$	...	$P_n M_{nn}$	$P_n C_n$	$P_n \Delta K_{n1}$	$P_n \Delta K_{n2}$	...	$P_n \Delta K_{nn}$	$P_n Q_n$
Labour input	$W_1 L_{11}$	$W_1 L_{12}$	...	$W_1 L_{1n}$						$W_1 L_1$
	...	...		...						...
	$W_h L_{h1}$	$W_h L_{h1}$	...	$W_h L_{h1}$						$W_h L_h$
Net returns to capital by industry										
1	$R_{11} P_1 K_{11}$	$R_{12} P_1 K_{12}$	...	$R_{1n} P_1 K_{1n}$						$P_1 \sum_j R_{1j} K_{1j}$
2	$R_{21} P_2 K_{21}$	$R_{22} P_2 K_{22}$	...	$R_{2n} P_2 K_{2n}$						$P_2 \sum_j R_{2j} K_{2j}$
$\vdots$	...	...		...						...
n	$R_{n1} P_n K_{n1}$	$R_{n2} P_n K_{n2}$	...	$R_{nn} P_n K_{nn}$						$P_n \sum_j R_{nj} K_{nj}$
Depreciation by industry										
1	$-p_1' P_1 K_{11}$	$-p_1' P_1 K_{12}$	...	$-p_1' P_1 K_{1n}$						$-\sum_j p_1' P_1 K_{1j}$
2	$-p_2' P_2 K_{21}$	$-p_2' P_2 K_{22}$	...	$-p_2' P_2 K_{2n}$						$-\sum_j p_2' P_2 K_{2j}$
$\vdots$	...	...		...						...
n	$-p_n' P_n K_{n1}$	$-p_n' P_n K_{n2}$	...	$-p_n' P_n K_{nn}$						$-\sum_j p_n' P_n K_{nj}$
Gross input	$P_1 Q_1$	$P_2 Q_2$	...	$P_n Q_n$	$\sum_i P_i C_i$	$\sum_i P_i \Delta K_{i1}$	$\sum_i P_i \Delta K_{i2}$	...	$\sum_i P_i \Delta K_{in}$	

simple set of such accounts is portrayed.[15] Since the Canadian version of these accounts is what is employed in our measures of multifactor productivity, particularly the new measures, care must be taken in understanding the construction and theoretical basis of these accounts.

Consider the portion of the table labelled "Intermediate input and output". The first row deals with the disposition of the first industry's gross output. Some of it flows to and is used as intermediate input in the second industry ($P_1 M_{12}$), some of it flows into the final demands of households ($P_1 C_1$), and some of it flows into the capital formation of the other industries. For example, Table 1-1 shows part of the gross output of the first industry flowing into the gross capital formation taking place in the nth industry, $P_1 \Delta K_{1n}$. Row 2 in Table 1-1 similarly allocates the gross output of the second industry, and in general, there will be as many rows as there are industries so that row n in the table apportions the gross output of the nth industry. Since the industries are restricted each to producing only one type of commodity, it is unlikely that all industries will be producing outputs for all dispositions. Some industries will be producing intermediate outputs, some mainly for households (what may be called consumer goods industries), and others will be mainly producing buildings and machines that appear as part of the capital formation of other industries (durable or capital goods industries).

When all the intermediate and final outputs for an industry are summed, one gets the value of the industry's gross output. Because of the assumption that each industry produces only one commodity or service, it will be observed that, along the rows, the prices will cancel out. From Table 1-1, summing the entries along row n, for example, we have

$$P_n M_{n1} + P_n M_{n2} + \cdots + P_n M_{nn} + P_n C_n + P_n \Delta K_{n1} + \cdots + P_n \Delta K_{nn} = P_n Q_n$$

$$(1\text{-}2)$$

Because P_n cancels, this can be written as

$$M_{n1} + M_{n2} + \cdots + M_{nn} + C_n + \Delta K_{n1} + \Delta K_{n2} + \cdots + \Delta K_{nn} = Q_n$$

The intermediate input rows and columns depict one aspect of the technological interdependence of the economy. If one reads along the nth row, one sees that the nth industry supplies many other industries with intermediate output. If one reads down the nth column, one notes that the nth industry employs intermediate inputs produced by many other industries.

The next set of rows in Table 1-1, called "Labour input", show the value of the different kinds of labour services used in the various industries. Once

---

[15] In Table I-1, households are treated alike – it is one of the simplifications that can be dropped in more complicated analyses.

again, along any row only one type of labour is employed. So for the hth kind of labour, one may write

$$W_h L_{h1} + W_h L_{h2} + \cdots + W_h L_{hn} = W_h \bar{L}_n \tag{1-3}$$

With prices cancelling,[16] this is

$$L_{h1} + L_{h2} + \cdots + L_{hn} = \bar{L}_h$$

The $\bar{L}_h$ indicates that the total amount of that kind of labour input is taken as a given (not constant, because over time the labour force may be growing or changing because wages may be changing) in the sense that, as an input, it is not produced by the economic system. If, however, the flow of labour service is treated as the flow of services of human capital, then such services (but not, of course, the people who own such capital) can be treated as part of the flow of the service of producible inputs since human capital is produced by the economy. Thus, if part of the flow of labour service is that of, say, scientists or musicians or doctors and if their productive services are obtained by investment in education in universities, schools of art, or institutes of medical research, then such services can be and sometimes are treated as producible by the economic system.

The rows of Table 1-1 denoted "Net returns to capital" show what may be called the net rentals being earned on the net capital stocks. In the first row, for example, the net rentals on capital goods of the type produced by the first industry are shown as part of the value of such inputs in the second industry, $R_{12} P_1 K_{12}$, where R_{12} is the net rate of return on the capital goods earned in the second industry, P_1 is the price of the first industry's output (now considered invariant to the using industry), and K_{12} is the capital goods of the type produced in industry 1 but used in industry 2. Again, along any row only one type of capital good is employed – more precisely, one type of the flow service of a capital good is "rented" – and for (say) the second capital good produced in the second industry, one can write

$$R_{21} P_2 K_{21} + R_{22} P_2 K_{22} + \cdots + R_{2n} P_2 K_{2n} = P_2 \sum_j R_{2j} K_{2j} \tag{1-4}$$

or, cancelling prices,

$$R_{21} K_{21} + R_{22} K_{22} + \cdots + R_{2n} K_{2n} = \sum_j R_{2j} K_{2j}$$

---

[16] In an economy in which labour moves freely from one industry to another, competition assures that the price of labour (of the same kind) will be the same in all industries. If there is some unspecified cost associated with the movements of labour, then of course, in any period of time it may be the case that the price of labour (of the same kind) will not be the same in all industries. That cost must, of course, be properly considered in any specification of what is meant by the same kind of homogeneous labour.

If it were assumed that the net rate of return on capital goods of the second type were the same in all industries (i.e., $R_{21} = R_{22} = \cdots = R_{2n} = R_2$), or if rates of return were equal across industries, then the net rates of return would cancel out as well. The symbol K_{2j} would continue to represent, however, both the stock of capital goods and the net service flow of such capital goods.

Finally, the rows of Table 1-1 called "Depreciation" may be similarly explained. Elements in the final row, for example, show the value of depreciation or capital consumption on capital goods of the type produced in the nth industry occurring in all the industries in which such capital goods are found. For example, $-p'_n P_n K_{n2}$ is the rate of change in price of the nth type of capital good because of depreciation times the value of such capital goods found in the second industry. Over all industries,

$$-p'_n P_n K_{n1} - p'_n P_n K_{n2} - \cdots - p' P_n K_{nn}$$
$$= \sum_j (-p'_n P_n K_{nj}) = P_n \sum_j (-p'_n K_{nj}) \tag{1-5}$$

If prices cancel, one has

$$-p'_n K_{n1} - p'_n K_{n2} - \cdots - p'_n K_{nn} = -\sum p'_n K_{nj}$$

The rows labelled "Net returns to capital" and "Depreciation" in Table 1-1 could be added together element by element to yield what could be called "Gross returns to capital." A representative element would be

$$R_{ij} P_i K_{ij} - p'_i P_i K_{ij} \quad \text{or} \quad (R_{ij} - p'_i) P_i K_{ij}$$

where $R_{ij} - p'_i$ represents the gross rate of return earned by capital of the type produced in the ith industry found in the jth industry and $P_i K_{ij}$ is the value of the corresponding net stock. The expression $(R_{ij} - p'_i) P_i K_{ij}$ is the gross rental being earned by the capital good K_{ij} of the type produced by the ith industry found in the jth industry. Once again, the symbol K_{ij} stands for the stock and service flows of the capital good.

The distinction drawn between gross (net) rentals and gross (net) rates of return must be emphasized. Neo-classical theory emphasizes the services of the capital goods (i.e., machine-hours) and the gross (or net) rentals earned by such capital goods. Capital service is treated as being "on all fours" with the services of labour and land. The theory behind the new multifactor productivity measures stresses that capital goods are ways in which the economic system transforms present consumption forgone into permanent consumption flows. The capital goods embody such services, and they earn rentals metered by the gross (or net) rates of return.[17]

---

[17] In an economy in which capital goods can be moved freely from one industry to another (rented automobiles, airplanes, and tank cars would be examples), competition assures

The value of gross inputs into the first industry will be equal to the value of intermediate inputs from other industries (e.g., $P_2 M_{21}$ is the value of the intermediate inputs coming from the second industry used in the first industry), the value of labour inputs, the net returns to all the capital found in the first industry (e.g., $R_{21} P_2 K_{21}$ is the net returns to capital on capital goods of the type produced in the second industry found in the first industry), and capital consumption allowances on all the capital found in the first industry. The value of gross input will be the same as the value of gross outputs. This may be expressed as

$$P_1 M_{11} + P_2 M_{21} + \cdots + P_n M_{n1} + W_1 L_{11} + \cdots + W_h L_{h1} + \cdots$$
$$+ R_{11} P_1 K_{11} + \cdots - p_1' P_1 K_{11} + \cdots = P_1 Q_1 \qquad (1\text{-}6)$$

and there will be n such identities for the n industries.

The final output columns may be summed to give the value of total consumption by households and the value of gross capital formation by all the various industries, as shown at the bottom of Table 1-1.

Simple input–output matrices: quantities

The information contained in the input–output accounts can be used to show important technological interdependence among industries.

Consider now the jth row of the intermediate part of Table 1-1. It is, as has been shown,

$$\sum_i P_j M_{ji} + P_j C_j + \sum_i P_j \Delta K_{ji} = Q_j \qquad (1\text{-}7)$$

The prices cancel, and we have

$$\sum_i M_{ji} + C_j + \sum_i \Delta K_{ji} = Q_j \qquad (1\text{-}8)$$

If we define intermediate input–gross output coefficients as $a_{ij} = M_{ij}/Q_j$, then the row may be expressed as

the price of capital services (in the neo-classical sense) of the same kind will be the same in all industries (salespeople from firms engaged in very different activities will pay the same rentals for the same cars at Canadian airports). The gross rentals would then cancel out along the rows. If there is some unspecified cost associated with the movements of capital, then again, as for labour, the rentals earned on capital goods (of the same kind) will not be the same in all industries. Even more importantly in the case of capital, the "adjustment" costs must be properly considered in any specification of what is meant by the same kind of capital. In an economy in which the ownership of capital, either directly or indirectly through the bond and stock exchanges, in any industry, is costlessly transferable, competition will assure that the price of waiting services will be the same in all industries, i.e., the same net rate of return will hold in all industries. Once again costs of transferring ownership must be incorporated into the analysis.

$$\sum_i a_{ji} Q_i + C_j + \sum_i \Delta K_{ji} = Q_j \tag{1-9}$$

The equations for the rows for all industries can be expressed compactly as

$$AQ + C + \Delta K = Q \tag{1-10}$$

Where A is a matrix (of order $n \times n$) of all the intermediate input–gross output coefficients, $A = [a_{ij}]$; Q is a column vector (of order $n \times 1$) of all the gross outputs of all the industries; and C and ΔK are similar vectors that pertain to consumption and gross capital formation. If A is real, then the matrix equation may be written as

$$C + \Delta K = [I - A]Q \tag{1-11}$$

or

$$[I - A]^{-1}C + [I - A]^{-1} \Delta K = Q \tag{1-12}$$

where the inverted matrix $[I - A]^{-1}$ shows the direct and indirect intermediate input requirements per unit of gross output of the n industries.

If the labour components of Table 1-1 are now examined and labour input–gross output coefficients are defined as $L_{hj}/Q_j = b_{hj}$, then for the hth kind of labour, $b_{hj}Q_j = L_{hj}$ and for all kinds of labour,

$$BQ = \bar{L} \tag{1-13}$$

where B is the matrix (of order $h \times n$) of the b_{hj}'s, Q is again the column vector of the gross outputs of the industries, and $\bar{L}$ is the column vector (of order h) of the given nonreproducible flows of labour.

The intermediate input and labour input equations can be combined to yield

$$B[I - A]^{-1}C + B[I - A]^{-1} \Delta K = BQ = \bar{L} \tag{1-14}$$

where a particular vector of final output of consumption and gross fixed capital formation will require a particular (vector of) labour input. In the equation, the matrix $B[I - A]^{-1}$ portrays the direct and indirect labour input requirements for each type of labour per unit of output of the n industries so that $B[I - A]^{-1}C$ could be a vector of the amounts of the different kinds of labour directly and indirectly required throughout the whole economic system to support a particular composition of final consumption by the households of the economy.

The net returns to capital may be similarly expressed. Thus, for the capital goods produced in the ith industry, one has [from identities (1-4)]

$$R_{i1}K_{i1} + R_{i2}K_{i2} + \cdots + R_{in}K_{in} = \sum_j R_{ij}K_{ij}$$

and defining the net capital service input–gross output coefficient as, $e_{ij} = R_{ij}K_{ij}/Q_j$, one also has $\sum_j e_{ij}Q_j = \sum_j R_{ij}K_{ij}$, and for all industries,

$$EQ = K \tag{1-15}$$

where E is a matrix (of order $n \times n$) of the capital service coefficients $E = [e_{ij}]$ and K is the $n \times 1$ vector of the capital services for each type of capital. Again it is possible to say that

$$E[I-A]^{-1}C + E[I-A]^{-1}\Delta K = EQ = K \tag{1-16}$$

so that the matrix $E[I-A]^{-1}$ is the set of coefficients showing the direct and indirect flows of net capital services of the n type of capital per unit of output of the n industries.

Consider finally depreciation. The discussion on depreciation or capital consumption allowances showed that identities 1-5 can be reconstituted, for the nth capital good, as

$$-p'_n P_n K_{n1} - p'_n P_n K_{n2} - \cdots - p'_n P_n K_{nn} = P_n \sum (-p'_n K_{nj})$$

Again, each capital good of the same type would have the same price so that prices cancel, and we write

$$-p'_n K_{n1} - p'_n K_{n2} - \cdots - p'_n K_{nn} = -p'_n \sum_j K_{nj}$$

and there are n such equations. Define the depreciation input–gross output coefficients as $\hat{d}_{ij} = -p'_i K_{ij}/Q_j$; then, where $\hat{D} = [\hat{d}_{ij}]$,

$$\hat{D}Q = \hat{K} \tag{1-17}$$

and $\hat{K}$ is the $n \times 1$ vector of capital consumption for each type of capital. Again,

$$\hat{D}[I-A]^{-1}C + \hat{D}[I-A]^{-1}\Delta K = \hat{D}Q = \hat{K} \tag{1-18}$$

so that the matrix $\hat{D}[I-A]^{-1}$ is the set of coefficients showing the direct and indirect flows of capital consumption of the n types of capital per unit of output of the industries.

In conclusion, a particular vector of final demand, $C + \Delta K$, by means of the input-output accounts, can be decomposed into

$$B[I-A]^{-1}[C+\Delta K] = \bar{L}$$
$$E[I-A]^{-1}[C+\Delta K] = K \tag{1-19}$$
$$\hat{D}[I-A]^{-1}[C+\Delta K] = \hat{K}$$

An equation such as

$$B[I-A]^{-1}[C+\Delta K] = \bar{L}$$

states that, given the vector of final demand $[C+\Delta K]$, we know the amount of labour services directly and indirectly involved in all the industries associated with such final demand requirements. Consider a component of the final demand vector, $C_j + \Delta K_j$, where the final demand or net output (gross output less intermediate output) of industry j is recorded and the final outputs of all other industries are set at zero. Then

$$B[I-A]^{-1}[C_j + \Delta K_j] = \bar{L}_j$$

are not only the services of labour directly involved in industry j – in producing industry j's final or net output – but also the services of labour in all the other industries associated indirectly with the level of activity of industry j. Industry j may indirectly call upon labour services employed in many other industries, and it is such indirect labour services as well as that at work directly in industry j that the vector $B[I-A]^{-1}[C_j + \Delta K_j] = \bar{L}_j$ captures.

From the equations

$$E[I-A]^{-1}[C + \Delta K] = K \quad \text{and} \quad \hat{D}[I-A]^{-1}[C + \Delta K] = \hat{K}$$

we see that analogous arguments about the direct and indirect uses of the services of capital and capital consumption can be developed.

A further simplification is possible. Recall the e_{ij} and $\hat{d}_{ij}$ were defined respectively as

$$\frac{R_{ij} K_{ij}}{Q_j} \quad \text{and} \quad \frac{-p'_i K_{ij}}{Q_j}$$

If we define

$$d_{ij} = \frac{K_{ij}}{Q_j}$$

and $D = [d_{ij}]$, the set of all capital output coefficients, and if rates of return and rates of depreciation all cancel out in a manner similar to prices, then the basic quantity equations can be expressed as

$$B[I-A]^{-1}[C + \Delta K] = L \qquad D[I-A]^{-1}[C + \Delta K] = K$$

This simple illustration of the technological interdependence among industries of modern economics can be seen in yet another way when we turn to price relations.

Simple input–output matrices: prices

If we return to the price equation for industry j, we have

$$\sum_i P_i M_{ij} + \sum_h W_h L_{hj} + \sum_i R_{ij} P_i K_{ij} - \sum_i p'_i P_i K_{ij} = P_j Q_j \qquad (1\text{-}20)$$

This may be written as

$$\sum_i P_i a_{ij} Q_j + \sum_h W_h b_{hj} Q_j + \sum_i P_i e_{ij} Q_j + \sum_i P_i \hat{d}_{ij} Q_j = P_j Q_j \qquad (1\text{-}21)$$

When the quantity equations were being considered, the prices cancelled out. When price equations are being considered, the gross outputs cancel out. For the jth industry, the price equation becomes

$$\sum_i P_i a_{ij} + \sum_h W_h b_{hj} + \sum_i P_i e_{ij} + \sum_i P_i \hat{d}_{ij} = P_j \qquad (1\text{-}22)$$

and for all n industries,

$$PA + WB + PE + P\hat{D} = P \qquad (1\text{-}23)$$

where P is a row vector (or order $1 \times n$) and W is a row vector (of order $1 \times h$, where there are h types of labour). One can immediately write

$$WB = P + PA - PE - P\hat{D}$$
$$= P[I - (A + E + \hat{D})]$$

or

$$WB[I - (A + E + \hat{D})]^{-1} = P \qquad (1\text{-}24)$$

Hence, the price equations say, as duals to the quantity equations, that given the h-order vector of wage rates for labour and given the $n \times n$-order matrices of net rates of return and rates of depreciation and knowledge of the direct and indirect primary input content of commodities as represented by the various matrices, the vector (of order $1 \times n$) of the prices of all the producible commodities is known.

In other words, one can say that P_j, the price of the output of industry j (a component of the vector P), can be expressed as being equal to the prices of labour of all kinds modified by the direct and indirect requirements for such labour *and* the rates of return to capital, which are in the E matrix, modified by the direct and indirect requirements for the services of capital *and* the rates of depreciation, which are in the $\hat{D}$ matrix. If the rates of return to capital were equal for all net capital stocks in all industries, then

$$E = RD$$

where R is *the* rate of return; if depreciation rates were the same for each capital good regardless of the industry using it, then $\hat{D} = \hat{\delta} D$, where $\hat{\delta}$ is the diagonal of such depreciation rates, and the price equation would be

$$WB[I - A - (R + \hat{\delta})D]^{-1} = P$$

so that the roles of real rates of return and depreciation rates associated with P would be more clearly seen.

In summary, simple input–output accounts depict the values of inputs and outputs in all industries in terms of quantities and prices and convey that information in such a way that the technological interdependence among the industries is simply depicted. Traditional measures of multi-factor productivity use the data on inputs and outputs by industry. The new estimates presented in this study require as well the knowledge of the interdependence among the industries. We will see that the measures of multifactor productivity are dynamic analogues to the static input–output accounts of this section. We now turn to measures of multifactor productivity, to dynamic rather than static accounting identities.

C   Advances in knowledge and dynamic identities

In this section, we show how the static identities can be expressed in terms of rates of growth or, more generally, rates of change.

The static account for industry j was

$$P_j Q_j = P_i M_{ij} + W_h L_h + R_{ij} P_i K_{ij} - p_i' P_i K_{ij} \tag{1-25}$$

When dealing discretely with differences between periods of time, changes in the value of gross output, V_j, can be expressed as

$$V_j = P_{j1} Q_{j1} - P_{j0} Q_{j0}$$

or, with $P_j = P_{j0} + \Delta P_j$ and $Q_{j1} = Q_{j0} + \Delta Q_j$, as

$$V_j = (P_{j0} + \Delta P_j)(Q_{j0} + \Delta Q_j) - P_{j0} Q_{j0} = P_{j0}\,\Delta Q_j + \Delta P_j Q_{j0} + \Delta P_j\,\Delta Q_j$$

where the subscripts 0 and 1 refer to two comparison periods of time, base (0) and current (1), so that the change in value is decomposed into three components: the change in the quantity of gross output times the price, $P_{j0}\,\Delta Q_j$, plus the change in price of gross output times the quantity $\Delta P_j Q_{j0}$ plus an interaction term, the change in price times the change in quantity, $\Delta P_j\,\Delta Q_j$.[18]

---

[18] One could also say that since $P_{j0} = P_{j1} - \Delta P_j$ and $Q_{j0} = Q_{j1} - \Delta Q_j$, the discrete difference would be

$$V = P_{j1} Q_{j1} - (P_{j1} - \Delta P_j)(Q_{j1} - \Delta Q_j)$$
$$= P_{j1}\,\Delta Q_j + \Delta P_j\,Q_{j1} - \Delta P_j\,\Delta Q_j$$

It will be noticed that the interaction term changes sign because the change in quantities and prices are now being "weighted" by current-period prices and quantities rather than their base-period counterparts. In the discrete sense, P_j and Q_j are the average prices and quantities in any period.

For purposes of conceptual discussion and simplicity of exposition, assume the components of the interaction terms are so small that their product is negligible. In other words, only instantaneous changes within a period of time are considered. Thus,

$$dV_j = P_j \, dQ_j + Q_j \, dP_j = P_j Q_j \left(\frac{dQ_j}{Q_j} + \frac{dP_j}{P_j} \right)$$

and

$$\frac{dV_j}{V_j} = \frac{dQ_j}{Q_j} + \frac{dP_j}{P_j}$$

so that the proportionate rate of change in the value of gross output in any time period is identically equal to the sum of the proportionate rates of change of the price P_j and the quantity of gross output Q_j.

For further economy of exposition, the proportionate-rate-of-change expression will be written as

$$v_j = q_j + p_j$$

where

$$v_j = \frac{1}{V_j} \frac{dV_j}{dt} = \frac{1}{V_j} \dot{V}_j;$$

that is, the lowercase letter stands for the proportionate rate of change of the variable in question.[19]

---

[19] If one assumes that an industry produces a number of products, k, so that

$$V_j = P_{kj} Q_{kj}$$

then $V_j = P_{kj0} \Delta Q_{kj} + \Delta P_{kj} Q_{kj0} + \Delta P_{kj} \Delta Q_{kj}$ as before, except that each term is a product of vectors rather than a product of scalars. Again, the formula will show the result of differences in the definition of change illustrated in note 18. One can construct Laspeyres and Paasche indexes of the prices and quantities of the gross output. The quantities indexes

$$\frac{P_{kj0} Q_{kj1}}{P_{kj0} Q_{kj0}} \quad \text{and} \quad \frac{P_{kj1} Q_{kj1}}{P_{kj1} Q_{kj0}}$$

are also related to Laspeyres – and Paasche – equivalent indexes of "the" quantity of gross output,

$$\frac{P_{kj0} Q^*_{kj1}}{P_{kj0} Q_{kj0}} \quad \text{and} \quad \frac{P_{kj1} Q_{kj1}}{P_{kj1} Q^*_{kj0}}$$

where Q^*_{kj1} is the set of outputs produced if, given "current" inputs and technology, the marginal rates of transformation across such outputs were equal to the relative "base"-period prices and Q^*_{kj0} is the set of outputs produced if, again given inputs and technology, the marginal rates of transformation were equal to the relative "current"-period prices.

In the case of industries made up of profit-maximizing firms, the behaviour of these indexes and their price counterparts will depend upon changes in tastes, income effects,

Consider now the expression $P_i M_{ij}/P_j Q_j$, that is, the value of inter-mediate inputs used in industry j as a proportion of its gross inputs or gross output. In the form of proportionate rates of change this is

$$\alpha_{ij}[(p_i+m_{ij})-(p_j+q_j)]$$

where p_i+m_{ij} is a column vector of the sum of the proportionate rates of change of intermediate input prices and quantities, p_j and q_j are similar measures for the output, and α_{ij} is a row vector showing the *share* of each intermediate input from industry i being used by industry j in the total value of all gross inputs used in industry j.

Such expressions can be said to hold for every component of the gross inputs for industry j, that is, for the returns to labour, net returns to capital, and depreciation. If one considers the net returns to capital in industry j, for instance, then one has

$$\tau_{ij}[(r_j+p_i+k_{ij})-(p_j+q_j)]$$

where r_j is the proportionate rate of change in the net rate of return on the capital goods owned and used in industry j, p_i is the proportionate rate of change in the price of the capital good made in industry i and owned and used in industry j, k_{ij} is the proportionate rate of change in the stock of that good, and τ_{ij} is the share of the net returns to such capital in the total value of all gross inputs used in industry j.[20]

For industry j, the identity can be rewritten as the *fundamental dynamic identity*:

$$p_j+q_j = \alpha_{ij}(p_i+m_{ij})+\beta_{hj}(w_{hj}+l_{hj})+\tau_{ij}(r_j+p_i+k_{ij})$$
$$+ \delta_{ij}\left(\frac{\dot{p}_i'}{p_i'}+p_i+k_{ij}\right) \tag{1-26}$$

and inputs being used by the firms, the neutrality and biases in input use associated with technical advance, and changes in the degree of competition in the various output and input markets. For further discussions of such output indexes, see W. E. Diewert, "The Theory of the Output Price Index and the Measurement of Real Output Change", eds. W. E. Diewert and C. Montmarquette, *Price Level Measurement* (Ottawa: Supply and Services, Government of Canada, 1983).

[20] In index number form, one would have as quantity indexes for, say, the intermediate inputs

$$\frac{P_{i0}M_{ij1}}{P_{i0}M_{ij0}} \quad \text{and} \quad \frac{P_{i1}M_{ij1}}{P_{i1}M_{ij0}}$$

in their Laspeyres and Paasche forms together with the matching price indexes. Again, one could construct, at the intermediate input level, Laspeyres – and Paasche – equivalent quantity and prices indexes.

Such Laspeyres and Paasche indexes can be constructed for the measurable inputs, separately, such as the set of all labour inputs or indeed all the measurable inputs taken together.

where

w_{hj} = proportionate rate of change of money wage rates of the labour of the hth kind used in industry j,

l_{hj} = proportionate rate of change of the quantity of such labour,

$\dot{p}'_i/p'_i$ = proportionate rate of change of the rate of economic depreciation of the capital good producible in industry i owned and used in industry j,

β_{hj} = share of wages for the hth kind of labour in the value of gross inputs for industry j,

δ_{ij} = similar share for depreciation or capital used up

and all other symbols are as previously defined.

Traditional measures of multifactor productivity

A manipulation of the fundamental dynamic identity for industry j may now be considered. Assemble on one side of the identity all the quantities and on the other side all the prices. The result will be the traditional measure of multifactor productivity for industry j:

$$q_j - \left[\alpha_{ij}m_{ij} + \beta_{hj}l_{hj} + \tau_{ij}k_{ij} + \delta_{ij}\left(\frac{\dot{p}'_i}{p'_i} + k_{ij}\right)\right]$$
$$= t_j$$
$$= [\alpha_{ij}p_i + \beta_{hj}w_{hj} + \tau_{ij}(r_{ij} + p_i) + \delta_{ij}p_i] - p_j \qquad (1\text{-}27)$$

The left-hand side of the identity shows the rate of change of the *quantity* of gross output less the share-weighted rates of change of the *quantities* of all the intermediate, labour, net capital service, and capital consumption factors or inputs. If the left side of the identity is positive, one would say that the rate of change of output per unit of multifactor input is positive or one would be observing, in activity j, an improvement in economic efficiency, multifactor productivity, or advances in knowledge *so defined*. *That* rate of change of multifactor productivity, t_j, is the traditional multifactor productivity measure.

It will be noted that the multifactor productivity measure can be easily decomposed into partial measures. Since

$$q_j = (\alpha_{ij} + \beta_{hj} + \tau_{ij} + \delta_{ij})q_j$$

because the shares sum to unity, the left-hand side of (1-27) can be written as

$$\alpha_{ij}[q_j - m_{ij}] + \beta_{hj}[q_j + l_{hj}] + \tau_{ij}[q_j - k_{ij}] + \delta_j\left[q_j - \left(\frac{\dot{p}'_i}{p'_i} + k_{ij}\right)\right] = t_j \qquad (1\text{-}28)$$

which shows the traditional multifactor productivity increases as equal to the weighted sums of the proportionate rates of growth of the intermediate input partial productivity measure, $q_j - m_{ij}$, the labour partial productivity measure, $q_j - l_{hj}$, the net capital service productivity measure, $q_j - k_{ij}$, and capital used up productivity measure, $q_j - (\dot{p}_i'/p_i' + k_{ij})$.

The right-hand side of identity (1-27) shows that the traditional measures of multifactor productivity can also be expressed as the share-weighted rates of change in the *prices* of all the intermediate, labour, net capital service, and capital consumptions factors or inputs less the rate of change in the *price* of gross output. It can also be written as

$$\alpha_{ij}[p_i - p_j] + \beta_{hj}[w_{hj} - p_j] + \tau_{ij}[r_{ij} + p_i - p_j] + \delta_{ij}(p_i - p_j) = t_j \qquad (1\text{-}29)$$

where the various rates of change of input prices are now expressed in own-product terms. For example, the expression $w_{hj} - p_j$ shows the proportionate rate of change of the *real* wage rate for labour of the hth kind, in this case *real* meaning not what the wage will buy but, in terms of the product, what it costs. Similarly, the expression $r_{ij} + p_i - p_j$ is the proportionate rate of change of the *own-product* net rental of the type of capital good reproducible in the ith industry but used in the jth industry.

Whether expressed in terms of the proportionate rates of change of the quantity of outputs relative to the quantity of inputs or the proportionate rates of change of the price of inputs relative to the prices of outputs, the fundamental dynamic identity captures the essence of traditional measures of multifactor productivity. It is of critical importance to realize that such measures treat all measured inputs in precisely the same way; no distinction is made between those inputs that are being or could be produced by the very economic system being examined and those inputs that, though dependent on the choice and behaviour of economic agents, are not being produced by the economic system, inputs that in that sense are nonproduced.

The traditional measures wish to distinguish those effects on gross outputs that arise from changes in measurable inputs of all kinds from those connected with advances in knowledge or changes in efficiency with which such inputs are combined. It does not matter for the traditional measures that some inputs are themselves produced more efficiently and some – the nonproduced inputs – are not. In performing the preceding traditional separation of movements along a production surface from shifts in the surface, one must not take the produced–nonproduced distinction into account.

The traditional measures are based on the concept of a production or transformation function in the context of profit maximization. Consider the problem for the firm in industry j, where all firms are alike, of maximizing profits with respect to output, intermediate inputs, labour, and capital services. One writes this as

$$\max \pi_j = P_{kj}Q_{kj} - P_i M_{ij} + W_h L_{hj} + \left(R_j - \frac{\dot{p}_i'}{p_i'} \right) P_i K_{ij}$$

with respect to $\quad Q_{kj}, M_{ij}, L_{hj}, K_{ij}$

subject to $\quad \phi_j(Q_{kj}, M_{ij}, L_{hj}, K_{ij}; T_j) = 0$

where ϕ is the statement of the technical possibilities of transformation between inputs and outputs.

With our simplification that industry j produces one product, one has

$$P_j \frac{\partial Q_j}{\partial M_{ij}} = P_i \quad \text{for all intermediate inputs}$$

$$P_j \frac{\partial Q_j}{\partial L_{hj}} = W_h \quad \text{for all labour input}$$

$$P_j \frac{\partial Q_j}{\partial K_{ij}} = \left(R_j - \frac{\dot{p}_i'}{p_i'} \right) P_i \quad \begin{array}{l} \text{for all gross service flows} \\ \text{of capital goods} \end{array}$$

as the first-order conditions for competitive profit maximization. One can further write, for example,

$$P_j \frac{\partial Q_j M_{ij}}{\partial M_{ij} Q_j} = \frac{P_i M_{ij}}{Q_j}$$

or

$$\frac{\partial Q_j M_{ij}}{\partial M_{ij} Q_j} = \frac{P_i M_{ij}}{P_j Q_j}$$

or, with respect to the intermediate input produced in industry i used in industry j, the partial elasticity of output with respect to that input will equal that input's cost share in the value of gross output.

Again, one could write

$$\frac{\partial Q_j K_{ij}}{\partial K_{ij} Q_j} = \frac{(R_j - \dot{p}_i'/p_i') P_i K_{ij}}{P_j Q_j}$$

or, with respect to the gross service flow of the capital good reproducible in industry i (a capital goods industry) used in industry j, the partial elasticity of output with respect to that input service will equal the cost share of the gross rentals on that capital service in the value of gross output of industry j.

The statement of transformation

$$\phi_j(Q_{kj}, M_{ij}, L_{hj}, K_{ij}; T_j) = 0$$

states that given the state of technical knowledge, T_j, there exists a relationship of feasibility among the inputs and the outputs. Given the inputs, there exists a feasible relationship between the various outputs such that more of one kind of output implies less of another kind. Under competitive conditions, the marginal rate of transformation between any pair of outputs will equal their relative price. With the assumption of only one kind of output, then, with profit maximization associated with efficiently combined inputs, there is a feasible maximum output. We may write this as

$$Q_j = Q_j(M_{ij}, L_{hj}, K_{ij}; T_j)$$

This can be reexpressed as

$$q_j = \frac{\partial Q_j M_{ij}}{\partial M_{ij} Q_j} m_{ij} + \frac{\partial Q_j L_{hj}}{\partial L_{hj} Q_j} l_{hj} + \frac{\partial Q_j K_{ij}}{\partial K_{ij} Q_j} k_{ij} + t_j$$

that is, the proportionate rate of change of the gross output of industry j equals the weighted rates of change of all the inputs (where the weight for each input is its partial elasticity of gross output) plus the rate of advance of technical knowledge or efficiency with which inputs are combined in the industry. Under competitive conditions, the partial elasticities are equal to the cost shares so that the reexpressed production function is exactly the same as the traditional measure of multifactor productivity in identity (1-27).[21] That is, with

$$\frac{\partial Q_j M_{ij}}{\partial M_{ij} Q_j} = \frac{P_i M_{ij}}{P_j Q_j} = \alpha_{ij}$$

and so forth, we have

$$q_j = \alpha_{ij} m_{ij} + \beta_{hj} l_{hj} + (\tau_{ij} + \delta_{ij}) k_{ij} + t_j$$

as on the left-hand side of identity (1-27) (where for simplicity the rate of depreciation is assumed constant).

From the maximization-of-profit approach, we learn that, ceteris paribus, a lower price, P_i, because, say, of technical progress in the ith industry, leads firms in the jth industry to substitute the ith intermediate input against other inputs. If *all* inputs are substitutes for one another and those other than from the ith industry are unchanged, we would have output in industry j higher by

$$dQ_j = \frac{\partial Q_j}{\partial M_{ij}} dM_{ij}$$

---

[21] Under competitive conditions, constant returns to scale prevail so that the partial elasticities and the ex post cost shares sum to unity.

and in terms of rates of change

$$q_j = \frac{\partial Q_j M_{ij}}{\partial M_{ij} Q_j} m_{ij}$$

Thus, identity (1-28) would show $q_j - l_n$, $q_j - m_{kj}$, and $q_j - k_{ij}$ all positive, $q_j - m_{ij}$ negative, and no change in t_j. That is, with M_{ij} being substituted for all other inputs because it was relatively cheaper, the result of the traditional measures would be that the partial productivity of M_{ij} would be lower and the partial productivities of all other inputs would be higher, the changes in the partial productivities being such that with their elasticity weights the total productivity of all the inputs, the measure of multifactor productivity, in industry j would be zero. The changing input structure would, in this case, be due to different productivity advances taking place in the industries supplying the intermediate inputs. Industry j would be shown, in general, as substituting the cheaper for the relatively more costly inputs, but the use of more of the cheaper intermediate inputs should not, in the traditional measures, be confused with advances in knowledge in the industry in question.[22]

The basic purpose of the traditional measures, then, is to distinguish movements along the production function, such as the substitution of one intermediate input for other intermediate and primary inputs, from shifts in the production function or improvements in the efficiency with which all the measurable inputs are being combined to produce an industry's output.

Intermediate inputs may be classified into those coming from (say) energy industries such as products of petroleum and coal, and capital inputs may be classified into energy-using buildings, machinery, and equipment. With the traditional measures one studies how changes in the relative prices of energy (the oil price shocks of the early 1970s) affect the utilization of energy intermediate inputs and energy-intensive capital inputs and how substitution away from such inputs affects the rates of growth of other inputs, outputs, and multifactor productivity in energy-using industries.

A solution of the maximization-of-profit problem may be a cost function,

$$C_j = C_j\left(P_i, W_h, \left(R_j - \frac{\dot{p}_i'}{p_i'}\right)P_i, Q_j; T_j\right)$$

---

[22] The traditional approach to the measurement of total factor productivity at the industry level has one of its most recent applications in D. W. Jorgenson et al., *Productivity and US Economic Growth* (Cambridge, Mass.: Harvard University Press, 1987).

For a brief statement of such new measures, see D. W. Jorgenson, "Productivity and Economic Growth", a paper presented at the 50th Anniversary National Bureau of Economic Research Conference on Research in Income and Wealth, 12–14 May 1988, Washington, D.C.

where the cost of production in industry j is said to be a function of the prices of the various inputs, the level of output of industry j, and, again, the state of technology or the efficiency with which inputs are used in the industry. If constant returns to scale are assumed, then $C_j = C_j(P_i, W_h, (R_j - \dot{p}_i'/p_i')P_i; T_j)$ shows that costs (now unit costs) can be interpreted as a function of the prices and the state of technology in the industry. Under competitive conditions unit costs are equal to the price of the industry's product, so

$$P_j = C_j\left(P_i, W_h, \left(R_j - \frac{\dot{p}_i'}{p_i'}\right)P_i; T_j\right)$$

From this formulation, it is clear that given the prices of the inputs, an improvement in technology should lower unit costs and the price of the gross output. One can, therefore, write

$$-t_j = p_j - \left[\alpha_{ij}p_i + \beta_{hj}w_h + (\tau_{ij} + \delta_{ij})\left(r_j - \frac{\dot{p}_i'}{p_i'} + p_i\right)\right]$$

or

$$\alpha_{ij}p_i + \beta_{hj}w_h + (\tau_{ij} + \delta_{ij})\left(r_i - \frac{\dot{p}_i'}{p_i'} + p_i\right) - p_j = t_j$$

as we saw in the right-hand side of identity (1-27). One would say therefore that a higher rate of increase in the price of some intermediate input, such as oil, unless it depresses rates of return in energy-using industries, would lead, without any effect on multifactor productivity in the energy-using industries, to a higher rate of increase in prices in such an industry. The traditional measures of multifactor productivity at the industry level are then used to study differences between substitution among inputs of all kinds in a given state of knowledge and changes in the efficiency with which inputs are combined as changes in knowledge occur.

We have discussed, in general, the traditional measures of multifactor productivity at the industry level.[23] How would such measures be gathered together and presented for the economy as a whole?[24] At one time, it was believed that the appropriate industry output measures were constant-price

---

[23] This study is *not* concerned with the further questions as to ways in which multifactor productivity measures can be decomposed into returns to scale, increases in economic efficiency, "true" technical progress, and the like. For a recent example of such work see P. W. Bauer, "Decomposing TFP Growth in the Presence of Cost Inefficiency, Nonconstant Returns to Scale, and Technological Progress", Federal Reserve Bank of Cleveland, Working Paper 8813, December 1988.

[24] It was assumed in the foregoing that all firms in each industry were identical so that the measure of multifactor productivity for each firm and for the industry would be identical. Where firms are different, there is a problem of aggregating over firms to get industry measures.

value added, or in Canadian terms, constant-price gross domestic product.[25] With value added as the output concept, the traditional measures of total factor productivity will always be greater than measures produced with gross output since all intermediate inputs are netted out.[26] If value added were the output concept, then the aggregate measure of multifactor productivity would be

$$t = \frac{V_j}{V} t_j^*$$

where t_j^* are the *value-added* measures of multifactor productivity by industry, V_j/V is the share of *current-price* value added of industry j in aggregate value added, national income, or domestic product.[27]

Traditional measures of multifactor productivity at the industry level are now aggregated to the economy level by the Domar–Hulten aggregation procedure.[28] The implications for the traditional measures of the aggregation procedure are important. A simple example demonstrates.

Consider an industry k, fully integrated, that produces nothing but intermediate output used solely by industry j. The static accounts are

$$P_k Q_k = W_{hk} L_{hk} + (R_k - p_i') P_i K_{ik}$$

$$P_j Q_j = P_k M_{kj} + W_{hj} L_{hj} + (R_j - p_i') P_i K_{ij}$$

In terms of quantities, the traditional measures of multifactor productivity, ignoring depreciation, at the industry level are

$$q_k - [\beta_{hk} l_{hk} + (\tau_{ik} + \delta_{ik}) k_{ik}] = t_k$$

$$q_j - [\alpha_{kj} m_{kj} + \beta_{hj} l_{hj} + (\tau_{ij} + \delta_{ij}) k_{ij}] = t_j$$

The rate of multifactor productivity for the two industries taken together (as if it were a two-industry economy) by the Domar–Hulten procedure is

$$t = \frac{P_k Q_k}{V} t_k + \frac{P_j Q_j}{V} t_j = \frac{V_k}{V} \frac{P_k Q_k}{V_k} t_k + \frac{V_j}{V} \frac{P_j Q_j}{V_j} t_j$$

where the weights for the two industries are now

25 In our simple discussion, no attention is paid to indirect taxes and subsidies so that there is no difference between domestic product measured at factor cost or market prices.

26 Constant-price output measures at the value-added level are now recognized as highly misleading, except in the most trivial circumstances. See T. K. Rymes, *On Concepts of Capital and Technical Change* (Cambridge: Cambridge University Press, 1971), ch. 7 on net output, and T. P. Hill, *The Measurement of Real Product* (Paris: OECD, 1971).

27 No distinction is considered in this simple exposition between gross and net domestic product, i.e., net of depreciation or capital consumption used up.

28 E. D. Domar, "On the Measurement of Technological Change", *Economic Journal*, LXXI, December 1961, 709–29, and C. R. Hulten, "Growth Accounting with Intermediate Inputs", *Review of Economic Studies*, XLV, October 1978, 511–18.

$$\frac{V_k}{V}\frac{P_kQ_k}{V_k} \quad \text{and} \quad \frac{V_j}{V}\frac{P_jQ_j}{V_j}$$

or simply P_kQ_k/V and P_jQ_j/V.

Since industry k is wholly integrated, $P_kQ_k = V_k$, but because industry j uses intermediate inputs from industry k, $P_jQ_j > V_j$. Thus, the weights in the aggregation procedure sum to greater than unity. Thus, it is perfectly possible for the aggregate measure of multifactor productivity to be greater than the respective industry measures. Why?

It is clear that $m_{kj} = q_k$, that is, the growth rate of intermediate inputs from k to j equals the growth rate of the gross output of k. Hence, the traditional formula for t_j may be reexpressed as

$$q_j - [\alpha_{kj}(\beta_{hk}l_{hk} + (\tau_{ik} + \delta_{ik})k_{ik} + t_k) + \beta_{hj}l_{hj} + (\tau_{ij} + \delta_{ij})k_{ij}] = t_j$$

or

$$q_j - [\alpha_{kj}(\beta_{hk}l_{hk} + (\tau_{ik} + \delta_{ik})k_{ik}) + \beta_{hj}l_{hj} + (\tau_{ij} + \delta_{ij})k_{ij}] = t_j + \alpha_{kj}t_k$$

This reformulation shows that the final output of the economy, which is the gross output of industry j, is being produced with increased efficiency by the primary inputs directly involved in industry j *and* the primary inputs in industry k indirectly involved in the production of such final output.

The Domar–Hulten aggregation procedure yields

$$t = \frac{P_kQ_k}{V}t_k + \frac{P_jQ_j}{V}t_j$$

and this is equivalent[29] to

$$t = \alpha_{kj}t_k + t_j$$

Thus, the Domar–Hulten aggregation procedure, in order to derive meaningful measures of multiproductivity advance at the aggregate level, implicitly takes into account that in the industry producing final output, the intermediate inputs it is using are being produced with ever-increasing efficiency in the supplying industry. The Domar–Hulten aggregation pro-

---

[29] Since

$$V = V_k + V_j$$
$$= P_kQ_k + (\beta_{hj} + \tau_{ij} + \delta_{ij})P_jQ_j$$
$$= P_kM_{kj} + (\beta_{hj} + \tau_{ij} + \delta_{ij})P_jQ_j$$
$$= (\alpha_{kj} + \beta_{hj} + \tau_{ij} + \delta_{ij})P_jQ_j$$
$$= P_jQ_j$$

then

$$t = \frac{P_kQ_k}{V}t_k + \frac{P_jQ_j}{V}t_j$$
$$= \alpha_{kj}t_k + t_j \qquad \text{Q.E.D.}$$

cedure means that the fact that intermediate inputs are being produced more efficiently outside the using or receiving industry is, in effect, being implicitly taken into account, whereas when the individual industry measures are prepared, the measurement of the interindustry interdependence of the improving technology is explicitly ruled out. This seems at best inconsistent.

The general treatment of reproducible inputs in the new measures of multifactor productivity in an economy characterized by technological interdependence is the matter to which we now turn.

D   New measures of multifactor productivity

The basic distinction between the traditional and the new measures of multifactor productivity advanced in this study is that the new ones take into account the producibility of capital inputs.

We investigate this distinction by examining the simplest of all possible cases. Reconsider identity (1-27),

$$q_j - \left[\alpha_{ij} m_{ij} + \beta_{hj} l_{hj} + \tau_{ij} k_{ij} + \delta_{ij} \left(\frac{\dot{p}_i'}{p_i'} + k_{ij} \right) \right]$$
$$= t_j$$
$$= [\alpha_{ij} p_i + \beta_{hj} w_{hj} + \tau_{ij} (r_j + p_i) + \delta_{ij} p_i] - p_j$$

and examine the flow of intermediate input into industry j *that comes from itself* – a flow known in National Accounting as intra-industry intermediate input and output. There are many examples of such flows: Telephone companies use their own services to produce their outputs, wheat farmers use wheat as seed inventory, coal mines use coal to produce coal, construction companies use their own activities to repair their own buildings, and so forth. Industry measures of gross output can be inclusive or exclusive of such intra-industry flows of intermediate inputs and outputs.[30] From a technical or transformation function viewpoint, it is essential that such inputs be treated as part of all the inputs being used by an industry. One of the components of $\alpha_{ij} m_{ij}$ will be $\alpha_{jj} m_{jj}$ because behind it lies the production function

$$Q_j = Q_j(..., M_{jj}, ...; T_j)$$

and in terms of prices, one of the components of $\alpha_{ij} p_j$ will be $\alpha_{jj} p_j$ because behind it lies the unit cost function

$$P_j = C_j(..., P_j, ...; T_j)$$

---

[30] Even at the level of the individual firm, intrafirm shipments are common. The measures of gross output by industry can then be gross of intrafirm as well as intra-industry flows.

If industry j improves its productivity, then it is immediately clear that its own-account intermediate inputs, M_{jj}, are being produced more efficiently than before. One would want to account for the fact that such intra-industry inputs would require fewer inputs than before to produce them. Indeed, since they are part of the gross output of the industry, appearing there as intermediate output, in the measurement of multifactor productivity, increases in the efficiency with which they are being produced is, in fact, *partially* taken into account by the traditional measures. The new measures take such advances *wholly* into account. They are constructed to do this! If one ignores all the other inputs, the new measure would be

$$q_j - [\alpha_{jj}(m_{jj} - h_j) + \cdots] = h_j = [\alpha_{jj}(p_j + h_j) + \cdots] - p_j$$

On the quantity side, one solves for h_j, and in this case

$$h_j = (1 - \alpha_{jj})^{-1} t_j$$

The new measure of the rate of multifactor productivity will be greater than the traditional measure if the industry has intra-industry or own-account intermediate inputs and outputs.[31] The new measures, as the term $m_{jj} - h_j$ indicates, adjusts the own-account intermediate inputs for the changing efficiency with which they are produced. The growth of all the inputs required to produce the intermediate inputs, $m_{jj} - h_j$, is less than

[31] If the traditional measures for industry j were prepared by the Domar–Hulten aggregation procedure, one would have

$$t_j^* = \frac{P_j Q_j}{P_j Q_j - P_j M_{jj}} t_j = (1 - \alpha_{jj})^{-1} t_j$$

so that the aggregation procedure yields traditional measures t_j^* identical to the new measures. In this case, the traditional measure *nets out* the intra-industry intermediate inputs and flows. If the gross output measure were constructed net of such flows, the traditional measure, ignoring depreciation, would be

$$\frac{q_j - \alpha_{jj} m_{jj} - [\alpha_{ij} m_{ij} + \beta_{hj} l_{hj} + (r_{ij} + \delta_{ij})k_{ij}]}{1 - \alpha_{jj}} = t_j^*$$

where, if the output final to industry j is growing at the same rate as its intermediate output, it would be

$$(1 - \alpha_{jj})^{-1} t_j = t_j^*$$

The theory behind the traditional measures being prepared with gross output measures net of intra-industry intermediate inputs and outputs is that profit-maximizing firms use own-account intermediate inputs up to the point where

$$P_j \frac{\partial Q_j}{\partial M_{jj}} = P_j$$

or that the marginal physical product of own-account intermediate inputs would, under competitive conditions, be unity.

the growth of the intermediate inputs, m_{jj}. With increases in efficiency, the growth of the prices of the inputs required to produce the intermediate inputs, $p_j + h_j$, will exceed the growth of the prices of the intermediate inputs themselves, p_j. Differentiation of the unit cost function gives results that make the identical point in a different but more illuminating way! One has

$$[\alpha_{jj} p_j + \cdots] - p_j = t_j$$

The change in the price of the output is expressed in terms of the change in the prices of inputs of the industry and the improvement in their productivity. That must be true as well for the price of the own-account intermediate input. The new measures would therefore show the change in the price of the inputs *primary* to the industry, or

$$[\alpha_{jj}(p_j + h_j) + \cdots] - p_j = h_j$$

so that again

$$(1 - \alpha_{jj})^{-1}[\alpha_{jj} p_j + \cdots] - p_j = (1 - \alpha_{jj})^{-1} t_j = h_j$$

The new measures, therefore, can be said to measure the improvement in the multifactor productivity of industry j when the factors are primary to that industry and adjust for the fact that the own-account intermediate inputs are themselves being produced with greater efficiency by the industry's primary inputs.[32]

The traditional measures are not invariant to the output concept (even when all components of gross output, final and intermediate) are changing at the same rate. That is, $t_j^* > t_j$, as we have seen. Suppose we construct the new measures for gross output restricted to exclude intra-industry flows. We would have

$$\frac{q_j - \alpha_{jj} m_{jj}}{1 - \alpha_{jj}} - \frac{[\alpha_{ij} m_{ij} + \cdots]}{1 - \alpha_{jj}} = h_j^* = \frac{[\alpha_{ij} p_j + \cdots]}{1 - \alpha_{jj}} - p_j$$

whereas if we prepared the new measures for the gross output concept *inclusive* of intra-industry intermediate outputs, we have

$$q_j - [\alpha_{jj}(m_{jj} - h_j) + \alpha_{ij} m_{ij} + \cdots] = h_j = [\alpha_{jj}(p_i + h_j) + \alpha_{ij} p_i + \cdots] - p_j$$

---

[32] When the traditional measures are prepared using prices of inputs and outputs, it would be immediately clear from

$$P_j = C_j(\ldots, P_i, P_j, \ldots, W_h, \ldots; T_j)$$

that one would want to solve for P_j and work with a net cost function

$$P_j = C_j^*(\ldots, P_i, \ldots, W_h, \ldots; T_j^*)$$

before estimating the change in the technology parameter.

so that

$$\frac{q_i - \alpha_{jj} m_{jj}}{1 - \alpha_{jj}} - \frac{[\alpha_{ij} m_{ij} + \cdots]}{1 - \alpha_{jj}} = h_j = \frac{[\alpha_{ij} p_i + \cdots]}{1 - \alpha_{jj}} - p_j$$

Thus, $h_j = h_j^*$. The new measures have, in this sense, a robust quality not shared by the traditional measures.

The new measures make such results general for all technologically interdependent industries. Restrict the discussion to intermediate inputs and outputs. For industry j, the new measures would be

$$q_j - \left[\alpha_{jj}(m_{jj} - h_j) + \alpha_{ij}(m_{ij} - h_i) + \beta_{hj} l_{hj} + \tau_{ij} k_{ij} + \delta_{ij}\left(\frac{p_i'}{p_i} + k_{ij}\right) \right]$$

$$= h_j = [\alpha_{jj}(p_j + h_j) + \alpha_{ij}(p_i + h_i) + \beta_{nj} w_{hj} + \tau_{ij}(r_j + p_i) + \delta_{ij} p_i] - p_j$$

There would be similar measures for all the other industries!

We see immediately that the new measures have an important data requirement not needed by the traditional measures. The new ones require knowledge of the to whom–from whom interindustry technological relationships provided by input–output accounts such as those produced by Statistics Canada.

What is the meaning again of such entries as $m_{ij} - h_i$ and $p_k + h_k$ in a measure of total factor productivity for industry j? The expression m_{ij} measures the rate of change of intermediate outputs from industry i used as inputs in industry j, h_i is an expression of the rate of change in the productivity of those factors *primary* to industry i, and $m_{ij} - h_j$ measures therefore the services of inputs primary to industry i used indirectly, through the use of the intermediate input–output technology, in industry j. The new concept of total factor productivity advanced here therefore deals with the increase in the productivity of primary nonproduced inputs used *directly* and *indirectly* in industry j.

On the price side, the expression p_k shows the rate of change of the price of the intermediate output produced in industry k used in industry j and h_k measures the rate of change in the productivity of those factors *primary* to industry k, so that $p_k + h_k$ measures the rate of change in the prices of primary inputs in industry k *used indirectly* in industry j. The new concept of multifactor productivity measures the rate at which the prices of primary inputs used directly *and indirectly* in industry j are transformed, via increases in their productivity, to rates of change in the price of industry j's output.

Consider again the two-industry example provided in the preceding with respect to the Domar–Hulten aggregation procedure. For simplicity ignore most of the nonintermediate inputs. The traditional measures are

$$q_k - [\cdots + \tau_{ik} k_{ik} + \cdots] = t_k = [\beta_{hk} W_h + \cdots] - p_k$$

and

$$q_j - [\alpha_{kj} m_{kj} + \cdots + \tau_{ij} k_{ij} + \cdots] = t_j = [\alpha_{kj} p_k + \beta_{hj} w_h + \cdots] - p_j$$

where again industry k, itself fully integrated, supplies industry j with intermediate inputs.

The new measures are

$$q_k - [\cdots + \tau_{ik} k_{ik} + \cdots] = h_k = [\beta_{hk} w_h + \cdots] - p_k$$

and

$$q_j - [\alpha_{kj} (m_{kj} - h_k) + \cdots] = h_j = [\alpha_{kj} (p_k + h_k) + \cdots] - p_j$$

The difference is immediate. *For the wholly integrated industry, the traditional and new measures are identical.* If, however, the traditional measures show no productivity advance in the using industry, that is, $t_j = 0$, but that industry is using relatively more of the intermediate inputs from the supplying industry, then $h_j > 0$, that is, the new measures will be showing that industry j, using primary inputs directly and *indirectly*, is experiencing an advance in productivity. What is that advance? It is clear that $h_j = \alpha_{kj} h_k = \alpha_{kj} t_k$.[33] *This is precisely the measure of multifactor productivity traditionally produced when an aggregate measure was required.*

The new measures are aggregated differently. The new measures are aggregated by means of each industry's contribution to total final output. In the example, all of industry k's gross output is intermediate output; it has no final output. The only industry with final output is industry j. Thus, for the two industries taken together the aggregate new measure of total factor productivity is

$$h = e_k h_k + e_j h_j$$

where e is the share of each industry's final output in total final output.

Since in our simple example $e_k = 0$ and $e_j = 1$, then

$$h = h_j = \alpha_{kj} h_k = \alpha_{kj} t_k$$

It will be noted that the new aggregate measures are based on each individual industry's interdependent measure and that the interdependence is

---

[33] That is,

$$q_j - [\alpha_{kj} m_{kj} + \cdots] + \alpha_{kj} h_k = h_j = \alpha_{kj} h_k + [\alpha_{kj} p_k + \cdots] - p_j$$

However,

$$q_j - [\alpha_{kj} m_{kj} + \cdots] = t_j = [\alpha_{kj} p_k + \cdots] - p_i$$

which are assumed to be zero.

in each industry's measure and is not, as it is in the traditional measures, implanted in the measures by an aggregation procedure.

For intermediate inputs, the aggregate new measure, at least for a closed economy, will be the same as the Domar–Hulten aggregate of the traditional measures of total factor productivity. The aggregate traditional measure arrives at that result by a process of aggregation that takes the intermediate input–output interdependent technology into account but does not take such interdependence into account in preparing any individual industry's measure. The new measures take the interdependence into account in preparing each individual industry's measure and do not impose it as an aggregation procedure.

If the two industries k and j were interdependent in a more complicated sense in that they would both supply each other with intermediate inputs, we would have, in matrix notation,

$$\begin{bmatrix} t_k \\ t_j \end{bmatrix} = \begin{bmatrix} 1 & 0 \\ 0 & 1 \end{bmatrix}\begin{bmatrix} h_k \\ h_j \end{bmatrix} - \begin{bmatrix} 0 & \alpha_{jk} \\ \alpha_{kj} & 0 \end{bmatrix}\begin{bmatrix} h_k \\ h_j \end{bmatrix}$$

or

$$\begin{bmatrix} t_k \\ t_j \end{bmatrix} = \left(\begin{bmatrix} 1 & 0 \\ 0 & 1 \end{bmatrix} - \begin{bmatrix} 0 & \alpha_{jk} \\ \alpha_{kj} & 0 \end{bmatrix} \right)\begin{bmatrix} h_k \\ h_j \end{bmatrix}$$

and the use of the input–output accounts, with respect to cost shares, now becomes clear. When $\bar{t}$ and $\bar{h}$ are n-row vectors of individual industry traditional and new measures of multifactor productivity, we have $\bar{t} = [I - A]\bar{h}$ when I is the identity matrix and A is the matrix of intermediate input–output cost shares, so that if $I - A$ permits, one has $[I - A]^{-1}\bar{t} = \bar{h}$.

The traditional aggregate measure of multifactor productivity using the Domar–Hulten procedure for a closed economy is

$$t = P\hat{Q}\hat{E}^{-1}\bar{t}$$

where $P\hat{Q}\hat{E}^{-1}$ is a n-column vector where each element is an industry's gross output, PQ, expressed as a share of *total* value added or final output for the whole economy, E.[34]

The new aggregate measure of total factor productivity is

$$h = e\hat{E}^{-1}\bar{h}$$

where $e\hat{E}^{-1}$ is a n-column vector where each element is an industry's final output, e, expressed as a proportion of total final output, E.

At the aggregate level and with respect *only* to intermediate inputs, the traditional and new measures are the same. The new measures take the

---

[34] The weights are also, as we have seen, $P\hat{Q}\hat{V}^{-1}\hat{V}\hat{E}^{-1}$, where each element is each industry's gross output as a proportion of its value added multiplied by its value added as a proportion of total value added or final output.

technological interdependence into account in preparing each industry's measure. The traditional measure takes the interdependence into account only as an aggregation procedure when it nets out the intermediate input–output flows to measure the aggregate productivity advance of primary nonintermediate inputs for the whole economy. The new measures focus always on the productivity advance of such primary inputs and therefore do not have to get multifactor productivity measures for such primary inputs by the aggregation procedure of "netting out" intermediate inputs.

The new measures, however, go beyond customary intermediate inputs in their treatment of producible inputs in a technologically interdependent set of industries. The accounts for industry j are, again,

$$q_j - \left[\alpha_{ij}(m_{ij} - h_i) + \beta_{hj}l_{hj} + \tau_{ij}(k_{ij} - h_i) + \delta_{ij}\left(\frac{\dot{p}_i'}{p_i'} + k_{ij} - h_i \right) \right]$$

$$= h_j$$

$$= [\alpha_{ij}(p_i + h_i) + \beta_{hj}w_h + \tau_{ij}(r_j + p_i + h_i) + \delta_{ij}(p_i + h_i)] - p_j \qquad (1\text{-}30)$$

Consider first the treatment of depreciation or capital consumption. It is straightforward because depreciation is merely another example of intermediate flows of inputs. If industry j uses up capital in its production and in the capital goods industries technological advances are taking place, then the production cost of the capital being used up in the production of Q_j measured in terms of the primary inputs required for its replacement is being reduced. The traditional measures ignore this; the new measures explicitly take into account the fact that ongoing technological advance in the capital-supplying industries means that the primary input replacement cost of capital consumption or depreciation is being reduced.

In matrix terms, we would have

$$\bar{\imath} = [I - A - \hat{D}]\bar{h}$$

so that

$$[I - A - \hat{D}]^{-1}\bar{\imath} = \bar{h}$$

where D is the matrix of capital consumption allowances that industry shares in gross output. Again

$$h = e^N E^{N-1}\bar{h}$$

where the weights are the shares of each industry in *net* final output.[35]

---

[35] With net final output (or net national income), which is, for the simple economy under review, consumption plus net (of depreciation) capital formation, the new measures are a measure of multifactor productivity by what E. F. Denison calls end-product total factor productivity. Compare E. F. Denison, *Estimates of Productivity Change in Industry: An Evaluation and an Alternative* (Washington, D.C.: the Brookings Institution, 1989). It assumes that each industry's multifactor productivity in the new sense provided in this study applies equally to its final as well as its intermediate output.

The new measures press on, however, into the most contentious areas of measurement. Consider the term $k_{ij} - h_i$. The expression k_{ij} is the rate of change of the services of the net stock of capital producible in industry i in industry j. The subtraction of the h_i term means that services are measured in terms of the rate of change of the primary inputs in the capital goods industry i capable of producing such capital goods. What, however, is the nonproduced primary input, similar to labour and land, associated with the capital input? It is the waiting or the postponement of potential consumption for which owners of the capital goods are paid! If the capital goods industries experience an advance in productivity, then not only is capital consumption in industry j being replaced more cheaply than before, but even more importantly, the services of the net stocks of capital in industry j are also producible currently more cheaply than before, but even more importantly, the services of the net stocks of capital in industry j are also producible currently more cheaply than before. The flow of waiting or consumption forgone that has to be undertaken to obtain and/or augment the net capital stocks and their flow of services is being reduced.

The new measures provide estimates of the multifactor productivity of the fundamental primary nonproduced inputs in industries each taken separately and all together in capital-accumulating technologically interdependent economies. The primary nonproduced inputs are the services of labour, land, and waiting. In a technically progressive economy primary inputs do not include the services of capital goods or the capital goods themselves for they are producible by the economic system. Increases in them are accounted for to a precisely measurable extent by technical progress. The producibility of traditionally conceived capital inputs is rigorously accounted for by the new measures. Since the primary inputs are labour, land, and waiting, the new multifactor productivity measures also reflect the rate at which the real incomes of the owners and providers of the services of labour, land, and waiting will be changing through time because of advances in knowledge.

Consider the "price side" of our new productivity measures, particularly with respect to the net returns to capital. For industry j, we have

$$[\cdots + \tau_{ij}(r_j + p_i + h_i) + \cdots] - p_j = h_j$$

In traditional terms, the expression $r_j + p_i$ measures the rate of change of the net rental $R_j P_i$ earned on the stock of capital goods that can be produced in industry i owned and used in industry j, the net rental being interpreted as the price of the service of the capital good. What the new measures need is the rate of change in the prices of the primary inputs associated with capital used in industry j. If there are advances in the productivity of the capital goods industries, then any waiting in industry j can result in a larger flow of capital goods and their associated services in industry j. The efficiency of waiting will be increasing, and therefore the price of waiting will be rising faster than the price or net rental of the services of the capital goods.

In matrix terms, we would again have

$$\bar{t} = [I - A - (E + \hat{D})]\bar{h} \qquad [I - A - (E + \hat{D})]^{-1}\bar{t} = \bar{h}$$

where E is the matrix of net returns to capital industry shares in gross output.[36] Again, the aggregate measure is

$$h = e^N E^{N-1} \bar{h}$$

with the industry weights continuing to be each industry's contribution to net final output.

New measures of total factor productivity that are different from traditional measures have been introduced and discussed in extremely simple terms in this chapter. Traditionally, one writes of the productivity of labour, land, and capital. One should write of the productivity of labour, land, and waiting or consumption forgone. An evaluation of the traditional and new measures and their major strengths and weaknesses, particularly of the new measures, is provided in Chapter 2.

Appendix I Multifactor productivity measures and nonexhaustible and exhaustible natural agents of production

The new measures of multifactor productivity change can incorporate the services of nonproduced natural agents of production such as land and ore bodies.

A schematic view of the static and dynamic accounts for such inputs is now presented.

Assume that there exist two types of natural agents of production: land and ore. From land, a flow of services can be said to originate that is inexhaustible; that is, the powers of the soil are God given and cannot by any economic activity be augmented or reduced. The land is therefore a Ricardian natural agent. There is as well an exhaustible natural agent such as a body of ore. As it is used, its supply and, therefore, the flow of potential services embodied in it are reduced and cannot be augmented by economic production.[37] The ore body is said to be subject to depletion.

---

[36] The shares $E + \hat{D}$ are therefore the shares of the gross returns to capital.

[37] In reality, of course, land is worn out by intensive use, but the services of land can be augmented by fertilization (an intermediate input or capital formation) and exhaustible natural agents (biological natural agents such as fish and forests) can be augmented by a production (again a form of an intermediate input or capital formation).

Consider the Ricardian land first. The accounts and matrices in Chapter 1 would be augmented by $RP_n N$, where (in any industry) N is the stock of the services of land and RP_n is the rental. In the case of capital goods we had RP_k as the (net) rental for a capital good. Here we have RP_n as the gross (equal to net) rental for the services of a homogeneous stock of land.

Then in the matrix of primary inputs for the quantity system, one has

$$N_1 + N_2 + \cdots + N_n = \bar{N}$$
$$T_1 Q_1 + T_2 Q_2 + \cdots + T_n Q_n = \bar{N}$$

where $T_j = N_j / Q_j$ for all j, or $TQ = N$. To the system outlined in the text we would add a third relationship,

to $\quad B[I-A]^{-1}[C+\Delta K] = \bar{L}$

and $\quad E[I-A]^{-1}[C+\Delta K] = \hat{K}$

we add $\quad T[I-A]^{-1}[C+\Delta K] = \bar{N}$

as the three primary inputs: services of labour L, waiting $\hat{K}$, and land N. With technical progress, however, because land is not producible, it can be treated in the same fashion as labour and waiting, or the way in which traditional measures of multifactor productivity treat "capital".

In industry j, a new entry would appear in the multifactor productivity identity as set out in Chapter 2. Focussing only on this new entry, we would have

$$q_j - [\cdots + \epsilon_{nj} n_j] = h_j = [\cdots + \epsilon_{nj}(r_j + p_n) + \cdots] - p_j$$

where ϵ_{nj} is the share of the rental on land in industry j's gross output, n_j is the rate of change in the quantity of the services of land (for many types of land, we would deal in vectors), and p_n is the rate of change in the stock price of land so that $r_j + p_n$ is the rate of change in the rental on land owned in industry j.

Consider now the ore body. Our accounts would be augmented by

$$RP_n^* N^* + \tau^* P_n^* N^*$$

where τ^* is the rate of depletion and the asterisks represent exhaustible natural agents. The depletion of the ore bodies cannot be inserted into the matrix of intermediate input flows because ore bodies are not produced in any part of the economy.

In addition, the static-quantity accounts have

$$rT^*[I-A]^{-1}[C+\Delta K] = rN^*$$

where

$$T^* = [t_{kj}] = \frac{[N_{kj}^*]}{Q_j}$$

The new dynamic identity for quantities for industry j would be

$$q_j - [\alpha_{ij}(m_{ij} - h_j)] + \beta_{ij} l_j + \tau_{ij}(k_{ij} - h_j)$$

$$+ \delta_{ij} \left[\frac{\dot{p}_i'}{p_i'} + (k_{ij} - h_i) \right] + \epsilon_j n_j^* + \tau_j^*(n_j^*) = h_j$$

where $\epsilon_j n_j^*$ is the share of rents (e.g., royalties) on exhaustible natural agents in industry j's gross output times the rate of change of the stock of such agents in industry j and $\tau_j^*(n_j^*)$ is the share of depletion of such agents in gross output times the rates of change in the rates of depletion and stocks of natural exhaustible agents of production in industry j.

For any industry, the stocks of "land" can be changing because the industry can be buying or selling land. Similarly, any industry can be buying or selling stocks of exhaustible natural agents.

The new dynamic identity for prices can be similarly constructed. In principle, therefore, the new measures of multifactor productivity can be augmented to show the changing efficiency of labour, waiting, and non-exhaustible and exhaustible natural agents of production.

With technical progress, however, the concept of the depleting stock of exhaustible natural agents becomes ambiguous since technical progress and learning would seem to involve the continual discovery, appearance, and subsequent using up of such inputs as well as the continual reduction in the cost of Ricardian natural agents such as land.

The important problem alluded to here is that what are "given" natural agents such as ore bodies cannot even be ascertained independently of the state of technology. Consider the case of oil. At one time, oil was not scarce and pools of oil reserves had no value – that is, no net rents accrued to oil reserves. (Indeed, at one time oil oozed out of the ground in certain places and impeded the work of horses in Canadian agriculture. Moreover, the complete stock or reserves of oil pools would be unknown since the lack of scarcity value of oil would make the acquisition of such costly information unprofitable.) Given the preferences of individuals, however, advances in technology – such as the invention of the internal combustion engine – made oil reserves scarce and therefore valuable. The emergence of rent accruing to such reserves arises from technical advance.[38] The ques-

---

[38] In general, of course, technical advance will see profits (and losses) arise in many activities unless the advances are perfectly foreseen. These profits, called quasi-rents, will be competed away so that net returns to capital in the various activities will not include such profits (or losses). Indeed, if care is taken in setting out "costs of adjustment" in all activities, it follows definitionally that such quasi-rents are everywhere and at all times competed away. In the case of natural agents, however, whose scarcity value arises because of technical advance, the net *rents* will not be competed away.

When a technical advance occurs that makes certain exhaustible natural agents scarce,

tion is: Should the depletion allowances – those charges arising from the using up or exhaustion of this now scarce resource – be charges against the gross product of the economy?

The problem is clear: Past technical advances created the scarcity value of the natural agents in question; indeed, without such technical advance the inputs in question would not be enumerated. Future technical advances, though unknown today, *may* undercut the scarcity of those very natural agents whose net rents are the result of past technical advances. Resource economic theory is concerned with the question of the optimum or efficient rate at which such ore bodies should be used up and must postulate the extent to which future technical advances will undercut the scarcity of such natural agents in the future in order to derive the optimal rate of exploitation.[39]

National accounting theory would suggest, however, that the depletion of ore bodies should be charged against gross output. Within the context so far developed and implemented, the contemporary net output of an economy is a concept that relates to the given state of technology and not to prospective technology, it being understood, of course, that current expectations and prices will be affected by contemporary views about prospective technology. If current changes in technology undercut the scarcity value of certain ore bodies (i.e., the rise in the value of oil reserves may have been associated with a fall in the value of coal reserves) such that it is no longer profitable to exploit them, then depletion allowances will fall to zero since the cessation of economical exploitation means that the ore bodies *are,* in fact, no longer being depleted. Yet the matter remains that what are exhaustible natural agents cannot be ascertained independently of technology, and changes in technology result in a changing inventory of such natural agents. Over time, improvements in technology will be associated with increasing volumes of such scarce exhaustible agents. Though not produced like capital agents, the volume (or constant-price value) of exhaustible natural agents will tend to increase along with improvements in technology. No allowance, however, should be made for this phenomenon to affect the new measures of multifactor productivity advances.

not all will be equally accessible to profitable exploitation. Certain pools of oil reserves will be exhausted first and others later. Thus, exhaustible natural agents, just like Ricardian lands, will have differential scarcities and rents according to their exploitation costs. The principle that net rents to exhaustible natural agents arise because of technical advance nonetheless remains.

[39] Private owners of ore bodies, determining how much of the ore capacity to sell, must also form a view as to how valuable the remaining ore body will be and the stock price of the ore body will therefore reflect expected rates of technical advance.

CHAPTER 2

An evaluation of the traditional and new measures of multifactor productivity

A   Introduction

The formula for multifactor productivity measurement can be expressed in either the traditional way [identity (1-27)], that is,

$$q_j - \left[\alpha_{ij} m_{ij} + \beta_{hk} l_{hj} + \tau_{ij} k_i + \delta_{ij} \left(\frac{\dot{p}_i'}{p_i'} + k_{ij} \right) \right]$$

$$= t_j$$

$$= [\alpha_{ij} p_i + \beta_{hj} w_{hj} + \tau_{ij}(r_{ij} + p_i) + \delta_{ij} p_i] - p_j$$

or in the new way [identity (1-30)], that is,

$$q_j = \left[\alpha_{ij}(m_{ij} - h_i) + \beta_{hj} l_{nj} + \tau_{ij}(k_{ij} - h_i) + \delta_{ij} \left(\frac{\dot{p}_i'}{p_i'} + k_{ij} - h_i \right) \right]$$

$$= h_j$$

$$= [\alpha_{ij}(p_i + h_i) + \beta_{hj} w_{hj} + \tau_{ij}(r_j + p_i + h_i) + \delta_{ij}(p_i + h_i)] - p_j$$

In successive periods of time, in general, not only will all rates of change of quantities of outputs and inputs and their prices be different for all industries, but also the cost shares by industry will change.

The changes in cost shares as weights result from substitution among inputs for a given technology and nonneutralities in advances in technical knowledge. Moreover, the net final output weights will also be changing year by year so that the new aggregate measures of multifactor productivity, as well as the traditional measures, will reflect substitution, nonneutral advances in technology, income effects, and changes in tastes. In the face of such complexity, it is useful to deal with examples where the differences between the traditional and new measures, particularly at the individual industry and aggregate levels, can be sharply drawn and explored. To focus on differences between the traditional and new measures, we explore cases where the cost shares for all the reproducible inputs do *not* change over time.

Consider the net returns to capital as a share of the cost of producing gross output in industry j. From

$$\tau_{ij} = \frac{R_j P_i K_{ij}}{P_j Q_j}$$

the change in τ_{ij},

$$\dot{\tau}_{ij}/\tau_{ij} = r_j + p_i + k_{ij} - (p_j + q_j) = 0$$

if

i. $r_j = 0$ and $p_i = p_j$ and $k_{ij} = q_j$; that is, the cost share will show no change when the net rate of return to capital is unchanged and all capital input prices show the same rate of change as output prices and the quantities of all capital inputs show the same rate of change as output quantities; or

ii. $r_j = 0$ and $p_i - p_j + k_{ij} - q_j = 0$; that is, the cost share will show no change when the net rate of return is unchanged and the *value* of the net capital stock–gross output ratio is unchanged; or

iii. $r_j > 0$, $p_i - p_j = 0$ and $k_{ij} - q_j < 0$ such that $r_j + k_{ij} - q_j = 0$; that is, the net rate of return is increasing whereas the quantity capital-output ratio is decreasing in an offsetting way or $r_j + p_i - p_j > 0$ and $k_{ij} - q_j < 0$ so that both the net rate of return and the price of the gross output of activity j are rising to offset the increase in the gross output of j relative to the capital input.

A similar taxonomy could be prepared for all the cost shares. The share of net returns to capital in industry j's gross output could be constant at the same time as advances in productivity in it and related supplying industries are such that the cost share of one kind of intermediate input is rising while that for a different kind is falling in an offsetting way. Furthermore, there is no reason to assume the static technology is such that when substitution among inputs occurs because their relative prices are changing, the cost shares will remain unchanged.

A focus on the net (and gross) returns to capital cost share is useful, however, for relating our examination of the two measures of multifactor productivity to the relevant economic theory.

Economic theorists would in general classify the first two cases, *dealing with capital producible inputs,* as Harrod neutral technical progress, and the third is related to Hicks neutral technical progress.[1] For both

---

[1] Hicks, *The Theory of Wages.* The Hicksian definition of neutrality refers to pairs of inputs and entails that the ratio of the marginal products of the inputs remain unchanged. If relative input prices meter relative marginal products and if relative input prices are unchanging, then so must relative input quantities (otherwise the cost shares will change) and the technical change would be Hicks neutral. If value shares are constant, however, then relative input–output prices must move in offsetting ways to relative input–output quantities in the manner outlined in the text for Hicks neutrality to apply. For a discussion of a concept of Hicksian neutrality in which relative input–output prices and relative input–output quantities do not move in offsetting ways, see C. Blackorby, C. A. K. Lovell, and M. C. Thursby, "Extended Hicks Neutral Technical Change", *Economic Journal,* LXXXVI, December 1976, 845–52.

Harrod and Hicks, neutral technical progress with respect to producible intermediate inputs shares would be

$$\dot{\alpha}_{ij} = p_i + m_{ij} - p_j - q_j = 0$$
$$= p_i - p_j = m_{ij} - q_j = 0 \quad \text{(for Harrod)}$$

and

$$p_i - p_j > 0 \quad \text{and} \quad m_{ij} - q_j < 0 \quad \text{(for Hicks)}$$

For nonproducible inputs, such as labour, one would have

$$\dot{\beta}_{hj} = w_h - p_j + l_{hj} - q_j = 0$$

where, for both Harrod and Hicks, neutral advance would entail $w_h - p_j > 0$ and $l_{hj} - q_j < 0$.

It will be noted that for *all* inputs the Hicks definition is the same. The fact that some inputs are produced and some are not plays no essential role in the Hicks definition. The Harrod conception of neutral technical progress was designed to take into account precisely this fundamental difference among inputs.

Consider Hicksian neutrality first. It would appear that for a single isolated activity the Hicksian concept is perfectly clear. For given amounts of intermediate inputs, labour and capital services and capital being used up, output would increase so that one would have

$$q_j - m_{ij} = q_j - l_{nj} = q_j - k_{ij} > 0$$

and in terms of prices, if the prices of the inputs are given to the activity, then the unit cost or price of its output will fall so that one would have

$$p_i - p_j = w_{hj} - p_j = r_j + p_i - p_j = p_i - p_j > 0$$

that is, in terms of Hicksian neutrality, one would expect the gross output per unit of every kind of input to rise at the same rate, and one would expect every own-product price to rise proportionately as well. Thus, for example, if the prices of all the inputs were given for industry j, one should expect competition to push down the price of the gross output of industry so that, for instance, $r_j + p_i - p_j$; the gross rental on each of the capital inputs in own-product terms would rise as the same rate as the own-product wage rate, $w_{hj} - p_j$. These apparently unambiguous[2] results depend upon the degree to which the activity is integrated. A nonintegrated activity is one that produces none of its own input. In the Hicksian

---

[2] If technical progress in industry j does not result in a decline in the unit cost and price of the gross output of industry j, then the net rate of return to capital in industry j must rise relative to other industries or the spot prices of existing capital goods in industry j will be increased in price, both leading to greater accumulation in industry j. The text maintains the symmetry of the Hicks definition of neutrality for both quantities and prices.

case, a neutral advance in technology means that no input is affected *in its production* by the technical advance.

If we consider, however, industry j as producing intermediate inputs for itself (again, the example of a coal mine using coal in its operations is typical), then the change in the cost share of such own-accounts intermediate inputs will be

$$p_j - p_j + m_{jj} - q_j$$

It is clear that $p_j - p_j = 0$; that is, the own-product price of something in its own units cannot vary. In order for $q_j - m_{jj} > 0$, however, the cost share should be decreasing. This implies that some or all of the other cost shares for industry j are changing, which contradicts the assumption of Hicksian neutrality. In order for the cost share to be unchanging, it must be the case that $m_{jj} - q_j = 0$. Industry j, experiencing "neutral" progress of the Hicksian type, will see its output rising relatively to all of its inputs, *except* those it produces for itself. The traditional measure of multifactor productivity, using prices first, would be

$$\alpha_{ij}(p_i - p_j) + \alpha_{jj}(p_j - p_j) + \beta_{lhj}(w_h - p_j)$$
$$+ \tau_{ij}(r_{ij} + p_i - p_j) + \delta_{ij}(p_i - p_j) = t_j$$

With Hicksian neutrality, in all cases the proportionate change in relative prices will be the same, *excluding the own-account inputs!* For the case of a completely nonintegrated industry, t_j would be the equal proportionate change in our product relative prices. For the case of a limited degree of integration, t_j would, however, be less than the equal change in relative prices so the concept and measurement of neutral Hicksian technical progress *is not independent of the degree of integration*. The same measure, using quantities, would be

$$\alpha_{ij}(q_j - m_{ij}) + \alpha_{jj}(q_j - m_{jj}) + \beta_{lhj}(q_j - l_{hj})$$
$$+ \tau_{ij}(q_j - k_{ij}) + \delta_{ij}(q_j - k_{ij}) = t_j$$

Again all output–input ratios would be increasing at the same rate, except one, Q_j/M_{jj}, which would be constant so that $q_j - m_{jj} = 0$. Once again, t_j would be less than the equal change in output relative to inputs, and the measurement of multifactor productivity in the Hicks neutral case would not be invariant to integration.

In Chapter 1, we saw that in this case the Domar–Hulten aggregation procedure eliminates this nonrobustness of the traditional measure by netting out the effects of the own-account intermediate inputs. From the production or transformation function sense of productivity measurement, however, there is no justification for the elimination of such intermediate inputs.

The effects of integration on the traditional measures do *not* depend on the assumption of neutrality. When productivity advance is occurring in the industry in question, economic theory suggests that own-product relative prices and own-product input–output relative quantities would behave differently than their non-own-product counterparts. Traditional measures of multifactor productivity would be affected by the degree of integration whether or not neutral technological change is occurring. The assumption of neutrality is employed simply to sharpen the distinction between the traditional and new measures of multifactor productivity and to focus on what distinguishes them.

As was shown in Chapter 1, the new measures are not affected by such limited integration. Indeed, what the new measures show is that an industry, if it is improving its productivity, will be producing and using more of its own-account intermediate inputs. The traditional measures treat such growth in own-account intermediate inputs as a separate source of growth in accounting for the change in the industry's gross output. It clearly is not – the growth in the intermediate input occurs primarily because of advances in technical knowledge and must be treated as such.

When the new measures are expressed in price form for this simple case, we have

$$[\alpha_{ij}(p_j + h_j - p_j) + \cdots] = h_j$$

and $p_j + h_j$ measures the rate of change of the prices of the *primary* inputs used in industry j to produce its output. With technical progress in the industry, the prices of its primary nonproducible inputs must be rising relative to the price of its output, which is the same in this case as the price of its own-account intermediate inputs, and this is precisely what the new measures of multifactor productivity will show.

That the new measures are invariant to differences in limited integration and the traditional measures are not is not so much a property of the assumption of neutrality (such an assumption is used to illustrate sharply the logic of the comparisons) as the property of the new measures to take into account rigorously technological interdependence involved in producible commodities being used as inputs. (In this case of limited integration, the technological interdependence is self-contained within an industry.) In traditional National Accounting terms, with own-product intermediate inputs, a distinction between gross outputs and intermediate inputs gross and net of *intra-industry* flows must be made. The new measures are not subject to a shift in output and input measures from ones that are gross of such intra-industry flows to those that are net of them. The traditional measures are, however, subject to such shifts in output concepts.

With no integration, the traditional and new measures are the same in the example provided. They would both show rates of productivity advance equal to the common increase in output per unit of inputs and the common increase in input prices relative to the price of output. The new measures remain the same; the traditional measures get lower the more important are own-account intermediate inputs.[3]

If the industry in question were engaged in the production of capital goods and produced some own-account goods, the same considerations would apply and the difference between the new and traditional measures would again follow and would depend upon the behaviour of the values of τ_{jj} and δ_{jj}, the cost shares of the net returns to capital and capital consumption allowances for own-account capital goods.

Consider another type of limited integration. Suppose again that there is neutral technical progress in both of two industries related in the following limited way. Industry i sells intermediate output to, and purchases intermediate input from, industry j but advances in multifactor productivity in all other industries may be ignored. For simplicity, the *intra*-industry flows, which we have just discussed, will also be ignored. Consider only the interindustry intermediate input flows that would apply for the traditional measures for industry i (in quantities),

$$\cdots + \alpha_{ji}(q_i - m_{ji}) + \cdots = t_i$$

and (in prices)

$$\cdots + \alpha_{ji}(p_j - p_i) + \cdots = t_i;$$

while for industry j

$$\cdots + \alpha_{ij}(q_j - m_{ij}) + \cdots = t_j$$

and

$$\cdots + \alpha_{ij}(p_i - p_j) + \cdots = t_j$$

The new measures for industry i would be

$$\cdots + \alpha_{ji}[q_i - (m_{ji} - h_j)] + \cdots = h_i$$

and

$$\cdots + \alpha_{ji}(p_j + h_j - p_i) + \cdots = h_i$$

and for industry j

[3] The traditional measures of multifactor productivity get lower and lower the more and more gross is the industry's output concept simply because more and more inputs are being taken into account. It is obvious that the more and more such factors are accounted for, the more and more will such factors account for the growth in the output and the less and less important, as a source of growth, will traditional multifactor productivity apparently be. This apparent reduction in the importance of productivity advance is the result of a conceptual artifact and arises due to the failure to distinguish between producible and nonproducible inputs, a failure to which the new measures are not subject.

$$\cdots + \alpha_{ij}[q_j + (m_{ij} - h_i)] + \cdots = h_j$$

and

$$\cdots + \alpha_{ij}(p_i + h_i + p_j) + \cdots = h_j$$

Assume that the two activities are experiencing the same rate of advance in productivity. If neutral, then $p_j - p_i$, $q_j - m_{ji}$, and $q_i - m_{ij}$ will be zero. Output per unit of input (and input prices relative to output prices) for all other inputs but the interconnected interindustry ones will be increasing for the two industries at the *same* rate of productivity advance *measured the new way*. That is, $h_i = h_j = h$.

In the case of the traditional measures, however, we will have

$$t_i = h_i - \alpha_{ji} h_j = (1 - \alpha_{ji})h$$
$$t_j = -\alpha_{ij} h_j + h_j = (1 - \alpha_{ij})h$$

The traditional measures will both be less than the new measures, and unless $\alpha_{ji} = \alpha_{ij}$, the traditional measures will be different! The equal rates of neutral multifactor productivity advance in the two industries shown by the new measures would be the *same* for the traditional measures if and only if the technological interconnectedness between the two industries is ignored. Once that interdependence is recognized and account of it taken (i.e., $\alpha_{ij} = \alpha_{ji} > 0$), the traditional measures not only fall below the new measures but do so in an arbitrary way. In general, different rates of multifactor productivity advance would be traditionally measured in a situation where, consistent with equal new rates, the relative prices (and quantities) of the commodities produced by the two industries should remain unchanged.

The difference would not be related in any way to differences (assumed nil for purposes of exposition) in productivity advance but would be simply a function of the observed difference in interindustry intermediate input cost shares. Even more interestingly, if the Harrod neutral rate of technical progress in industry i exceeded that for j, that is, $h_i > h_j$, then if $\alpha_{ij} = \alpha_{ji}$, though the traditional measures would be less than the new measures, their ranking would be the same; that is, $t_i^* > t_j^*$. If, however, $\alpha_{ji} > \alpha_{ij}$ sufficiently, not only would the traditional measures be lower but the ranking would be reversed; that is, $t_i^* < t_j^*$. If productivity advance were greater in industry i compared to j and the cost share of inputs from industry j into i exceeded the cost share of inputs from industry i into j, it could be the case that the traditional measures would show the relative productivity advances reversed simply because of the limited interindustry integration involved.

An example will make this point clear. Assume that all other inputs save the intermediate input flows between the two industries are primary. In both industries, output per unit of primary inputs is growing at the same rate. In quantity terms, we would then have for the two industries the traditional measures

$$\beta_i(q_i - l_i) + \alpha_{ji}(q_i - m_{ji}) = t_i$$
$$\beta_j(q_j - l_j) + \alpha_{ij}(q_j + m_{ij}) = t_j$$

and for the new measures,

$$\beta_i(q_i - l_i) + \alpha_{ji}[q_j - (m_{ji} - h_j)] = h_i$$
$$\beta_j(q_j + l_j) + \alpha_{ij}[q_j - (m_{ij} - h_i)] = h_j$$

Harrod neutral technical progress at the same rate in the two interconnected industries implies $q_i - l_i = q_j - l_j > 0$ and $q_i - m_{ji} = q_j - m_{ij} = 0$. Then

$$t_i = \beta_i(q_i - l_i) \qquad t_j = \beta_j(q_j - l_j)$$

Again, $\beta_i = 1 - \alpha_{ji}$ and $\beta_j = 1 - \alpha_{ij}$, β_i and β_j are less than 1, and there is no reason for $\beta_i = \beta_j$. From

$$t_i = \beta_i(q_i - l_i) = h_i - \alpha_{ji}h_j$$

and

$$t_j = \beta_j(q_j - l_j) = -\alpha_{ij}h_i + h_j$$

The new measures are

$$h_i = q_i - l_i = q_j - l_j = h_j$$

that is, as postulated to be the case, the new measures reveal the rate of multiproductivity advance in the two activities to be the same. Even in simple cases of interdependence the relationship between the traditional and new measures of multifactor productivity are interesting and reveal their conceptual differences.

When solving for h_i and h_j in such simple cases, one has

$$h_i - \alpha_{ji}h_j = t_i = \beta_i(q_i - l_i) + \alpha_{ji}(q_i - m_{ji})$$
$$\alpha_{ij}h_i + h_j = t_j = \beta_j(q_j - l_j) + \alpha_{ij}(q_j - m_{ij})$$

or

$$h_i = \frac{t_i + \alpha_{ji}t_j}{1 - \alpha_{ji}\alpha_{ij}} \qquad h_j = \frac{\alpha_{ij}t_i + t_j}{1 - \alpha_{ji}\alpha_{ij}}$$

In the simple case $t_i = \beta_i(q_i - l_i)$ and $t_j = \beta_j(q_j - l_j)$ and $q_i - l_i = q_j - l_j$; that is, the rate of increase in output per unit of primary nonreproducible inputs in the two industries is the same. If h_i and h_j are zero (i.e., there *are* no advances in technical knowledge recorded in the basic statistics of outputs and inputs), then of course, t_i and t_j will also be zero.

What of the case, however, where *overall* Harrod neutrality is not occurring at the same rate in both activities? Suppose, in the traditional sense, that while there is multifactor productivity advance in industry j, there appears to be none in industry i. It does not follow, however, that if $t_i = 0$ and $t_j > 0$, $h_i = 0$, since

$$h_i = \frac{\alpha_{ji} t_j}{1 - \alpha_{ji} \alpha_{ij}}$$

Why is this? The new measure for industry i records positive technical advance when the traditional measure does not. The new measure explicitly takes into account the fact that the produced inputs that industry i obtains from industry j are being produced with increased efficiency and that industry i is using indirect primary inputs more efficiently than before.

The new measure, in the case $t_i = 0$, would be

$$h_j = \frac{t_j}{1 - \alpha_{ji} \alpha_{ij}}$$

The significance of the coefficient $\alpha_{ji} \alpha_{ij}$ should be noted. Industry j is producing its output more efficiently. Some of that output flows to industry i and some of i's output flows back to industry j so indirectly some of the producible inputs used by industry j are in fact being produced more efficiently by itself and *should* therefore show up as part of the measured productivity advance in industry j. The more important is the interdependence, the larger is $\alpha_{ji} \alpha_{ij}$ and the more will h_j stand above t_j.

The logic of $\alpha_{ji} \alpha_{ij} > 0$ is simply, of course, a more complicated aspect of the fact that industry j is *indirectly* producing some of its own input. If either $\alpha_{ji} = 0$ (so that industry j supplied industry i with no inputs) or $\alpha_{ij} = 0$ (so that industry j used no inputs from industry i), then of course, $t_j = h_j$. Actual economies are generally characterized by such interdependence, and measures of multifactor productivity that distinguish between nonproduced and produced inputs must take such interdependence into account.

Return to the example and industry i. In the case being considered, the new measures would show positive productivity advance, the traditional measures none. The traditional measures would not say that the efficiency of primary inputs in industry i have not increased; rather the traditional measures would say that the combined efficiency of primary inputs *and* those inputs produced elsewhere (in industry j) have not increased. The traditional measure for industry i would be

$$\beta_i(q_i - l_i) + \alpha_{ji}(q_i - m_{ji}) = t_i = \beta_i(w_i - p_i) + \alpha_{ij}(p_j - p_i)$$

In this case $q_i - l_i = w_i - p_i$ would be positive; that is, output per unit of primary inputs would be rising as would own-product primary input prices (e.g., real wage rates in terms of industry i's output would be increasing). With cost shares unchanged, the movements in output per unit of intermediate input and the own-product price of such inputs would be offsetting; that is, $q_i - m_{ji} = p_j - p_i$ would be equal and negative.

Traditional theory would say that in response to a relative cheapening of intermediate inputs (because of the technical advance in industry j), industry i will substitute such intermediate inputs for primary inputs and the *partial* primary input productivity in industry i would be enhanced. The rise in primary input prices relative to the output price of industry i would be accounted for by the fall in the intermediate input price relative to the output price of industry i. In this simple example it is possible to say what the movement in relative input–output prices would be. From the prices approach we have

$$\beta_i(w_i - p_i) + \alpha_{ji}(p_j - p_i) = h_i - \alpha_{ji}h_j$$
$$\beta_j(w_j - p_j) + \alpha_{ij}(p_i - p_j) = -\alpha_{ij}h_i + h_j$$

Even though the primary inputs in the two industries may be growing at different rates, if the primary inputs are the same, in competitive price systems their prices should be the same if the primary inputs are "free" to move from industry to industry. Then $w_i = w_j = w$. As a consequence, we would have

$$\beta_i w - [p_i - \alpha_{ji}p_j] = h_i - \alpha_{ji}h_j$$
$$\beta_j w - [-\alpha_{ij}p_i + p_j] = -\alpha_{ij}h_i + h_j$$

or

$$\begin{bmatrix} \beta_i \\ \beta_j \end{bmatrix} w - \begin{bmatrix} 1 & -\alpha_{ji} \\ -\alpha_{ij} & 1 \end{bmatrix}\begin{bmatrix} p_i \\ p_j \end{bmatrix} = \begin{bmatrix} 1 & -\alpha_{ji} \\ -\alpha_{ij} & 1 \end{bmatrix}\begin{bmatrix} h_i \\ h_j \end{bmatrix}$$

or

$$\begin{bmatrix} \beta_i \\ \beta_j \end{bmatrix} w - \begin{bmatrix} 1 & -\alpha_{ji} \\ -\alpha_{ij} & 1 \end{bmatrix}\begin{bmatrix} h_i \\ h_j \end{bmatrix} = \begin{bmatrix} 1 & -\alpha_{ji} \\ -\alpha_{ij} & 1 \end{bmatrix}\begin{bmatrix} p_i \\ p_j \end{bmatrix}$$

or

$$\begin{bmatrix} 1 & -\alpha_{ji} \\ -\alpha_{ij} & 1 \end{bmatrix}^{-1}\begin{bmatrix} \beta_i \\ \beta_j \end{bmatrix} w - \begin{bmatrix} h_i \\ h_j \end{bmatrix} = \begin{bmatrix} p_i \\ p_j \end{bmatrix}$$

from which it follows, since $\beta_i = 1 - \alpha_{ji}$ and $\beta_j = 1 - \alpha_{ij}$, that

$$\begin{bmatrix} w \\ w \end{bmatrix} - \begin{bmatrix} h_i \\ h_j \end{bmatrix} = \begin{bmatrix} p_i \\ p_j \end{bmatrix}$$

Thus, when primary input prices in the two industries are the same, the new measures of multifactor productivity are predictions of relative output prices. Then the movements in the relative prices and quantities of the producible intermediate inputs are, in a technologically interdependent system, determined by the movements in primary input prices and the relative efficiencies with which such primary inputs are employed in the various interrelated industries. The movements in relative prices of producible intermediate inputs will not, in general, be predicted by the traditional measures of multifactor productivity. Indeed, the predicted movement in the relative prices of gross output could be quite different. That is, since

$$p_i - p_j = w - h_i - [w - h_j] = h_j - h_i$$

one has

$$p_i - p_j = \frac{\alpha_{ij} t_i + t_j}{1 - \alpha_{ji} \alpha_{ij}} - \frac{t_i + \alpha_{ji} t_j}{1 - \alpha_{ji} \alpha_{ij}}$$

$$= \frac{(\alpha_{ij} - 1) t_i + t_j (1 - \alpha_{ji})}{1 - \alpha_{ji} \alpha_{ij}}$$

Then $p_i - p_j = t_j - t_i$ if and only if α_{ji} and α_{ij} are zero and the technological interdependence between the two industries is ignored.

Moreover, it is the measured increases in the new concept of productivity that is associated with the rise in primary input prices (in own-product terms) in the two industries. Again, for the two industries,

$$\beta_i (w_i - p_i) + \alpha_{ji} (p_j - p_i) = h_i - \alpha_{ji} h_j$$

$$\beta_j (w_j - p_j) + \alpha_{ij} (p_i - p_j) = -\alpha_{ij} h_i + h_j$$

If $w = w_i = w_j$, then since $h_j - h_i = p_i - p_j$, one has

$$\beta_i (w - p_i) = \beta_i h_i \qquad \beta_j (w - p_j) = \beta_j h_j$$

or

$$w - p_i = h_i \quad \text{and} \quad w - p_j = h_j$$

as before.

The new measures show by how much prices of primary inputs can rise in own-product terms in the two industries.

In the two basic cases of Harrod neutral progress for industries related to each other through intermediate input and outputs where the rates of progress were the same and where they were different, the new measures of multifactor productivity would seem to have logical content. They predict movements in relative prices. They explain why own-product primary input prices can rise for an industry for which traditional measures of productivity advance show no advance. Essentially the new measures capture the producibility of the intermediate inputs displayed in the technological interdependence of the industries as reflected in their input–output statistics – the traditional measures do not.

It is common in the literature on economic growth to find arguments that Hicksian and Harrodian concepts of neutral technical change are related via the concept of the elasticity of substitution between and among inputs.[4] In one-sector models of economic growth it is argued, for instance, that Hicks and Harrod neutral technical advances are the same if and only if the elasticity of substitution between capital and labour is unity. As this chapter demonstrates, *the static concept of the elasticity of substitution has nothing whatever to do with the distinction between the two concepts of technical advance.* The Hicksian concept makes no distinction between produced and nonproduced inputs; the Harrodian concept does, and in modern economies where so many inputs are producible, the distinction matters both theoretically and, as our study shows, empirically in the measurement of multifactor productivity.

The discussion is bordering on taxonomy – a mere classification of observed changes. One needs but does not have a theory of technical progress. The new measures, although in the general case doubtless exhibiting nonneutral multifactor productivity advance, have the enormous analytically attractive property of continually taking into account the producibility of the intermediate inputs displayed in the technological interdependence among activities as it affects "growth accounting" for intermediate inputs.[5]

The theoretical discussion has so far dealt with two interrelated activities that produce intermediate inputs for each other. What characterized the inputs, however, was not so much their intermediate nature but the fact that these were produced. They could just as well have been fixed capital inputs and the analysis would have been the same. One would have had to ask once more what are the primary inputs lying behind those capital inputs, the commodity capital inputs again being producible.

Consider a special case of an economy of two simple industries: one that produces consumption goods and another that produces capital goods. The previous notation can be repeated. For quantities,

---

[4] For an early exposition of the point, see, for example, R. W. Jones, "'Neutral' Technological Change and the Isoquant Map", *American Economic Review*, LV, September 1965, 848–55.

[5] Readers may find more illuminating a less abstract example provided as an appendix to this chapter.

$$\beta_i(q_i - l_i) + \alpha_{ji}[q_i - (k_{ji} - h_j)] = h_i$$
$$\beta_j(q_j - l_i) + \alpha_{jj}[q_j - (k_{jj} - h_j)] = h_j$$

The difference in notation reveals that in this case, a two-sector model, industry j (the capital goods sector) gets no inputs from industry i (the consumption goods sector), all of the output of which flows into the final consumption of households. The capital goods sector produces its own capital goods and those used by the consumption goods sector. The capital goods sector has the limited integration earlier discussed – it uses as an input some of its own output.

Once again special cases illustrate the logic of the differences between the two measures of multifactor productivity. From the growth literature, it is known that in steady-state equilibrium,

$$q_i - k_{ji} = q_j - k_{jj} = 0 \quad \text{and} \quad q_i - l_i = q_j - l_j = q - l$$

Thus

$$\beta_i(q_i - l_i) = t_i = h_i - \alpha_{ji} h_j$$
$$\beta_j(q_i - l_i) = t_j = -\alpha_{jj} h_j + h_j$$

Again, because of the extraordinary simplicity of the example, one can solve h_j for industry j (the capital goods sector) without reference to any other industry. Clearly, $q_j - l_j = h_j$, and since $k_{jj} - h_j$ is the proportionate rate of growth of the *nonproduced* capital input, called waiting, in industry j, it follows that waiting is increasing at the same rate as labour. Thus, technical progress is neutral in Harrod's sense. Similarly, $q_i - l_i = h_i$, the primary inputs of labour and waiting, directly and indirectly involved in the production of the consumption good, are increasing in efficiency in the Harrod neutral way. Thus, the new measures of multifactor productivity reflect exactly what economic theory has meant by steady-state technical progress in a two-sector economy. Just as before, however, the traditional measures will understate the rate of technical progress. Thus,

$$\beta_i(q_i - l_i) = t_i \qquad \beta_j(q_j - l_i) = t_j$$

and there is no a priori need for them to be equal. From the price *dynamic identities*, one would have

$$\beta_i(w - p_i) + \alpha_{ji}(r_j + p_j + h_j - p_i) = h_i$$
$$\beta_j(w - p_j) + \alpha_{jj}(r_j + p_j + h_j - p_j) = h_j$$

Once again, the limited integration involved in the capital goods sector implies, of course, that the price of its own capital in its own output terms cannot be changing. Steady-state equilibrium also requires that the net rate of return to capital in both activities be constant, $r_i = r_j = 0$, so that again $h_j = w - p_j$; thus the own-product prices of labour and waiting in the capital goods activity would be rising at the new rate of technical progress. Similarly, $h_i = w - p_i$ and steady state implies $h_j = w - p_j = w - p = w - p_i = h_i$.

Real wage rates would be rising at the same time in both activities. So would the real return to "waiting". By this, one means that the owners of capital goods (or claims upon them) would be experiencing a rising level of "real income" or permanent consumption along with owners of labour without altering the rates at which they are forgoing present consumption any more than owners of labour are altering the rates of which they are forgoing (the present consumption good value of) leisure. The working and waiting are the two primary inputs whose efficiency is increasing in both industries at the same rate.

Outside of steady-state analysis, there is, of course, no reason to suppose that advances in productivity as captured by the new measures would reflect neutrality or the same rates of technical progress in the two industries. However, the need to take always into account that capital goods (or the services of such capital goods) are themselves being produced and reproduced with ever-changing efficiency – a need always captured by the new measures and neglected by the traditional measures – would remain.

An even greater simplification permits a comparison of the measures in a further illuminating way. Suppose the economy can be represented as if it were a one-commodity economy. For such an economy no problem of aggregation (across commodities) can arise. For such an economy, the traditional measures would be

$$\alpha(q-m) + \beta(q-l) + \tau(q-k) + \delta\left[q - \left(k + \frac{\dot{p}'}{p'}\right)\right]$$

$$= t$$

$$= \alpha(p-p) + \beta(w-p) + \tau(r+p-p) + \delta(p-p)$$

The new measures are

$$\alpha[q-(m-h)] + \beta(q-l) + \tau[q-(k-h)] + \delta\left[q - \left(k + \frac{\dot{p}'}{p'} - h\right)\right]$$

$$= h$$

$$= \alpha(p+h-p) + \beta(w-p) + \tau(r+p+h-p) + \delta(p+h-p)$$

and either for quantities or prices the h can be obtained. Once again, neutrality and steady-state growth would entail

$$\beta(q-l) = t = \beta(w-p)$$

in the traditional case and

$$q - l = h = w - p$$

in the new case.

Generally speaking, in one-commodity growth models the intra-industry flow of intermediate inputs is ignored. The intra-industry flow of capital goods (treated in such models as depreciation, or capital used up, and the services of the one-commodity stock of capital) is treated, however, in the traditional measures as if the goods were inputs similar to labour. It is the services of waiting that are similar to the services of labour, not capital used up or the flow of services of the stock of capital. If the cost shares are recomputed for a one-commodity economy in which the *intra*-industry gross flows of intermediate inputs and outputs are ignored, then the revised traditional measures will be correspondingly higher whereas, of course, the new measures will be invariant. Indeed, if one takes a measure of output in which the value shares of reproducible inputs are made smaller and smaller, the traditional measures will get higher and higher approaching in the limit the new measures.[6]

If no technical progress occurs, that is, if $h = 0$, then the traditional analysis applies. Thus, if the individuals of the economy should decide to wait more, to save at a higher rate, one would observe, given traditional assumptions and *neglecting the problem of Keynes,* there will be an increase in q relative to l and offsetting changes in k relative to q (with nonneutral effects on the rate of capital consumption and cost shares – the shares being interpreted as partial elasticities of production with respect to the inputs).

On the side of prices, again on traditional assumptions, the rise in the own-product wage rate, $(w - p) > 0$, would be offset by the fall in the gross and net rate of return to capital so that the dynamic identities would reflect the rise in the price of working relative to the primary nonreproducible capital input as the ratio of waiting to working – the ratio of capital to labour – rose. Further, if such changes were superimposed on technical advances as captured by the new measures, such changes would still be manifest in the numbers so that even though working and waiting were becoming more efficient in Harrod-efficient units one would measure a rise in waiting *relative* to working.

The simple one-commodity model also permits diagrammatic representation of the differences between the new and traditional measures. In

---

[6] For an example, see E. F. Denison, *Accounting for United States Economic Growth, 1929–1969* (Washington, D.C.: The Brookings Institution, 1974), 133–5. See the comments on Denison's procedure in T. K. Rymes, "More on the Measurement of Total Factor Productivity", *Review of Income and Wealth,* XXIX, September 1983, 314.

Quantities:

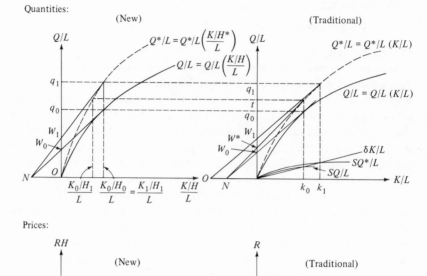

Figure 2-1. Measures of multifactor productivity advance in a one-commodity, two-"factor" economy.

Figure 2-1[7] the distinction between produced and induced changes in output and capital in the case of a once-over improvement in technology is described. The figure is standard in the economic growth theory literature.

The top of the figure refers to quantities, and the right-hand side shows the traditional analysis. For neutral advance, the ratio of capital to labour remains unchanged, whereas the wage rate and net rate of return to capital rise in the same proportion. This is illustrated by the proportional

[7] Figure 2-1 is based on Figure 5.1 in T. K. Rymes, *On Concepts of Capital and Technical Change,* and Figure 1 in T. K. Rymes, "More on the Measurement of Total Factor Productivity", *Review of Income and Wealth,* XXIX, September 1983, 300. A related argument appears in F. Reid, "Comment", eds. S. Maital and N. M. Meltz, *Lagging Productivity Growth: Causes and Remedies* (Cambridge, Mass.: Ballinger Publishing, 1980), and in R. Landau, "Technology and Capital Formation", eds. D. W. Jorgenson and R. Landau, *Technology and Capital Formation* (Cambridge, MA: MIT Press, 1989).

increase in the wage rate from OW_0 to OW^* and the proportional increase in the gross rate of return by the increase in the slope of line NW_0, which extended is tangent to $(Q/L)(K/L)$ (showing that output per unit of labour is a function of capital per unit of labour), to the slope of line NW^*, which extended is tangent to $(Q^*/L)(K/L)$. An unchanging propensity to save results in the very increase in technology producing more capital,[8] and the traditional measures treat such accumulation as a "separate source of growth". The increase in output per unit of labour from q_0 to q_1 is divided into two parts: $q_0 t$ (the increase owing to technical progress or "shift in the production function") and the remainder tq_1 (accumulation in the *new* state of technology or "movement along the production function"). The new measures, illustrated on the left-hand side, show the entire increase in output per unit of labour from q_0 to q_1 as being due to technical progress because the very act of technical advance reduces the primary input content of the given commodity capital; that is, for a given ratio of commodity capital to labour, with $H_0 = 1$, the ratio K_0/L can be represented as $(K_0/H_0)/L$. With technical progress $H_1 > 1$ and $(K_0/H_1)/L$ represent a fall in the ratio of waiting to labour as the primary inputs necessary to reproduce and maintain the given commodity capital have fallen.

The amounts of labour and, given the savings relation, waiting supplied have remained unchanged, and the extra commodity capital accumulation is *produced not induced* by the technical advances. Thus, the effect of the burst of technology is to reduce the waiting–labour ratio from $(K_0/H_0)/L$ to $(K_0/H_1)/L$ (or a fall in what Joan Robinson called the "real" capital/labour ratio).[9] The flow of waiting has, however, remained unchanged, and further commodity capital accumulation is produced until the ratio $(K_1/H_1)/L$ equals $(K_0/H_0)/L$; that is, the measured ratio of waiting to labour is unchanged. In the Harrod–Robinson case, all the proportionate increase in output per unit of labour is attributed to once-over improvement in technology.

The bottom of Figure 2-1 illustrates the same analysis in terms of prices. In the traditional case, the factor price frontier, $P(R, W)$ is drawn in terms of the net rate of return and the real wage rate. A particular technique from the given technology is chosen resulting in wage rate W_0 and net rate of return R. An improvement of technique [the shift in the factor

---

[8] The steady-state equilibrium condition can be written as $s(q'(k) - \delta)q(k) = \delta k$, $s' > 0$, where s is the fraction of output saved such that the once-over advance in technology, because it is associated with an initial rise in $q'(k)$, *induces* as well extra accumulation. For a *given* schedule of saving propensities, the very act of technological advance *produces* accumulation.

[9] J. Robinson, *The Accumulation of Capital* (London: Macmillan, 3rd ed. 1969), 121.

price frontier from $P(R, W)$ to $P^*(R, W)$] of the neutral type will show R and W increasing in the same proportion, but the accumulation that results would increase W and lower R until R is unchanged and the wage rate is W_1. (The "movement" along the factor price frontier matches the movement along the production "function".) Thus, tangents to the shifting factor price frontiers rotate with a constant rate of return and a rising wage rate. For new measures, the primary input price frontier is drawn in terms of the prices of working and waiting, W and RH. For a given technology, $H_0 = 1$ and the primary input price frontier is the same as the factor price frontier. An improvement in technology of the neutral type, however, shifts the primary input price frontier out to $P^*(RH, W)$ in the same proportion to the old and shows equiproportionate increases in real wages W and the real price of waiting, RH.

The symmetry in the new measures is now readily seen. Nonproduced inputs can only be changed by induction, not by production. The Harrod–Robinson–Read quantities diagram shows equiproportionate increases in output per unit of working and waiting, whereas the Harrod–Robinson–Read price diagram shows equiproportionate increases in the real prices of working and waiting. Technical advances raise the efficiency and price of primary inputs. It cannot do so for inputs that are simultaneously outputs or are produced by the very inputs said to be increasing in efficiency or price.

B   Aggregation and multifactor productivity measurement

We have set out and compared *industry* measures of multifactor productivity of the traditional and new types. We now briefly deal with certain problems of aggregation involved in the traditional and new measures.

We have already seen that the new measures take into account the extent to which industries are technologically interdependent. In empirical work, the drawing of a boundary line between two industries is sometimes arbitrary so that what are intermediate outputs flowing from industry i as intermediate inputs into industry j can, to some extent, be a statistical artifact. To the extent that industry classifications are arbitrary, the new as compared to the traditional measures of total factor productivity at the industry level appear strengthened. In practice, industries (and firms) produce more than one commodity. The new measures assume that the improvement in productivity of an industry pertains to all the commodities being produced by that industry. The industry technology assumption (as distinct from the commodity technology assumption, a distinction of importance in modern input–output accounting) is discussed in the empirical section of our study.

With respect to aggregation over industries, we have already discussed the Domar–Hulten aggregation procedure by which the traditional measures of multifactor productivity by industry are aggregated to an economywide measure. We have, as well, pointed out that the new measures of multifactor productivity by industry are aggregated by using each industry's contribution to net final output.[10] At the aggregate level, when *dealing only* with intermediate inputs, the two measures of multifactor productivity are, as we have seen, the same.

For the traditional approach, the aggregation procedures involve a change in the industry measures. For example, the aggregate measure of multifactor productivity for total manufacturing would be different than the traditional measures for major groups within manufacturing, such as foods and beverages, products of petroleum and coal, and so forth. The measure for each of the major groups would themselves differ from those for the three-digit industries composing such groups if there were intra-group flows of intermediate inputs *and* outputs.

The new individual industry measures are not themselves affected by the relative final output weights. The major group aggregates, the manufacturing aggregates, and aggregate measures of multifactor productivity of the economy as a whole would not, of necessity, get larger and larger as the various aggregations were performed since the economywide interdependence of technology is always being taken into account in any individual industry's new measure of multifactor productivity.

The output of industries is sometimes taken to be value added or gross domestic product. With the traditional multifactor productivity approach it is, however, increasingly recognized that sector measures calculated with an output concept in terms of value added or gross domestic product lead to what are called "incorrect" measures of productivity advance, which are said to be biased upward compared to the "correct" measures based on the gross output concept.[11] With gross output measures, the traditional aggregate is constructed by applying weights of gross output to aggregate final output, such weights summing to greater than 1. The

[10] It is assumed that depreciation or capital consumption allowances are being treated as intermediate inputs so that the weights in the Domar–Hulten procedure will be each industry's gross input as a share in total *net* final output and the weights for the new measures will be each industry's share in net final output. Again, the sum of the weights in the Domar–Hulten aggregation procedure exceed unity so that the interindustry advances in productivity reflected in the intermediate flows of inputs and outputs are being accounted for in the aggregate, even though they do not appear in the individual industry traditional cases.

[11] See, e.g., P. S. Rao and R. S. Preston, "Inter-factor Substitution, Economies of Scale and Technical Change: Evidence from Canadian Industries", *Empirical Economics,* IX, 1984, 87–111, and M. Bruno, "Raw Materials, Profits, and the Productivity Showdown", *Quarterly Journal of Economics,* XCIX, February 1984, 1–19.

aggregate index will be the same as when traditional industry measures with domestic product as the individual industry output concept are weighted together by means of each industry's share in the aggregate domestic product. (Each industry's share in domestic product is not the same as each industry's share in final output.)

As we have seen, however, the traditional measures are lower the more gross is the output concept employed and higher the more intermediate or reproducible are the inputs that are "netted" out. It is not a question of which traditional measure is more correct. What matters is that only the new measures rigorously take into account the interdependence and produced nature of the intermediate inputs in productivity measurement.

With traditional industry measures based on the gross output concept (and one must be clear whether the gross output concept includes or excludes *intra*sector flows, i.e., whether one is working with unduplicated or duplicated gross output), it is now being argued that aggregate multifactor productivity measures be constructed by the Domar–Hulten means of weighting together the sectoral measures by the ratio of each sector's gross output to total or aggregate value added or aggregate gross domestic product. Since the weights will clearly sum to a number greater than unity, the aggregate measure will in general exceed the individual sector measures. In this case the traditional aggregate measures seek to take into account the fact that technical progress in a sector producing intermediate output contributes to advances in efficiency in those sectors using such output as intermediate inputs. This interdependence is of course also taken into account by the new measures, but in a rigorously consistent way.

In principle, if an industry's output is redefined to be more and more of a gross concept, moving, for example, from net domestic product to gross domestic product (including depreciation) to gross unduplicated output (excluding intra-industry intermediate flows) to gross duplicated output (including such intermediate flows), the traditional measure of total factor productivity for the industry could be reduced to something almost vanishingly small. Multifactor productivity as a residual would be almost totally accounted for simply because more and more reproducible inputs are being incorporated into the output measure.

The aggregate measure of multifactor productivity, with the Domar–Hulten aggregation procedure, could conceivably record substantial rates of productivity advance even if each industry's measure were negligible. Why? Simply because the weights attached to all the vanishingly small individual industry measures could sum to a very large number indeed, such as 1, 1,000, 10^x, or whatever. The more and more gross is the output concept used for the individual industry measures, the greater and greater would be the sum of the weights.

The new measures are not subject to this aggregation phenomenon!

The individual industry new measures are aggregated by the shares in final output, such shares summing to unity. The new measures take into account, however, the fact that the net capital stocks of each industry and at the aggregate are themselves being produced with increased efficiency when the capital goods industries are experiencing advances in technical knowledge. The new measures will always exceed the traditional measures when such productivity advance is occurring. It will be remembered that the h_j's take into account the changing efficiency of not only those primary nonreproducible inputs measured and classified as being directly involved in industry j but also those primary inputs indirectly involved in all related industries.[12]

A particular industry need not have any final output. Its gross output could be entirely intermediate output used by other industries. The number of industries contributing directly to final demand could be less than the total number of industries. However, the changing efficiency of the industries not contributing directly to final demand is not missed in any aggregation because the h_j's for the included industries take into account such changing efficiency because the included industries use intermediate inputs from the industries not recorded as directly contributing to final output.

Traditional measures are then subject to arbitrary nonrobustness when aggregation over industries is performed. The method of aggregation for the new measures provides a consistent aggregation measure of multifactor productivity as well as a method of capturing measures of improvements in productivity of Pasinetti's vertically integrated sectors. Two important new conceptual additions to National Accounting, the new measures of multifactoral productivity advance in this study and Pasinetti's concept of vertically integrated sectors, are thus shown to be linked.

C On measures of multifactor productivity and capitalization of inputs

What is or is not a nonproduced input is not always clear. It sometimes appears, even for natural agents such as land, that the services of land can be produced. With, for example, fertilization, the flow of services of

---

[12] The aggregation procedure for the new measures also gives us a measure of multifactor productivity that aggregates over Pasinetti's hypervertically integrated sectors. See Pasinetti, *Structural Change and Economic Growth,* ch. VI, "The Empirical Significance of Vertically-Integrated Analysis". See also his "The Notion of Vertical Integration in Economic Analysis", ed. L. L. Pasinetti, *Essays in the Theory of Joint Production* (New York: Columbia University Press, 1980).

a given stock of homogeneous land can not only be maintained but also be increased. Yet it is the increased service of the fertilizer that improves the flow of services from the land. If the land with fertilization was rented, then the rents will include a return on the investment of fertilizer. The distinction between the services of fertilizer and the nonproduced services of the land would be preserved. When it comes to labour services, however, the distinction becomes less sharp. A worker can be said to have invested in "human capital", either obtained on the job or through some formal institution of instruction. Scientists, graduates of tertiary and secondary schools, and workers trained "on the job" or that have simply acquired skills by repetition may be said to embody investment in human capital.

Therefore, rather than treat their incomes as wages or payments for the nonproduced services of labour, the rewards of such agents can be treated as returns to capital. In a technically progressive economy, an industry hiring or using such human capital will find the capital embodied in them growing more rapidly than if they were treated as standard units of labour. If we let K_{hj} be the stock of human capital employed in industry j, then $(R_{hj} - \dot{p}'_{hj}/p'_{hj})P_h K_{hj}$ will be the gross returns to human capital of the hth type used in industry j. Contrast this with $W_h L_{hj}$, the value of the wages earned by the hth type of labour in industry j. When technical progress in the provision of human capital takes place, the gross rental, $(R_{hj} - \dot{p}'_{hj}/p'_{hj})P_h$, will tend to remain unchanged relative to a rising W_h, whereas K_{hj}, the stock of human capital, will tend to rise relative to L_{hj}, the labour in whom the human capital is embodied.[13]

---

[13] If wage payments are capitalized (if industries are said to treat the payment for the services of scientists as investments in the accumulation of "research and development") and if real wage rates are rising, then the same result holds: The stock of human capital (the stock of research and development) will grow relative to the labour inputs (scientists) measured as nonreproducible inputs.

Let $W(t)L(t) = W(0)\exp(n't)L(0)\exp(nt) = W(0)L(0)\exp(n'+n)t$ be the salaries of scientists to be capitalized, where n' is the rate of improvement in the real salary rate of scientists and n is the rate of growth of the number of such scientists. By the Goldsmith–Redfern method of perpetual inventory (ignoring depreciation), the value of the stock of human capital will be

$$V(t) = \int_{-\infty}^{0} W(0)L(0)\exp(n'+n)t \, dt$$
$$= \frac{W(0)L(0)\exp(n'+n)t}{n'+n}$$

The instantaneous change in the stock will be

$$\dot{V}(t) = W(0)L(0)\exp(n'+n)t$$

The proportionate rate of growth of the stock will be

The consequences for the traditional measures of multifactor productivity are immediate. Consider again the simple measures for any industry where we ignore in the subscripts the industry in question, where α_i represents the cost share of intermediate inputs flowing from industry i and where all other inputs are ignored for simplicity,

$$\beta(q-l)+\alpha_i(q-m_i) = t = \beta(w-p)+\alpha_i(p_i-p)$$

Suppose that part of the returns to nonproduced inputs are treated as returns to capital and appear as part of capital produced by the industry (part of the wage bill is capitalized as on-the-job investment in training or research and development). Then the simple measures for activity j, ignoring depreciation, are replaced with

$$\beta^*(q-l)+(\beta-\beta^*)(q-k)+\alpha_i(q-m_i)$$
$$= t^*$$
$$= \beta^*(w-p_j)+(\beta_j-\beta_j^*)(r+p-p)+\alpha_i(p_i-p)$$

where $\beta-\beta^*$ is that part of the cost share of labour that is capitalized, k is the rate of growth of the stock of human capital produced and used in the industry, and r is the proportionate rate of change in the rate of return to human capital.

The previous discussion suggests that $k>l$, that is, the stock of human capital will be rising relative to the labour input in the industry. All other measures remain unchanged – all that has happened is that some nonproduced inputs have been reclassified as produced inputs. Compare the traditional measures of productivity in quantity terms before and after such reclassification:

$$t-t^*= \beta(q-l)+\alpha_i(q-m_i)+\beta^*(q-l)-(\beta-\beta^*)(q-k)-\alpha_i(q-m_i)$$
$$= (\beta-\beta^*)[q-l-q+k] = (\beta-\beta^*)k-l$$

Since the revised weights entail $\beta-\beta^*>0$ and we have seen that $k-l>0$, it follows that $t-t^*>0$. Thus, the traditional measured rate of multifactor productivity has been reduced by the simple reclassification of labour input to capital inputs. This is surely a meaningless result. The mere reclassification of inputs from labour to capital by some simple capitalization procedure should not, in principle, change the measured rate of

$$\frac{\dot{V}(t)}{V(t)} = n'+n$$

The stock of human capital will be growing at a rate $n'+n$ that exceeds the rate of growth of the number of scientists, n, if the real salary rate of scientists is increasing over time.

multifactor productivity. This reflects again the lack of robustness of the traditional measures of multifactor productivity. The price approach yields

$$t - t^* = \alpha(w-p) + \alpha_i(p_i - p)$$
$$- [\beta^*(w-p) + (\beta - \beta^*)(r + p - p) + \alpha_i(p_i - p)]$$
$$= (\beta - \beta^*)[(w-p) - (r + p - p)]$$
$$= (\beta - \beta^*)[w - (r + p)]$$

With wages rising relative to gross rentals on human capital, the mere capitalization of nonproduced inputs lowers the traditional measures of multifactor productivity.

Consider now the difference between the new measures. With respect to quantities, before the capitalization of certain labour inputs, the new measures would be

$$\beta(q - l) + \alpha_i[q - (m_i - h_i)] = h$$

and after such capitalization, they would be

$$\beta^*(q - l) + (\beta - \beta^*)[q - (k - h^*)] + \alpha_i[q - (m_i - h_i)] = h^*$$

where k_j is the growth rate of the human capital of the jth type and h_j is the productivity advance in the industry "producing" such capital.

The difference between the two measures, $h - h^*$, is then

$$(\beta - \beta^*)[(q - l) - (q - (k_j - h_j) - l)]$$

By assumption, $\beta - \beta^* > 0$, so that the new measure with capitalization of some of the nonproduced input will be less (greater) than the new measure without capitalization if $k_j - h_j > l$ ($< l$).

If the capitalization inputs were "own account", then, of course, $k_j - h_j = l$, and the mere capitalization of input such as labour "learning while doing" would not affect the new measures of multifactor productivity. Of course, $k_j - h_j = l$ is a special case, but although in general capitalization of nonproduced inputs would affect the new measures of multifactor productivity, no a priori sign can be attached to the effects. In the traditional case, however, capitalization of inputs *always* reduces the measure of multifactor productivity.[14]

---

[14] When traditional measures of multifactor productivity advance are considered as residual measures of ignorance, the mere capitalization of inputs, previously considered as nonproduced, because it lowers the measure, would seem to account for some of the measured advances in productivity. Of course, it does no such thing; the lowered measure of productivity growth results merely from the fallacy involved in the symmetric treatment of produced and nonproduced inputs by the traditional measures. The new measures, logically, treat such inputs differently, which is why the new measures are more robust than the traditional counterparts.

The argument generalizes. One can argue that all advances in technical knowledge are costly and must be procured by investment of one kind or another. One can seek to "explain" more and more productivity growth by capitalizing more and more inputs previously treated as nonproducible. One can in fact argue that all technical advance is produced in a costly way and in the limit treat all inputs as producible or capital inputs. Then if the weighted average of all the capitalized inputs is growing at the same rate as output, the traditional measures of productivity advance will be lower and lower – in the limit showing no advance at all. The new measures can be expected to be invariant, in the sense outlined, to such reclassifications, again illustrating the strength of the new measures.[15]

Appendix II   Multifactor productivity measurement and industrial technological interdependence: An example

Coke is an input used in the production of steel (and the complexity that steel may be used indirectly in the form of machines in the production of coke will be ignored).[16] Suppose there is an advance of productivity in the production of coke and the price of coke falls relative to the price of steel. Where the cost share of coke in steel production remains unchanged so that the degree to which coke in steel production is substituted for other inputs offsets the decline in coke's own-product price (i.e., the price of coke in terms of steel), the traditional argument would be that the rise in the gross output of steel is accounted for by the substitution of coke for other inputs because of the decline in the relative price of coke. The Harrodian argument would say that of the primary inputs engaged in steel production, those *indirectly* engaged (i.e., those in coke production) have improved in their productivity, and by means of using more of the coke output, those directly engaged have their own productivity enhanced. The traditional measure would argue that the substitution of coke for other inputs in steel production raises the marginal physical products of those inputs, which offsets the fall in the marginal physical product of coke. In

---

[15] Elsewhere it has been shown that the procedure of reclassifying nonproduced into produced inputs, which in the limit reduces measured technical progress to zero, is the same as arguing as if the economy is a von Neumann economy, unable to deal with technical change. See Rymes, *On Concepts of Capital and Technical Change,* 104. For a similar argument, see Pasinetti, *Structural Change and Economic Growth,* appendix to ch. VI, "A Criticism of the von Neumann-Type of Dynamic Models as Applied to Economic Systems with Technical Change". For a discussion of how this capitalization problem affects the interpretation of research and development expenditures as a source of economic growth, see T. K. Rymes, "Technical Progress, Research and Development", ed. G. Feiwel, *Joan Robinson and Modern Economic Theory* (London: Macmillan, 1989).

[16] T. K. Rymes is indebted to Fred Gruen and Michael Carter of the Australian National University for discussions about the example in this appendix.

the case of unchanging cost shares, the average physical product of the directly employed primary inputs rises and the average physical product of coke falls in proportions that match the changes in marginal physical products. The traditional approach would say that no productivity advance has occurred in steel production, the rise in the marginal and average products of the direct primary inputs being offset by the decline in the marginal and average products of the coke inputs.

The new measures would show that the reason why coke inputs have increased is precisely because the primary inputs engaged in coke production and therefore indirectly engaged in steel production have improved in productivity and that substitution of coke for other inputs entails a technology that permits substitution of indirect for direct primary inputs, enhancing the productivity of the primary inputs directly employed in steel production. If, in fact, coke production were integrated as part of the process of steel production, then the primary inputs involved in steel production would exhibit productivity advance. This is precisely what the new measures are constructed to show and to cut through the apparent disintegration of coke–steel production by rigorously taking into account the technological interdependence between coke and steel production.

Suppose, however, that the nature of the technology is such that more limited substitution possibilities exist.[17] The cheapening of coke relative to steel leads to some – in the limiting case, no substitution of coke for other inputs in steel production such that the coke cost share falls and the shares for the other inputs rise. (Some of the primary inputs, many in number, may be complementary to coke such that their cost shares may also fall.) Take the limiting case of no substitution whatsoever. The traditional measure would show no multifactor productivity advance in steel production. (In the case of a zero elasticity of substitution, marginal physical products are not well defined.) The new measure would, however, continue to show multiproductivity advance in steel production because the primary inputs used indirectly in steel production have improved productivity.

In terms of the previous notation, the ith sector is coke and the jth sector is steel. The traditional measures of multifactor productivity in terms of quantities would be

$$\beta_i(q_i - l_i) = t_i \quad \text{and} \quad \beta_j(q_j - l_j) + \alpha_{ij}(q_j - m_{ij}) = t_j$$

In the case of such substitution where the β's remain unchanged, the measured increases in the average products of the primary inputs directly employed in steel production, the positive $q_j - l_j$, would be offset by the

[17] For a discussion of the many kinds of static technologies that can only be arbitrarily approximated, see R. G. Chambers, *Applied Production Analysis: A Dual Approach* (Cambridge: Cambridge University Press, 1988), ch. 5, "Flexible Forms and Aggregation".

decrease in the average product of coke in steel production, the negative $q_j - m_{ij}$. Thus, whereas $t_i > 0$, $t_j = 0$. In the case of no substitution, $q_j - l_j = q_j - m_{ij} = 0$, that is, none of the input–output coefficients would show change, and again $t_i > 0$ and $t_j = 0$. In terms of prices the traditional measures of multifactor productivity would be

$$\beta_i(w_i - p_i) = t_i$$
$$\beta_j(w_j - p_j) + \alpha_{ij}(p_i - p_j) = t_j$$

The negative $p_i - p_j$ would be offset by the positive $w_j - p_j$. In the case of limited or no substitution, however, α_{ij} would fall and β_j would rise. This would not affect the measures of multifactor productivity because changing weights attached to the changing relative input–output and own-product prices do not affect the instantaneous measured rates of productivity advance. In terms of quantities, the new measures would be

$$\beta_i(q_i - l_i) = h_i$$
$$\beta_j(q_j - l_j) + \alpha_{ij}[q_j - (m_{ij} - h_j)] = h_j$$

In this simple case, of course, $t_i = h_i$, that is, there would be no difference in the traditional and new measures of multifactor productivity in coke production, but $h_j > t_j$, that is, the new measures of productivity advance in the steel activity would be greater than the traditional measures. The computation of h_j is simple in this case:

$$\alpha_{ij}h_i = \alpha_{ij}\beta_i(q_i - l_i) = h_j$$

In terms of prices, the new measures would be

$$\beta_i(w - p_i) = h_i$$
$$\beta_j(w - p_j) + \alpha_{ij}(p_i + h_i - p_j) = h_j$$

With or without substitution,

$$p_j = \beta_j w + \alpha_{ij} p_i$$

and

$$\beta_j[w - (\beta_j w + \alpha_{ij} p_i)] + \alpha_{ij}[p_i + h_i - (\beta_j w + \alpha_{ij} p_i)] = h_j$$

or

$$\alpha_{ij}h_i = \alpha_{ij}(q_i - l_i) = h_j$$

As before, for the quantities, the instantaneous rate of change of the new measure of multifactor productivity would not, however, be invariant to the elasticity of substitution between direct and indirect primary inputs. That is, even if there were no instantaneous change in $\beta_i(q_i - l_i)$ or t_i, if α_{ij} were changing, then h_j would change. In symbols,

$$\dot{h}_j = \beta_i(q_i - l_i)\dot{\alpha}_{ij}$$

or the observed acceleration or deceleration in the new measure of multi-factor productivity would reflect changes in α_{ij}, the value of the indirect primary inputs in steel production.

So far the cases of elasticities of substitutions lower than those sufficient to preserve α_{ij} unchanged have been considered. In the fixed coefficient case, despite the relative improvement of the productivity of the indirect primary inputs in coke production, the movement of the cost share of such indirect primary inputs in steel production reflects the fact that the nature of technical change and choice is bringing about *less* integration between the coke and steel activities. The new measure of multifactor productivity in the production of steel would appropriately be falling. In the limit, with advancing productivity in coke production, if the value of α_{ij} fell to zero, there would be no integration – no technological interdependence between coke and steel production. None of the primary inputs at work in coke production could therefore be treated as primary inputs indirectly involved in steel production. The new measures of multifactor productivity in the steel activity would fall – in the limit – approaching the traditional measures that do not take into account the producibility of the coke used in the production of steel.

Rising cost shares such that the degree of integration between coke and steel production would be increasing could also be observed. Steel production would be observed to be using techniques of production linking it more closely to the coke activity, whose primary inputs are experiencing relatively higher advances in productivity improvement. In the case where the degree of integration is falling, the Harrod technical progress in steel production would be described as biased against indirect primary inputs or as indirect primary input saving (direct primary input using). In the case where the degree of integration is increasing, the Harrod technical progress would be said to be biased against direct primary inputs or as indirect primary input using (direct primary input saving). The Harrod conception of neutral technical change is associated with a given or unchanging degree of integration because in economic theory there is no reason to suppose that indirect primary inputs will be increasing or decreasing in their economic efficiency relative to direct primary inputs in a technologically interdependent economy.

CHAPTER 3

Some critical evaluations
of the new measures

In this chapter, we set out the major conceptual difficulties confronting our new measures in ascending order of importance.

As will be outlined later, there are many problems in ascertaining, in constant prices, the gross outputs and intermediate inputs by industry. The new and traditional measures are expressed in this study in terms of quantities; we have not checked our estimates by expressing them, identically, in terms of rates of change of prices.

Many data difficulties and imperfections are common to both the new and traditional measures of multifactor productivity. Such common problems do not need reiteration in this chapter as they are dealt with in Part II.

Of particular relevance to the new measures is the problem of imported intermediate and capital goods and the measurement of quality change for reproducible inputs and outputs.

A   Imports

With respect to the problem of imports, some industries in Canada import intermediate inputs. Lacking input–output tables linked between Canada and its trading partners, we are at this stage unable to take account of the fact that such inputs are being produced abroad more efficiently over time. Thus, if nonresident primary inputs increase in their technical efficiency relative to those domestically resident in Canada, one would predict that with respect to intermediate inputs, the terms of trade would turn in Canada's favour,[1] that Canadian industries would tend to substitute the relatively cheaper imported intermediate inputs for those domestically produced, so that Keynesian problems of the maintenance of aggregate demand set aside, total gross output per unit of domestic primary inputs would tend to be higher.

---

[1] Such terms of trade effects are not the same as those of a relative cheapening of imported consumption goods. Those in the text permit higher output to be produced whereas the lower priced consumption goods entail a rise in real incomes. A more general view is outlined later.

We would like to show that the multifactor productivity of Canada's domestic inputs has increased because they are co-operating with foreign primary inputs whose productivity is also increasing.[2] Unfortunately, we are not able to extend our new estimates by industry and for the aggregate private Canadian economy to account for the improvement in the productivity with which imported intermediate inputs are produced. As a consequence, our new estimates are biased downward; the extent of the bias can be appreciated by examining the weights for imported intermediate inputs in our measures. *To this extent,* our measures are similar to the traditional ones.[3]

It follows immediately that another drawback connected with the new measures is their failure to take into account that in the rest of the world advances in knowledge are taking place in the production of capital goods imported into and added to the Canadian domestic stock of capital. Here the terms-of-trade effect is of a more customary kind. An improvement in the efficiency with which imported capital goods are produced means that for Canada as a whole fewer resources have to be devoted to exports to finance the same flow of imported capital goods. In constant prices, the consumption that must be forgone to permit the same growth in the domestic capital stock is reduced because the imported component of that stock is now produced more cheaply. Although we cannot take such advances in knowledge into account in our measures, we do, however, take them into account with respect to the domestically produced components of the Canadian stock. With respect, therefore, to the import components of the capital stock, our new measures treat the capital stock component of inputs in the same way as the traditional measures do. We say, therefore, that our measures of multifactor productivity by industry and for the Canadian economy are biased down relative to what we believe, with an ideal data system, should be estimated.[4]

---

[2] A two-country case, with Canada as industry *j* and (say) the United States as industry *i*, would have the same analysis as that of Chapter 2.

[3] The traditional measures would be lower than the new estimates, even with this flaw, if the older measures are produced with intermediate imports treated as an input in the customary aggregate production function sense, i.e., if the gross output of the Canadian economy were taken to be personal and government consumption expenditure, business and government capital formation, and exports and the inputs as labour, capital imports, and intermediate imports. If the Domar–Hulten aggregation procedure is employed (or if, in fact, the aggregate old measures are employed with constant-dollar gross domestic product as the output concept), then again with respect to intermediate inputs the new and old measures should be the same.

[4] We have not adjusted our measures for the changing terms of trade among imported and domestically produced intermediate input and capital goods as a device to get around this problem. See Postner and Wesa, *Canadian Productivity Growth,* and A. Cas, W. E. Diewert, and L. A. Ostensoe, "Productivity Growth and Changes in the Terms of Trade

It is important to note that regardless of changes in the terms of trade, our new measures of multifactor productivity, because they fail to take into account the increased productivity of nonresident primary inputs, are biased downward. Thus, the term of trade in produced inputs could be turning against Canada, and our estimates of Canadian industry and aggregate multifactor productivity advance might still be too low.

B Quality change

Another major empirical problem is the measurement of quality change, particularly with respect to capital goods. Consider advances made in the design of computers or robots. If the new generation of computers has, relatively to the older machines, more of those characteristics for which purchasers pay higher prices, then standard quality-adjusted constant-price measures for the output of computers will show larger increases than (say) a mere count of computers. If equilibrium prevails, the characteristic prices of the computers will be equal to unit costs of such characteristics, and a quality-adjusted constant-price gross output index of computers will show the same change regardless of whether the quality adjustment is done in terms of characteristics or costs of production.[5]

Better machines in characteristic terms are the same as more machines in cost terms. If, however, application of the characteristic price approach to quality adjustments leads to more rapid increases in the constant-price gross output of computers than would application of the relative-costs-of-production approach,[6] then multifactor productivity in the computer-

in Canada", ed. R. C. Feenstra, *Empirical Methods for International Trade* (Cambridge, Mass.: Massachusetts Institute of Technology Press, 1988).

[5] "One would expect that in equilibrium the marginal cost of producing a quality change must approximate the incremental value of it to the user – otherwise a reallocation of resources would take place. Thus, real differences in the magnitude of the quality adjustments one gets from user-value and resource-cost adjustments presumably reflect shifts in functions, interference with competitive allocation, or wrong data", p. 305 from J. Triplett, "Concepts of Quality in Input and Output Price Measures: A Resolution of the User-value Resource-cost Debate", ed. M. F. Foss, *The U.S. National Income and Product Accounts: Selected Topics* (Chicago: University of Chicago Press for the National Bureau of Economic Research, 1983). See also J. E. Triplett, "Price Index Research and Its Influence on Data: A Historical Review", paper presented to the Fiftieth Anniversary Conference on Research in Income and Wealth, 12–14 May 1988.

For early arguments that under equilibrium conditions the two approaches to the quality-change problem in the measurement of the quantity and price of produced inputs and outputs lead to the same results, see D. Jorgensen, "The Embodiment Hypothesis", *Journal of Political Economy,* LXXIV, February 1966, 1–17, and Rymes, *On Concepts of Capital and Technical Change,* ch. 6.

[6] Such a possibility is said to arise if there is a "costless" improvement in the quality of a commodity or service. If there simply is more of a relatively high priced characteristic,

producing industry would be shown as rising at a faster rate and that in the computer-using industries, because of the higher rate of growth of the constant-price stock of computers, would be shown as rising at a lower rate.[7] Differences in the two methods of quality adjustment lead then to reallocations of multifactor productivity, measured in the traditional way, between capital-producing and capital-using industries.[8]

Differences in the quality-adjusted capital output and input measures arise because of the way in which the characteristics approach imbeds in the output series the "disequilibrium" profits resulting from the advances in knowledge in the capital-goods-producing industries whereas the cost-of-production approach leads to the advances in knowledge showing up in the capital-using industries.

To reiterate, if application of the characteristics approach leads to different results than the cost-of-production approach,[9] it does so because "disequilibrium" profits are being embedded in the new commodities and services. The constant-price output of industries *producing* such commodities and services and their multifactor productivity will be higher. If such industries produce final output such as personal expenditure on goods and services or business gross capital formation, then the total measured real final output of the economy will be growing more rapidly. If the industries produce intermediate output and, as part of gross capital formation, additions to capital stocks, then in the industries using such output as intermediate inputs or capital stock inputs, their inputs will be shown as rising more rapidly and their traditional measures of multifactor productivity less rapidly. In summary, application of the cost-less quality improvement characteristics approach to the construction of price and quantity indexes in an interindustry input–output System of National Accounts affects traditional multifactor productivity measures by industry in dramatic ways.

then the characteristics and cost-of-production approach must yield the same results. If there is an increase in current-period profits arising from producing more highly desired characteristics, then the current-period characteristics and cost-of-production approaches again must yield the same results. The fact that the base-period characteristics and cost-of-production approaches might yield different results compared to the current period is merely another aspect of the well-known index number problem.

[7] The former approach would lead to a fall in the price of computers relative to that resulting from the cost-of-production approach so differences in quality adjustments would affect measured price movements as well. The price indexes of computers using the characteristics approach would fall relative to those produced by the cost approach!

[8] For a graphic description of such results in the U.S. growth accounting systems, see Denison, *Estimates of Productivity Change in Industry*.

[9] The classic advocacy of the cost-of-production approach is found in E. F. Denison, "Theoretical Aspects of Quality Change, Capital Consumption and Net Capital Formation", *Problems of Capital Formation: Concepts, Measurement and Controlling Factors* (Princeton: Princeton University Press for the National Bureau of Economic Research, 1957).

The new measures of multifactor productivity advanced in this study would not reallocate productivity among industries in the same way.

From

$$[I-(A+E+D)]^{-1}t = h$$

we know that the new measure for any industry may be expressed as a linear combination of the traditional measures of the productivity advance of all related industries, the immediate industry, and those directly and indirectly supplying produced inputs to the industry in question.

If the measured constant-price inputs into a using industry are higher because of the application of the costless characteristic approach to quality improvement measurement of the outputs of the producing industries, the new measures of productivity in the using industry tend to remain unchanged because they show that the primary inputs indirectly employed in the using industries are experiencing increases in their productivity. The traditional measures of multifactor productivity in the using industries are lower because the constant-price produced inputs are so measured to be rising faster.[10]

The point can be simply seen. Using the quantities formulation, the new measure of multifactor productivity for industry j will be

$$q_j - [\cdots + \tau_{ij}(k_{ij} - h_i) + \cdots] = h_j$$

If the costless quality adjustment is made to the capital goods produced in industry i and employed in industry j so that the constant-price rate of growth of the net capital stock, k_{ij}, is raised to k_{ij}^*, then the traditional measure for industry j,

$$q_j - [\cdots + \tau_{ij}k_{ij}^* + \cdots] = t_j^*$$

will be reduced, that is, $t_j^* < t_j$. The productivity advance in industry i will, however, be increased by the quality adjustment. Thus, $q_i - (\cdots) = t_i$ will be changed to $q_i^* - (\quad) = t_i^*$ so that $t_i^* > t_i$ by exactly the increase in the measured growth rate of the output of the producing industry owing to the quality adjustment. The new measures of productivity advance for the producing industry, ignoring any produced inputs in that industry, will be the same as for the traditional measures. Thus, $h_i^* > h_i$ and $h_i^* - h_i = t_i^* - t_i$. The new measure of productivity advance in the receiving or using industry will, however, be unaffected. That is,

$$q_j - [\cdots + \tau_{ij}(k_{ij}^* - h_i^*) + \cdots] = h_j^*$$

Since $k_{ij}^* - k_{ij} = q_i^* - q_i = t_i^* - t_j = h_i^* - h_i$ then

---

[10] If the costless characteristic approach leads to higher traditional measures of multifactor productivity in industries producing consumer goods, then the new measures for such industries will also be higher.

$$k_{ij}^* - h_i^* = k_{ij} + h_i^* - h_i - h_i^* = k_{ij} - h_i$$

and $h_j^* = h_j$.

Thus, the new measures of multifactor productivity in the using industries would tend to be invariant with respect to National Accounting conventions in the assessment of the qualitative improvement in produced inputs.

Using the rates of change of prices formulation, the new measures will be $[\cdots + \tau_{ij}(r_j + p_i + h_i) + \cdots] - p_j = h_j$. If the constant-price quantity indexes of new capital stocks produced in i and used in j are raised because of the quality change adjustment, then the price index, that is, the net rental index, must be lowered. The traditional measures of productivity would be correspondingly lowered, $[\cdots + \tau_{ij}(r_j + p_i^*) + \cdots] - p_j = t_j^*$, where since $p_i^* < p_i$, $t_j^* < t_j$. The new measures would reflect the convention that the primary input prices in the supplying industries would not be falling to the same extent as is the price of the output being produced by them. The new measures would then be $[\cdots \tau_{ij}(r_j + p_i^* + h_i^*) + \cdots] - p_j = h_j^*$, and since $p_i + h_i = p_i^* + h_i^*$ and $p_i^* < p_i$ but $h_i^* > h_i$, again the new measures of multifactor productivity in the using or purchasing industries or those "downstream" from the costless innovation would tend to remain invariant to the quality change adjustment in the output and productivity of the producing or "upstream" industries.

C   Rented capital

With respect to rented capital goods, it is reasonable to argue that for the measurement of multifactor productivity, one wants the constant-price net stock of capital and capital consumption allowances appearing as inputs in the lessor or owning, not in the lessee or using, industries. The gross rents paid should appear as part of the gross output of the owning or lessor industry and as part of the intermediate inputs purchased by the lessee industry. Such a procedure ensures that the *net returns to capital* associated with the rented capital stocks will accrue in the owning or lessor industry, and since as well, the net capital stocks will appear in the owning industry, meaningful ex post estimates of the net rates of return to capital by industry can be prepared. Empirically speaking, it is difficult to get estimates of rented capital stocks by industry of use: Rental cars and industrial rental cars are rented from one industry to another, often within the same day; bits and pieces of multistory office buildings are rented out to many different firms in many different industries; and so forth. Thus, it would appear virtually impossible to allocate net stocks and capital consumption allowances associated with (say) rental cars and warehouses by "using" industry. If the gross rentals paid and received data exist, attempts to allocate stocks by using industry are not necessary. Gross rents paid by the using industry will cover all of the other inputs, for example, administration expenses necessary to provide the services of the rented capital goods. When multifactor productivity measures are attempted, the problem of rented capital goods illustrates clearly how one has to go "behind" the services of the capital goods. In this case, the gross services of the capital goods by themselves in the traditional sense are engaged in the using or lessee industries. The new measures of multifactor productivity would take into account the changing productivity of the lessor industries in any attempt to measure productivity advance in the lessee industries. The new measures would furthermore account for the changing productivity of the capital goods industries or those industries supplying the lessor industries with the capital goods whose services are in turn being leased out.

The important thing to note again is that the complete industry application of gross rents paid and received as being intermediate inputs into the lessee industry and as the intermediate part of the gross output of the lessor industries focusses attention on the requirement that the net returns and capital consumption allowances on the capital goods proper are, as near as can be done,[11] allocated to the owning industries. Why is the ownership important? This question gets us into the heart of the controversy about waiting being the fundamental primary input associated with the factor income – net returns to capital.

D   Utilization

Traditional measures of multifactor productivity sometimes are adjusted for changes in the utilization of capital stocks. The problem of adjusting measures of the services of "fixed" capital goods for changes in the utilization of capital goods is complex. There are routine maintenance expenditures connected with such capital goods that prolong their useful lives by maintaining the flow of their services (e.g., supervision of custodians, oiling of machines). Such expenditures are captured in regular data on labour and intermediate inputs. Capital goods used more intensively (e.g., plants are worked for longer hours, trucks are driven harder and faster without preventative maintenance) experience what Keynes described as

---

[11] Rented capital goods appearing as purchase, sale, and lease-back managements are now common. In some agreements of this type, the ownership of the capital goods reverts back to the lessee industries after agreed contract stipulations have been met. The extent to which lease arrangements contain financing arrangements as well is not easily ascertained, but the conceptual basis that suggests that net capital stocks and capital consumption allowances should be allocated on the basis of ownership, i.e., to the lessor industry, remains clear.

marginal user cost.[12] Data for such user costs do not, in general, exist. If capital goods in some industry are used more intensively, then ideally one would have data that would show an increase in constant-price capital consumption allowances, revealing a speed-up in the rate of depreciation or a temporary shortening in the economic lives of the capital goods in the industry as they are used more intensively. In industries where capital goods are used less intensively, if changes in the utilization of capital are an interindustry phenomenon, then ideally the constant-price capital input data would show effects opposite to those just described. Our fixed capital stock data do not show such temporary utilization changes. It should be remembered that a part of the capital input data, those reflecting inventories of finished goods and raw materials, which play the role of buffer stocks, will reflect changes in utilization as reflected by differences between production and sales of final goods and purchases and utilization of storable intermediate inputs. Such buffer stocks illustrate clearly the concept of waiting as the capital input that lies behind the new measures of multifactor productivity in this study. Such buffer stocks must be carried, they play no immediate technical role in production, and yet they are essential for production and consumption must be forgone to carry them. If changes in aggregate demand should cause capital to be underutilized and the measures of capital input are not adjusted, then measures of multifactor productivity will show smaller increases and, as our empirical work suggests, may even show negative changes. How does one interpret negative changes in advances in knowledge? If the capital stocks are adjusted for such changes in utilization, then the traditional measures would likely not show negative changes. Arguments can be made, however, that the utilization adjustment should not be made since changes in aggregate demand, in the Keynesian sense, cause the economy as a whole to lose efficiency in the sense that the unadjusted stocks show that the flow of services of the capital goods and, importantly, necessary consumption forgone to maintain such capital stocks are, because of insufficiency in aggregate demand, producing less than before. We have not made any utilization adjustments to our capital stock inputs. If we had, we should be attempting to measure the utilized flow of the services of capital goods. Rather we are attempting to measure the flows of waiting or consumption forgone associated with the capital

[12] J. M. Keynes, *The General Theory of Employment, Interest and Money*, VII, *The Collected Writings of John Maynard Keynes* (London: Macmillan for the Royal Economic Society, 1973), Appendix on User Cost. See also M. Kim, "The Structure of Technology with Endogenous Capital Utilization", *International Economic Review*, XXIX, February 1988, 111–30, and R. R. Betancourt and C. K. Clague, *Capital Utilization: A Theoretical and Empirical Analysis* (Cambridge: Cambridge University Press, 1981).

inputs. Under utilization, then, of the constant-price net stocks of capital results, we argue, in an inefficient use of the nonproduced capital inputs.

E   Waiting

Waiting is the input that is the nonproduced capital input in our study. We believe it to be clear that in a technically progressive economy, where there are advances in productivity in the capital goods industries, the flow of primary input services required to produce and reproduce capital goods is being reduced. If it were the case that labour and labour alone[13] were the only primary input, then capital goods would be but the product of labour, and measures of multifactor productivity advance would reduce merely to measures of the increase in productivity of labour, directly and indirectly involved, through the interdependence of industries, in the production of the final output of the economy.[14] Labour is, however, not the only class of primary nonproduced inputs in the economy. We argue, holding aside the Keynesian difficulties discussed, that in addition to labour or working there is the fact that for capital to be accumulated, some saving, some postponement or forgoing of present consumption, some waiting, is necessary. For capital to be maintained, for the various stocks of capital goods to be carried forward undepleted through time, waiting is again required.

As a telling illustration of how fundamental the capital measurement problem is, consider the measurement of labour inputs. During any period, individuals are endowed with so much time, only a fraction of which is rented into the marketplace.[15] Such time, commonly expressed in terms

[13] We ignore land and all other natural agents of production. See the Appendix to Chapter 2 for a discussion of how such inputs may be incorporated in multifactor productivity measurement.

[14] This impression is strengthened in the literature by references to Harrod-neutral technical progress as being labour augmenting. For an example of this argument, see L. L. Pasinetti, *Structural Change and Economic Growth* (Cambridge: Cambridge University Press, 1981).

[15] Our measures of multifactor productivity, both old and new, take no account of advances in economic efficiency that occur outside the market, whether in the government sector, such as the Public Administration and Defence Industry, or in "households", such as churches and private households. This creates a difficulty in the interpretation of our numbers illustrated by the following example. Improvements in household technology will change the extent to which households will hold inventories of pantry stocks. The profitability of different kinds of retail stores, with varying inventory policies, will be affected – as will be the measurement of multifactor productivity in the retail trade industry. For a study of how measures of multifactor productivity may be affected by their failure to deal with nonmarket activities, see K. Acheson and S. Ferris, "Problem of the Measurement of Multifactor Productivity in Trade and Service Industries", paper presented at the Conference on Multifactor Productivity Measurement at Carleton University in October 1987, and *Retail and Wholesale Trade Services in Canada* (Vancouver; Fraser Institute, 1988).

of years or hours in our measures of labour, is an imperfect indicator of the flow of labour services. It takes no account of the intensity of the effort (a manager, e.g., during his years of work, might be productive at a highly intensive level only in periodic outbursts while on other occasions could apparently be doing nothing). People who rent their services by the hour must be monitored to prevent shirking. Some labour is measured in terms not of input but of output, as in piece work. More importantly, work or human labour as an input in the process of production encounters the difficulty that a standard unit of labour is unknown; what most people rent is the services of their human capital, such capital acquired by investment in the acquisition of skills through various types of formal education and training or through on-the-job experience. Thus, it is probably better to measure, for multifactor productivity measurement purposes, the flow of services not of labour, but of human capital. However, the services of human capital and the stock of human capital, in all their manifestations, are reproduced. The problem then of what constitutes the primary input of capital in multifactor productivity measurement cannot be escaped. It is a fundamental conceptual and empirical problem.

A once-over improvement in technology that permits buildings, machinery and equipment, inventories, and human capital to be more cheaply produced means that, ceteris paribus, if individuals should maintain their *rates* of savings absolutely unchanged, further capital accumulation will take place. The extra capital accumulation that results is accountable for by the improvement in technology and is not a separate "source of growth" of the increased output of the economy.

If increased or decreased rates of saving accompanied (or were even induced by) the improvement in technology, then the changes in accumulation associated with the changed waiting would affect the recorded growth of the economy. However, that capital accumulation and growth that occurs because of the improvement in technique can be separated from that which is not produced or induced by the better technique. That distinction is what this study attempts to measure.

Consider one of the simplest of all possible models, the neo-classical one-commodity model. In steady equilibrium, we have

$$gk = \dot{k} = sq(k) - \delta k = 0$$

where, given the flow of working or labour, net capital accumulation gk, where g is the net growth rate, is greater or less than zero if the fraction of output (with output a function of working and capital) saved exceeds or falls short of depreciation. If the fraction of output saved (one measure of waiting) were greater, then the economy would accumulate further capital until again steady equilibrium might prevail. The fraction of output saved might be a function of capital, or wealth (which would include the capitalized value of the returns to working), or the ratio of consumption to wealth, and so forth. The crucial point is that whether one is concerned with the gross or net services of capital, where, for example, $\partial q/\partial k - \delta$ would be the net marginal product of the services of capital or the stock of capital if one distinguishes the services of a stock from the stock itself, all these capital inputs are endogenous in two senses: First, the services and the stocks of capital are produced by the economy, and second, these services and stocks depend upon the willingness of the economic agents to refrain from present consumption, to save or to wait. The stock of capital not only indexes the services of capital goods proper but also the services of waiting.

In the stationary equilibrium we can write

$$sq(k, T) = \delta k$$

and solve for the equilibrium k so that $k = k(s, \delta, T)$, that is, the equilibrium flow of capital services or the stock of capital will be some function of the propensity to save, the rate of depreciation, and the state of technology.[16] If we take the rate of saving as a measure of the flow of waiting, then the flow of services of capital goods proper and the flows and stocks of such goods are being maintained by the rate of saving or waiting. The waiting cannot be produced or reproduced by the economy. The waiting is the primary input and not the services of the capital goods proper or the goods themselves.

---

[16] Suppose we write the production function as Cobb–Douglas, or

$$Q = T \cdot L^{\alpha} K^{\beta}$$

i.e., the gross output is equal to the flow of labour and "capital" services as modified by their respective elasticities and the state of technology. Where $q = Tk^{\beta}$, the steady-state condition is

$$sTk^{\beta} = \delta k$$

so that

$$k = [s(T\delta)^{-1}]^{1/(1-\beta)}$$

and

$$q = T[s(T\delta)^{-1}]^{\beta/(1-\beta)}$$

Given β, δ, and T, i.e., the coefficients and the state of technology, stationary output per unit of working is determined by s, the fraction of gross output saved, one measure of the flow of waiting. If $T^* = 2T$, then if $s^* = \frac{1}{2}s$, so that $s^*T^* = \frac{1}{2}s(2T) = sT$, then the flow of capital services and output would be unchanged whereas the flow of waiting services would be reduced. In order to maintain the same flow of "capital" services, the members of the economy could wait less; they could reduce their fractions of income and output saved.

If there were, ceteris paribus, a once-over reduction in waiting, the stock of capital would not be being maintained and the steady-state equilibrium would be disturbed. Output will be less since the flow of services of the capital goods proper will be less. Output and the capital stock will be lower and remain lower where the lower waiting is matched by the lower capital requirements. That is, one has a new steady state,

$$s^*q(k^*, T) = \delta k^*$$

where $k^* = k(s^*, \delta, T)$, the lower capital stock, $k^* < k$, reflects the lower rate or flow of waiting, $s^* < s$.

One-commodity models are not, as the Cambridge capital controversy revealed, robust. We must reconsider those cases where the "capital" input in the traditional measures of multifactor productivity is, in reality, a complex of many kinds of capital goods.

From Keynes[17] we know that in temporary equilibrium the spot price

$$-P_{K0} + \frac{P_{C0}(1+p)(\partial C/\partial K) + P_{K0}(1+p'_K+p''_K)}{(1+R)(1+p)} = 0$$

of *any* capital good, new or used, P_{K0}, must be such that the following conditions are met: The present value, when the one-period interest rate i equals the one-period real rate R modified by the one-period expected rate of inflation in the price of a bundle of consumption goods, p [i.e., $1+i = (1+R)(1+p)$], of (a) the consumption value of the gross marginal physical product of the capital good one-period hence [i.e., $P_1(\partial C/\partial K) = P_0(1+p)(\partial C/\partial K)$] *and* (b) the one-period hence expected spot price of the capital, P_{K1}, will reflect the expected rate of depreciation, p'_k (i.e., p'_k is the expected rate of decline in the price of the capital good, given its utilization, as it ages one period[18]), and will also reflect other influences, such as the expected rate of inflation. Indeed the present value should reflect all the events expected to play upon the expected rate-of-change value of a capital good, p''_K, over its remaining economic life, save its aging. Hence

$$P_{K1} = P_{K0}(1+p'_K)(1+p''_K) = P_{K0}(1+p_{K1}+p''_K)$$

---

[17] J. M. Keynes, *The General Theory of Employment, Interest and Money*, VII, *The Collected Writings of John Maynard Keynes* (London: Macmillan for the Royal Economic Society, 1973), ch. 17, "The Essential Properties of Interest and Money".

[18] The conceptual basis for the calculation of depreciation is clear. It simply amounts to a comparison of the spot prices of capital goods *identical* in *all* respects save age. In practice, of course, the calculation is arbitrary. (The problem of the quality change exhibited by capital goods as new vintages replace old is discussed in the preceding text.)

Immediately, one has

$$RP_{K0} = P_{C0}\frac{\partial C}{\partial K} + (p'_K + p''_K - p)P_{K0}$$

and[19]

$$R = \frac{P_{C0}}{P_{K0}}\frac{\partial C}{\partial K} + p'_K + p''_K - p$$

Assume that the prices of capital goods in terms of a bundle of consumption goods is not expected to change, that is, $p''_K = p$. Then

$$R = \frac{P_{C0}}{P_{K0}}\frac{\partial C}{\partial K} + p'_K$$

or the real net rate of return equals the net marginal rate of transformation between present and permanent streams of consumption, since $\partial C/\partial K/(P_{K0}/P_{C0}) + p'_K$ is the ratio of what any capital good is expected marginally to contribute to permanent consumption to the cost of the capital good in terms of present consumption forgone, all adjusted for the depreciation rate. It is equally clear that

$$RP_{K0} = P_{C0}\frac{\partial C}{\partial K} + p'_K P_{K0}$$

is the net rental earned by the machine while

$$(R - p'_K)P_{K0} = P_{C0}\frac{\partial C}{\partial K}$$

is the gross rental. Furthermore, if we return to the more general formula

$$R + p = \frac{P_{C0}}{P_{K0}}\frac{\partial C}{\partial K} + p'_K + p''_K$$

we see that the net *nominal* rate of return includes the nominal capital gains expected to be earned from possession of the capital good.

[19] Such formulae appear in Keynes and in C. Bliss, *Capital Theory and the Distribution of Income* (Amsterdam: North-Holland, 1905); D. M. Nuti, "On the Rates of Return on Investment", eds. M. Brown, K. Sato, and P. Zarembka, *Essays in Modern Capital Theory* (Amsterdam: North-Holland, 1976), and in M. F. Mohr, "The Theory and Measurement of the Rental Prices of Capital in Industry Specific Productivity Analysis: A Vintage Rental Price of Capital Model", ed. A. Dogramaci, *Measurement Issues and Behaviour of Productivity Variables* (Boston: Kluwer Nijhoff, 1986). In Mohr's study, the effects of taxes on income, taxes on capital gains, and tax allowances for depreciation are also considered.

A further simplification is the one-commodity model just discussed, since $P_{C0}/P_{K0} = 1$. Then

$$R = \frac{\partial C}{\partial K} + p_K'$$

Temporary equilibrium entails that the spot prices of all capital goods must be such that the same competitive net rate of return applies to all. If not, if it were possible to transform from present into permanent consumption streams at a higher marginal rate through the acquisition or continued ownership of one capital good compared with another, then the spot price of the former would be higher and the latter lower until marginal rates of transformation were equalized.[20]

Behind the traditional measures of multifactor productivity lies the concept of the services of the capital goods as inputs in production functions, and these services have as prices the rentals

$$[R - p_k' - (p_k'' - p)]P_k = P_C \frac{\partial C}{\partial K}$$

In National Accounting, the related measures, as we have seen, are $(R - p_k')P_K$, all of which are in ex post terms and capital gains or losses have been eliminated by the measurement of R.

If there is an advance in the productivity with which the capital goods in question are being or can be produced, then it is clear that the services of the capital goods are themselves being produced more cheaply – more cheaply, of course, in terms of the primary inputs such as labour and waiting or in terms of the consumption that must be forgone to produce or reproduce such services.[21]

---

[20] At any time, the net rates of return, the marginal rates of transformation, may be consistent with positive or negative net investment and saving as the economy moves through a sequence of temporary equilibria with the possible, but not necessary, outcome being the full *steady*-state equilibrium. Costs of adjustment, such as renovation of existing capital goods and movements among existing industries, could be taken into account by (say) incorporation of complimentary inputs such as labour and materials in the statement of the net marginal physical product of the capital good. See Bliss, *Capital Theory and the Distribution of Income.*

[21] It is the capacity to be produced that is important. The capital goods being used or used up may have been produced earlier. Raw materials used up may be being withdrawn from inventories previously accumulated. The services of the capital goods may be from those produced many years ago. The rental on such services will reflect, of course, the cost of replacement of such vintage capital goods that will be the same, in temporary equilibrium, as the spot prices of the various vintages. All services of capital are metered in terms of current rentals and prices, i.e., in terms of current reproduction cost. The conditions under which the capital goods were produced (say) many years ago are utterly irrelevant for the measurement of multifactor productivity by either the traditional or new approaches.

It is the individuals, privately or collectively, who provide the waiting, who forgo the present consumption, which results in the various capital goods and their services one sees currently in existence and use. If the primary inputs, working and waiting, required currently to produce such goods and their services are reduced, then the amount of waiting necessary to maintain (and augment) such capital goods has been reduced. The efficiency of working and waiting, if increased, will result, with the same flow of services of waiting, in a greater stock of capital goods proper and their services.

In the one-commodity case, one sees the point if the flow of the waiting service is conceived as the fraction of output saved. In the case of many capital goods, the need for savings or the willingness to wait remain clear in order for there to be capital accumulation. Such waiting takes the form of accumulation and maintenance of many kinds of capital goods. Saying that the economy can produce or reproduce such capital goods and these services more efficiently is the same as asserting that a given flow of waiting in a heterogeneous capital goods economy *may* result in larger stock of such capital goods and a larger flow of their services. The efficiency of waiting has advanced.[22]

One may approach the problem from a strictly National Accounting view.

Consider the simple net rental price of the services of capital goods, RP_k. Consider now the price system approach to multifactor productivity measurement. For any industry for each capital good, we will have, in the traditional measure, $r + p_k - p$, which shows the proportionate rate of change in the own-product rental of each capital good owned in any industry.[23]

The price system approach clearly reveals the fundamental problem with the traditional measures. From the price side, productivity measures

---

[22] For economies with *unchanging* technologies and heterogeneous capital goods, a higher rate of savings or more waiting will result in a lower real rate of return, but there is no reason for the aggregate stock of capital to be higher or lower; i.e., there is no reason to expect some aggregate constant-price measure of the flow of services of the capital goods to be higher or lower.

    A simple Cambridge model illustrates. In steady states, the initial economy is represented by $P_k gK = s\pi RP_k K$ or $g = s\pi R$. A comparison economy has the configuration

$$P_k^* gK^* = s_{\pi^*} \cdot R^* P_K^* K^* \quad \text{or} \quad g = s_{\pi^*} \cdot R^*$$

so that if $s_{\pi^*} > s_\pi$, then $R^* < R$. There is no reason, however, to expect $P_k(K^* - K)$ or $P_k^*(K^* - K)$ to be greater or less than zero or equal to zero. See Harcourt, *Some Cambridge Controversies in the Theory of Capital.*

[23] It is instructive to note that rentals actually paid by any lessee industry will be treated as intermediate inputs and so, in the traditional approach, aggregated out by the Domar-Hulten procedure in aggregate measures of multifactor productivity.

are the rate of change of *input* prices less the rate of change of *output* prices. In $r + p_k - p$, r is the proportionate rate of change in the net rate of return – clearly an input price – whereas p is equally clearly an output price growth rate. What, however, is p_k? It is the proportionate rate of change of the price of the net capital stock, or the price of the capital good when it appears as the output of the capital goods industry from which it is drawn or reproducible. Clearly, then, P_k and its proportionate rate of growth, p_k, are output prices. They are not the requisite input prices. The traditional multifactor productivity measures are then inconsistent with respect to capital goods. With respect to the growth rate of what should be input prices, they present both input and output prices. The new measures are $r + p_k + h - p$. The question is: What is $p_k + h$? It stands for the proportionate rate of growth of the prices of *outputs* of the capital goods industries *plus* the growth rate of the new multifactor productivity measures in the capital-goods-producing industries, which equals the rate of growth of the *prices of the primary input prices* in those industries.

Thus, $r + p_k + h$ gives us the proportionate rate of changes of the primary input, r, associated with the transform of present into permanent streams of consumption in the immediate capital-good-owning industry plus the proportionate rate of change of the prices of the primary inputs, $p_k + h$, associated with the increasing efficiency, if any, in the capital-good-supplying industries and, of course, all industries directly and indirectly supporting such industries. The new measures then correctly express multifactor productivity advance in any industry in terms of the rate of growth of input prices minus the rate of growth of output prices.

National accountants will now see immediately the consequence when multifactor productivity measures are expressed in terms of proportionate rates of growth of outputs minus proportionate rates of growth of inputs.

Any value index is expressible in terms of quantity times price indexes.

It follows immediately with respect to the value of the net rentals for capital goods, $RP_k K$, that the value index $r + p_k + k$, when decomposed properly for multifactor productivity purposes, will appear as $r + p_k + h + k - h$ when, as just explained, $r + p_k + h$ is the *input price* index and $k - h$ is the *input quantity* index. Thus it can be seen that the new measures of multifactor productivity are also the correct way in which the current-price National Accounts, either at the industry or aggregate levels, are decomposed into quantity and price indexes for both outputs and inputs and productivity measurement.

F   On vertical integration

How do the new measures of multifactor productivity relate to Pasinetti's concepts of vertically integrated sectors and productivity aggregated by end use?[24] It will be recalled that with respect only to intermediate inputs the new and traditional industry measures, when aggregated to provide a measure for the entire economy, give the same result. The traditional measures take into account (though not at the individual industry level), by the Domar–Hulten aggregation procedure, the essential producibility of intermediate inputs in the context of interindustry technological interdependence. The new measures take account of that crucial aspect of intermediate inputs and outputs for each industry's measure and aggregate by net output or final demand weights.[25]

Reconsider the simple static input–output accounts. Ignoring depreciation, we have the quantity equations

$$B[I+A]^{-1}[C+\Delta K] = \bar{L}$$

for the vector of the direct and indirect labour requirements associated with the vector of net final demands $[C+\Delta K]$ and

$$E[I-A]^{-1}[C+\Delta K] = K$$

for the vector of the direct and indirect "capital" requirements.[26]

The matching price system was $P = WB[I-A-E]^{-1}$.

One can rewrite the net capital formation component of the vectors of final demand as

$$\begin{bmatrix} \dot{K}_1 \\ \dot{K}_2 \\ \vdots \\ \dot{K}_N \end{bmatrix} = \begin{bmatrix} \dot{K}_{11} + \dot{K}_{12} + \cdots + \dot{K}_{1N} \\ \dot{K}_{21} + \dot{K}_{22} + \cdots + \dot{K}_{2N} \\ \vdots \quad \vdots \quad \quad \vdots \\ \dot{K}_{n1} + \dot{K}_{n2} + \cdots + \dot{K}_{nN} \end{bmatrix}$$

or as

$$\begin{bmatrix} \dot{K}_1 \\ \dot{K}_2 \\ \vdots \\ \dot{K}_N \end{bmatrix} = \begin{bmatrix} G_{11}K_{11} + G_{12}K_{12} + \cdots + G_{1N}K_{1N} \\ G_{21}K_{21} + G_{22}K_{22} + \cdots + G_{2N}K_{2N} \\ \vdots \quad \vdots \quad \quad \vdots \\ G_{n1}K_{n1} + G_{n2}K_{n2} + \cdots + G_{nN}K_{nN} \end{bmatrix}$$

[24] See Pasinetti, *Structural Change and Economic Growth;* T. K. Rymes, "More on the Measurement of Total Factor Productivity", *Review of Income and Wealth,* XXIX, September 1983, 297–316; I. Steedman, "On the 'Impossibility' of Hicks-neutral Technical Change", *Economic Journal,* XCV, September 1985, 746–58, and Denison, *Estimates of Productivity Change in Industry.*

[25] It is assumed that capital consumption allowances are treated as intermediate inputs, in which case for the new measures the final demand weights are each industry's contribution to net domestic product or net final output whereas for the traditional measures the weights are each industry's gross output divided by *total* net final output.

[26] It will be recalled that E is a matrix with elements $e_{ij} = R_j K_{ij} Q_j^{-1}$, the net rate of return earned in the jth industry times the net stock of capital produced or producible in industry i owned in industry j divided by the gross output of industry j.

where $G_{ij}K_{ij}$ is the growth rate of the net capital stock producible in industry i owned in industry j times that capital stock.

Consider now the matrix F with elements

$$G_{ij}K_{ij}Q_j^{-1}$$

and rewrite the quantity equations as

$$B(I-A-F)^{-1}C = \bar{L}$$

and as

$$E(I-A-F)^{-1}C = \hat{K}$$

Consider now the final consumption vector C. Each element would be the output of a Pasinetti hypervertically integrated sector. Associated with any element of the vector, say, C_j, would be the vector of labour directly and indirectly associated with that final consumption, the labour not only directly involved in industry j but also indirectly involved in the production of intermediate inputs involved in j's output as well as in all the capital goods industries indirectly called upon to produce the growing capital stock. That is, since

$$AQ + C + FQ = Q$$

then

$$BAQ + BC + BFQ = BQ = \bar{L}$$

or the vector of labour inputs can be expressed in terms of three components: labour involved in the production of intermediate output, BAQ; labour involved in the production of final consumption, BC; and labour involved in the production of net capital accumulation, BFQ.

The same representation can be made for the capital input. If we consider Pasinetti sectors, we note, first, that sectors are not "naturally" observed collections of input and output statistics as are industries; rather they are formal constructs stemming from input–output accounts. In the case where some industries produce no final output, where they produce, that is, only intermediate output, the number of industries will exceed the number of sectors. Second, productivity measures at the aggregate level for all Pasinetti sectors will be the same for the traditional aggregate measures, using the Domar–Hulten aggregation procedure, because both measures "net" out intermediate inputs and outputs. These measures will not be the same for the new measures. Productivity measures for each Pasinetti sector will be the same as productivity measures by net final output or end use. Third, the new productivity measures advanced in this study always consider such advance in an interdependent interindustry technology and so capture the notion of integration so vividly expressed in the Pasinetti sector concept. Finally, the new productivity measures are by "observed" industries and use net final outputs as weights for aggregation procedures. If C_j is the component of net final output being considered (the output of the jth Pasinetti sector), then the relevant productivity measure by final output or end use is h_j, *not* the productivity measures, denoted v_j, calculated for the Pasinetti sectors. Why? The productivity measure for the Pasinetti sector j takes account of the produced nature of the intermediate inputs and the primary inputs required for their production used directly and indirectly in the production of C_j but *neither* takes account of the changing productivity of the industries producing the capital inputs, which will result in the aggregate v measures being the same as the Domar–Hulten aggregated t measures, *or* nets out capital inputs entirely on the grounds that labour is the only primary input (abstracting from natural agents) in production.

Our new measures of productivity advance provide the measures by end use or by Pasinetti's vertically integrated sectors without encountering the Domar–Hulten aggregation problem or going to the extreme of reducing all primary inputs to labour alone.

In the first part of this study, we have reviewed the basic theory lying behind the new measures of multifactor productivity advance and have compared them conceptually with the traditional measures. We now turn to our empirical work where the two measures, constructed from the same input–output data base, are presented, examined, and compared.

Measures of multifactor productivity, Canada, 1961–1980: Introduction to the experimental estimates

Part I of this study presented and compared the theoretical arguments behind the traditional and new measures of multifactor productivity. The new measures take into account the produced nature of capital inputs and, at the industry level, the technological interdependence involved in the production of outputs and inputs in a technically progressive world. The traditional measures do not.

Part II sets up two empirical models, one for the derivation of feasibility estimates of traditional multifactor productivity measures and the other for the new measures using an expanded input–output data base from Statistics Canada. Both measures should be regarded as experimental, for not all data problems have been resolved. The study demonstrates the potential in the use of an input–output data base for empirical studies of productivity and the feasibility of preparing Canadian estimates of the new measures of multifactor productivity.

The content of Part II is as follows.

Chapter 4 describes the input–output accounts and data base, which are the basis of the empirical model. It also defines and specifies the accounting concepts employed and limitations of the data. It goes on to present the modified input–output (I/O) model used and derives, from two different versions, the traditional and the new measures of multifactor productivity. The basic difference between these two measures lies in the measurement of the intermediate and capital inputs; that is, produced inputs. The new measure adjusts each produced input for the change in efficiency in its industry of origin, whereas the traditional measure does not. The result of this adjustment is an interdependent set of linear equations where the measures of multifactor productivity for all industries are simultaneously solved. By comparison, for the calculation of the traditional multifactor productivity measures, an industry's measure is independent of all others and can be solved by itself, because it measures only the productivity change stemming from the more or less efficient use of its inputs alone.

Chapter 5 presents the results of the estimation of the multifactor productivity measures. The multifactor productivity measure (MFP) is defined as the Törnquist index of output minus the Törnquist index of all inputs. The measures of MFP are derived for each pair of years using a time series of input–output data and other input data from 1961 to 1980. The discrete index number approximation used to estimate the continuous Divisia indexes of outputs and inputs are Törnquist indexes. The advantages of using these indexes are well known in the economic literature.[1] The share of each input in total output is defined to be the average of the value shares in each pair of years [e.g., $S_t = (S_t + S_{t-1})/2$]. The resulting year-to-year percentage changes in MFP were used to estimate the average of annual percentage rates of growth of MFP for period analysis. The relationship between the traditional and new measures is explored, and for any industry, the new measure is shown to be a linear combination of its own traditional measure and the measures of the industries that produce its inputs. Thus, given a vector of traditional industry measures, there is associated with it a vector of new industry measures that shows the total impact of the dispersion of the traditional measures through an interdependent industry production system, or, in other words, the direct and indirect effects of productivity change. Hence, an industry's new MFP measure can be decomposed into the sum of its own traditional productivity plus the indirect effects. The indirect effects can be further decomposed into either their industries of origin or the type of inputs in which they are embedded. The traditional measure of MFP is also decomposable into the formula of the individual rate of growth of output minus the share-weighted rate of growth in inputs. These results are also presented.

Domar[2] shows that, for an industry, the Leontief[3] measure of structural change and the traditional MFP measure are the same when the discrete terms in the structural change formula are replaced by their continuous analogue derived from constant-returns-to-scale production functions. Chapter 6 contains a proof of this result in the context of the Canadian I/O model and shows that when Törnquist quantity indexes are used as the discrete approximations to the underlying continuous data, the

[1] See W. E. Diewert, "Exact and Superlative Index Numbers", *Journal of Econometrics,* IV, May 1976, 115–45.

[2] E. D. Domar, "On the Measurement of Technological Change", *Economic Journal,* LXXI, December 1961, 709–29.

[3] W. Leontief, *Studies in the Structure of the American Economy* (Oxford: Oxford University Press, 1953).

equality carries through even for discrete data. Hence, the index of MFP (whether traditional or new) *is* an index of structural change and can therefore be expressed and decomposed into a weighted sum of the rate of change in the I/O coefficients explicitly disregarding changes in output.

Solow[4] showed for the aggregate economy that the rate of change of labour productivity could be decomposed into changes in the contribution of capital per unit of labour and changes in MFP. Chapter 6 also applies the preceding methodology to an industry and shows that the rate of growth of labour productivity is invariant with respect to the measure of MFP. Hence, it is only the distribution of the contributions of the produced inputs and of MFP that is affected (their sum is unchanged) when either the traditional or new concepts are used. In general, the new rate of MFP contributes more than the traditional rate to the rate of growth of labour productivity, and the produced inputs, taken together, contribute just that much less.

Tables associated with the various chapters present the results of the year-to-year changes for both traditional and new MFP indexes, and the decomposition analysis shows the results for the periods 1961-80, 1961-71, 1971-80, 1961-73, and 1973-80. The results for these last two periods confirm the post-1973 productivity slowdown.

There is a well-known aggregation problem between industry measures of MFP that should be based on a gross output concept and a measure for the entire economy that should be based on a net output (gross domestic product, GDP) concept. Chapter 7 calculates the overall economy's MFP rate and argues that, for the new measures, the weights should be the share of each industry's final output in the economy's final output. The rate of growth of MFP for industries producing intermediate inputs has already been incorporated into the MFP of the industries buying them. However, the traditional measures will tend to underestimate the economy's measure if final output weights are used. In this case, it is best to use the rule developed by Domar and to use as weights the ratio of an industry's gross output to the economy's final output. This adjustment is equal to the ones discussed by Hulten[5] and Denison.[6]

In this study, the new industry measures are aggregated to the economy's measure using final output weights; whereas for the traditional measures the weights used are the ratio of an industry's gross output to the economy's net output (for these latter weights, their sum exceeds unity).

[4] R. M. Solow, "Technical Change and the Aggregate Production Function", *Review of Economics and Statistics,* XXXIX, August 1957, 312-20.
[5] C. Hulten, "Growth Accounting with Intermediate Inputs", *Review of Economic Studies,* XLV, October, 1978, 511-18.
[6] Denison, *Estimates of Productivity Change in Industry.*

However, in spite of smaller industry weights at the economy level, the new measure still yields a larger rate of growth of MFP, for it takes into consideration all direct and indirect effects and feeds them into the affected industries in a manner resembling the Pasinetti concept of vertical integration.

We provide a final chapter that clearly states the relationship among all measures presented and the underlying concepts.

We finish this introduction with a word of caution in the use of I/O tables for MFP studies. The advantages of using an I/O framework are clear. The current-dollar I/O production accounts provide a detailed breakdown of an industry's current-dollar expenditures on intermediate and primary inputs and indicate the industry to which payments for the purchase of intermediate inputs were made. The value of total inputs or current-dollar cost of production is, of course, equal to the value of the total industry output. The constant-dollar tables offer information on the "quantities" of intermediate inputs bought, expressed in the prices of the base year, and of real gross domestic product or value added estimated by the method of double deflation. However, for the purpose of this study double-deflated GDP is of limited value; therefore, it has been replaced by information on the "quantities" of primary inputs used by industries, namely, hours worked, capital consumption allowances, and net capital stocks. When these expanded constant-dollar I/O tables are related to the payments of the factors of production contained in the current-dollar I/O tables, the implicit input prices are obtained, and all the necessary ingredients to derive industry-based MFP measures in terms of quantities and prices are in place. The current-dollar values are used to derive the input weights whereas the constant-dollar data yield the rates of growth of inputs.

The disadvantage of using the I/O industry production accounts should be equally obvious, for they are based on actual data reported by industries on their purchases of inputs and sales of output. Hence, the data reflects all shocks, maladjustments, and partial adjustments to which real industries are subjected in an uncertain world. Therefore, the resulting MFP measures should be loosely interpreted as barometers of economic efficiency or as true residuals and not in the stricter sense of measures of technical change. This is especially so in years when the economy underwent massive price shocks and/or was working at levels well below the full employment and utilization of inputs. Furthermore, the compilation of I/O data responds to institutional requirements that are at times far removed from the neatly defined economic concept of cost functions most appropriate for the derivation of MFP measures.

CHAPTER 4

Canadian input–output accounts and data base for MFP

A   Introduction

The Canadian input–output tables provide the most complete detailed accounting of economic activity in Canada for the business, personal, and government sectors. These tables are fully integrated within the Canadian System of National Accounts. They provide a conceptual framework or structure within which are fitted and arranged data of economic activities that are both collected and statistically estimated. The input–output tables are an invaluable source of data, quite apart from their use in standard I/O analysis.

Unfortunately, the emphasis on these tables is on the flows of currently produced outputs and inputs in the economic activities of Canada. Consequently, the tables are very rich in the representation of current output flows through the economic system – as intermediate outputs or final demand outputs. They are very poor on their accounting of the flows of the services of primary inputs such as labour and capital. Only the payments to these factors of production appear as aggregate values in the tables. In the case of produced capital inputs, the tables neither establish the relationship between stocks and flows nor calculate the yearly changes in the stocks of capital coming from the investment or capital formation flows that they record.

Thus, there is abundant information on the commodity outputs of industries and their interindustry flows in the industry production accounts of the I/O tables that are of interest to this study. This is contained in matrices with 191 industries and 595 commodities. However, there are no matrices (not even vectors) of capital stocks or labour input by industry associated with these tables. This study maintains the lowest possible level of aggregation in the I/O data compatible with other statistical series (such as capital stocks and labour inputs existing in Statistics Canada) required for the derivation of MFP measures at the industry and economy level. We now describe the basic structures and concepts of the I/O tables and the changes introduced.

Table 4-1. *Canadian I/O accounting framework*

	Commodities	Industries	Final demand	Total
Commodities		U	FD	q
Industries	V			g
Primary input		Y	YF	
Total	q'	g'	e'	

U is a matrix of the values of the intermediate inputs of industries;
V is a matrix of the values of the outputs of industries;
FD is the matrix of final demands;
Y is the matrix of primary inputs of industries;
YF is the matrix of primary inputs of final demand categories;
f is a vector of the values of total final purchases;
y is a vector of the values of total primary inputs of industries;
q is a vector of the values of total commodity outputs, q' is the transpose of q;
g is a vector of the values of total industry outputs, g' is the transpose of g;
e is a vector of the values of total inputs of final demand categories.

B   Input–output accounts

The accounting framework of the Canadian I/O tables consists of two sets of accounts (see Table 4-1): the production accounts, made up of the make or production matrix (V) and the use or intermediate input matrix (U), and the primary input matrix (Y). The disposition account is made up of the make, use, and final Demand (FD) matrices. All these matrices are rectangular; the U and V matrices list, for 191 industries, the use and production (respectively) of 595 commodities. The FD matrix identifies 136 final demand sectors and their expenditures for 595 commodities; the Y matrix shows the payments of 191 industries to seven primary inputs.[1]

The fundamental identity of the industry production account is that the value of total output (obtained from the make matrix) equals the value of total inputs (obtained from the U and Y matrices). The disposition accounts identity shows the value of total output by commodity equal to the total disposition of commodities (obtained from the U and FD matrices). The total disposition of commodity output can also be expressed in industry space. The following equalities therefore hold: An industry's value of total output equals the total disposition of its output,

[1] For a more detailed description see Statistics Canada, 15-201E, *The Input–Output Structure of the Canadian Economy* (Ottawa: Minister of Supply and Services, 1984).

which in turn equals the value of the total inputs to that industry.[2] These I/O accounts are the starting block towards the development of the MFP data base.

C   Industry aggregation

The final level of industry aggregation established for this study, 37 industries, is the most disaggregated level that our data requirements could support. We make use of existing published and unpublished data sources at Statistics Canada. The following data for business sector industries in current and constant dollars were required:

> Data on gross outputs and intermediate inputs. These exist as yearly time series since 1961 for 183 I/O industries.
>
> Data on capital stocks and capital consumption allowances (CCAs). These series exist back to 1926 for about 40 industries.
>
> Data on the returns to capital input. These exist as a residual class in the primary input matrix of the I/O tables since 1961 for 183 I/O industries.
>
> Data on total annual hours worked by industry. These exist for only about 20 industries since 1946.
>
> Data on payments to labour. These exist for the 183 I/O industries since 1961.
>
> Data on the stocks of inventories. These exist since 1971 for 183 I/O industries and from 1961 to 1971 were put together for the relevant industries for this study.

The derivation of the new measures requires knowledge of the industry of origin (or production industry) for each of the produced inputs, that is, for the intermediate inputs produced in the year, for capital consumption allowances treated in this study as if they were produced in the current year like any other intermediate input, and for the capital stocks and inventories so that they can be corrected for changes in efficiency of their *current* industry of origin.

Clearly only I/O data can fulfil this last set of requirements. The investment submatrix of the FD matrix has the commodity composition for investment expenditures for 36 industries, and this was the information used to make the correction for changes in efficiency of the industry producing such capital goods. It was decided that the measures could be

---

[2] Because of the three-way equality, the reader should keep in mind that throughout this study any rearrangement made of the Y matrix has to be matched by a corresponding one to the FD matrix even though it may not be explicitly stated.

derived for 37 industries.[3] Two sets of aggregation parameters were then constructed: One set aggregates the 183 I/O industries to 37 and another aggregates the 40 industries for which there is constant-dollar net capital stock and capital consumption allowances data to the same 37.[4] The two aggregation parameters are given in Appendices 1 and 2. Traditional MFP measures could have been easily obtained for the 40 industries for which there are capital stocks. However, for comparison purposes, the same industry aggregation was used for both measures.

D   Industry classification

Canadian establishments are assigned to industries using the Standard Industrial Classification (SIC) industry divisions and its definitions. The I/O industry classification corresponds closely to the three-digit level SIC with the exception of some industries that are groupings at that level or lower.

The industries included in the I/O tables are in the domestic business sector, producing goods and services for sale at prices intended to cover production costs. However, there are exceptions. A few of these industries, such as railways, receive heavy government subsidies and others are not "true" industries. The resulting measures of MFP for these few need further discussion, which is provided in Chapter 5.

There is a group of eight so-called dummy industries with a corresponding number of dummy commodities that were removed from the I/O industry classification for this study. The use of dummy industries is a technique for routing groups of commodities, such as office supplies, as inputs into industries when their precise commodity content is unknown. Commodity inputs to these industries were made equal to zero after distributing their values over the using industries according to their purchases of the dummy commodity, whose value was subsequently also set at zero. Table 4-2 lists the private business sector industries included in this study. Crown corporations are part of the business sector in the relevant industries. Nonprofit organizations are excluded.

The "post office" industry was also removed from the I/O business industries because it was impossible to obtain data on its capital stock. The value of its total output and total input were added to the columns

[3] The extra industry was obtained by separating the clothing and knitting mills industries that are aggregated into one in the investment matrix, keeping the same breakdown for the commodity composition of investment.

[4] To get a closer matching of the capital stock industries and the I/O industries, we obtained some confidential and unpublished capital stock data from the National Wealth and Capital Stock section of the Science, Technology and Capital Stock Division, Statistics Canada.

Table 4-2. *Multifactor productivity industry classification*

01	Agriculture and fishing
02	Forestry
03	Mines, quarries, and oil wells
04	Food and beverages
05	Tobacco products
06	Rubber and plastic products
07	Leather
08	Textiles
09	Knitting mills
10	Clothing
11	Woods
12	Furniture and fixtures
13	Paper and allied industries
14	Printing, publishing, and allied industries
15	Primary metals
16	Metal fabricating
17	Machinery
18	Transportation equipment
19	Electrical products
20	Nonmetallic mineral products
21	Petroleum and coal products
22	Chemical and chemical products
23	Miscellaneous manufacturing
24	Construction
25	Air transportation and other utilities and transportation
26	Railway transportation and telegraph
27	Water transport
28	Motor transport
29	Urban and suburban transportation
30	Storage
31	Broadcasting
32	Telephones
33	Electric power
34	Gas distribution
35	Trade
36	Finance, insurance, and real estate
37	Commercial services

"government revenue" and "government expenditure", respectively, in the FD matrix. The expenditures of industries on the post office commodity were removed from the intermediate matrix and added to the row "government goods and services" in the Y matrix.

The finance, insurance, and real estate industry includes government royalties on natural resources (I/O industry classification number 167) and owner-occupied dwellings (I/O number 166). These industries should have been removed from the classification "Finance, Insurance and Real Estate Industries". They are fictitious industries, without a true production structure. Royalty payments can be regarded either as taxes levied by governments on the exploitation of natural resources and/or land or as a rental payment from the users to the "owners" of the natural resources but certainly not as an industry. The royalty payments should be related to the stocks of natural resources and/or land. However, we have no knowledge of these stocks by industry. Therefore, they should be excluded from the industry classification and added to the matrix of primary inputs. Owner-occupied dwellings can be left as a separate industry whose output is the imputed rent of owner-occupants, even though the input vector into this industry and therefore its productivity is difficult to determine and measure.

The construction industry included in this study represents a point of departure from the criteria used to define industries, and it corresponds more closely to the concept of the construction activity. It consists of the output of the construction industry plus the output of construction labour forces in the other industries on so-called own-account construction. All inputs into the construction activity have been adjusted to correspond to the output concept used, except for the capital stock and depreciation, which remain on an industry basis. This implies that the capital stock of the industries engaged in own-account construction is overstated and that of the construction activity understated. Intermediate input payments and wages and salaries are adjusted by applying the input coefficients of the construction industry. A similar adjustment could, in principle, be made to the capital stocks of industries engaged in own-account construction by using capital–output ratios of the construction industry. However, the I/O tables do not explicitly include capital stocks, and to adjust the time series of capital stocks constructed for this study is difficult, as the required information is not readily available. This solution will not, in any case, be satisfactory. The consistent treatment of all industries calls for the reconstruction of construction as an industry rather than an activity and the restoration of construction outputs and input bundles to the industries doing own-account construction. In practice, the industries affected are mainly the utilities: telephones, electric power, and gas distribution.

E   Industry valuation

The valuation of the I/O tables is in producer prices. These can be defined as the selling price at the boundary of the producing establishment, excluding sale and excise taxes and also transportation, trade, and delivery charges, or levies after the final stage of production when they are not charged by the producer. These prices are from the point of view of the producer; they represent the payment made to them. The value of output is net of commodity indirect taxes, for example, sales and excise taxes, and all trade and transportation margins incurred in delivering the output to consuming sectors. The value of inputs includes indirect commodity taxes and all trade and transportation charges incurred in the purchases of intermediate inputs by industries. However, these additional cost elements incurred by the purchaser are recorded as separate purchases of commodities, called margins. Purchasers' prices or the prices paid by the buying industry are then equal to the sum of producers' prices plus the costs associated with the delivery of goods and the indirect taxes paid on these.

F   Industry output

The concept of output used in this study is duplicated gross output, that is, the total output produced by an industry in the current period including intra-industry purchases (or use) of its own output. The measurement of output in industries where the price–quantity relationship is difficult to establish and/or observe can present problems. In addition, there are specific output measurement problems for some industries in the Canadian I/O tables due to the following special conventions:

i.   The treatment of interest and dividends in the I/O data base entails that interest and dividends are included in the paying industry *rather* than the receiving industry. This presents obvious problems for the finance industry where interest received is the main operating revenue of the industry. The I/O convention looks at interest and dividends only as distribution of income rather than as the (rental) price associated with a (capital) service. This last view would be more consistent with production theory.[5]

ii.   Input–output attempts to relate output sales to final consumers. Industries that simply "move" output or intermediaries such as trade or transport break this link. The I/O tables create the concept of "margins" to reestablish it.

iii.   The I/O convention treats vertically integrated operations in the same manner as unintegrated ones. The output of vertically integrated sectors must be specially dealt with. In the Canadian case

---

[5] For an alternative viewpoint, see T. K. Rymes, "The Theory and Measurement of the Nominal Output of Banks, Sectoral Rates of Saving and Wealth in the National Accounts", eds. R. Lipsey and H. Stone Tice, *The Measurement of Saving, Investment, and Wealth* (Chicago: University of Chicago Press for the NBER, 1989).

this affects mainly the mining industry in relation to the smelting and refining.

We now discuss main problem areas.

G   Finance

Financial institutions provide a range of services to consumers for which specific charges are made. These services present no measurement problem; they are accounted as output of the industry. However, financial institutions also provide services for which no direct charges are made. All or part of the cost of providing these services is hidden in the interest rate differential between lenders (deposits) and borrowers (loans). The I/O data base imputations are made to value these services and include them in output of financial institutions. The imputation consist in (i) raising the actual (or estimated) interest payment made by banks and similar institutions to their depositors (this is increased to correspond to the imputed value of the services output purchased by their depositors) and (ii) decreasing the actual (or estimated) interest payment received by the banks from borrowers to correspond to the imputed value of the service output purchased by borrowers. The adjustment affects the distribution of GDP among industries by increasing that of financial sector and decreasing by a lesser amount the combined GDP of the industries that purchase the imputed services from the banks. That is, the economy's GDP after the banking imputation is bigger because part of the imputed service output of the financial institutions is consumed by borrowers and depositors in final demand sectors. The transactions, therefore, do not cancel as would purely interindustry transactions.

H   Wholesale and retail trade

In the I/O convention the output of the trade industry is defined as the total value of goods sold minus the total cost of goods purchased for resale. This difference, called the "trade margins", represents the values that appear in the gross output vector for these industries and that are then purchased by other industries and final demand sectors.

I   Construction

The output of construction is defined as the sum of the output of the construction industry plus the construction output of industries doing own-account construction. This concept of output corresponds to that associated with an activity rather than an industry, and it represents a clear departure point from the methodology used in the I/O tables previously discussed.

J   Base metal mining and related smelting and refining

Firms in this sector present a problem because of the high degree of vertical integration exhibited between non-ferrous-metal mines (in MFP industry 03) and the smelting and refining industry (in MFP industry 21). The I/O treatment appears, in this case, as the more useful one for productivity analysis. The value of output of a vertically integrated establishment is split into its mining and smelting-refining components and allocated to the respective industries. The smelting and refining industry is shown buying the output of mines along with the inputs required to transform it.

K   Real estate rents and industries

There are two different treatments of real estate rents depending on whether they originate in the corporate or in the unincorporated sector. If the establishment receiving real estate rents is in the corporate sector, the value of gross rent appears in the output vector of the industry in question. If the establishment is part of the unincorporated sector, the gross rents are transferred to the finance, insurance, and real estate industry and appear as part of its output. This differential treatment of real estate rents is common to all parts of the system of National Accounts and is due to a lack of information about the unincorporated sector in general. For owner-occupied dwellings, the imputed rents are the gross output of that industry.

L   Industry inputs

The rearrangements to inputs in the industry production accounts were mainly of two kinds. The first concerns the split between intermediate inputs (U matrix) and primary inputs (Y matrix); all inputs that are not the output of a domestic business industry are treated, for the purpose of this study, as primary inputs and are transferred to the primary input matrix. The second arrangement is the explicit incorporation into the Y matrix of quantity vectors of labour and capital inputs.

M   Intermediate inputs

In the Canadian I/O tables intermediate inputs consist of the purchased inputs used by an industry that are the current-period output of another industry. This means that commodities bought but not yet used are treated as additions to raw materials inventories, a final demand category. Similarly, used inputs that are not purchased but withdrawn from inventories are shown as intermediate inputs and as negative capital formation. Commodities produced and used within an establishment are not shown as intermediate inputs, although the labour and other materials used in their production are recorded. This is not the most appropriate treatment for our purpose. Ideally, for measures of MFP, intraestablishment use of its own output should be recorded both in the gross output vector and in the intermediate input vector. Otherwise, MFP measures particularly, the traditional measures, will not be invariant to the degree of changes in vertical integration of the establishments of an industry. Unfortunately, the internal use of own output is not recorded and is therefore difficult to estimate.

All imported intermediate inputs were removed from the use matrix and the final demand matrix using the import share assumption.[6] Hence, the use matrix or matrix of intermediate inputs in this study is more restrictive; it contains only the use of purchases of the current-period output of domestic (business sector) industries by (business sector) industries.

Note that whenever a special definition of output is used for an I/O industry, it is other industries' purchases of that special output that is shown as intermediate input in the use matrix. For example, industries are shown as buying cars from the car-producing industries and retail margins from the car retail industry. This is the treatment for all so-called margin industries. Similarly, the intermediate inputs that these margin-producing industries buy exclude "goods"; therefore, they are depicted as highly value added industries.

N   Primary inputs

The primary input matrix was expanded to include all inputs removed from the use matrix. Four extra rows were added: noncompeting imports[7] (I/O commodity classification numbers 588-93); unallocated imports and exports (commodity 594); competing imports; and government goods and services (commodity 595). Noncompeting imports consist of a group of commodities that are not produced domestically in Canada, such as

---

[6] The share of imports is defined as the ratio of imports of a commodity to its total domestic use.

[7] Noncompeting imports consist of commodities 588-93 in all years; commodity 275 in 1979; commodity 461 in 1968 to 1974 and 1978; commodity 491 in 1961. Numbers come from the commodity classification in Statistics Canada, *The Input–Output Structure of the Canadian Economy.*

cotton. In addition to these, there are a few commodities that were not domestically produced in some years, so in effect they became noncompeting imports and were added to that commodity row in those years. The total value of imported intermediate inputs by industry removed from the use matrix was also added, as an extra row, to the primary input matrix. The primary input matrix Y of this study contains all inputs used by the Canadian business sector industries that are not the output of that sector, that is, everything exogenous to it.

The value of imports in the I/O tables excludes import duties in order to approximate the concept of producers' value used for domestic intermediate inputs. It represents the price of an imported good at the point of entry into Canada, that is, the price at which it leaves the producing country. Transportation and other services at the Canadian border are added to the price, and so are custom duties, due when imports enter the country.

The value of government goods and services, such as water charges or airport landing fees, purchased by the business sector industries are also included in the primary input matrix. These values represent costs to business but do not normally cover production costs incurred by the government.

Indirect taxes, another category of the primary input matrix, consists of all tax items deducted as expenses by businesses. They are subdivided into commodity indirect taxes and other indirect taxes. The former are paid on the values or quantities of commodities produced or sold; the latter consist of fixed costs, such as property taxes, business taxes, or licenses, unrelated to the level of productive activity.

The incorporation into the primary input matrix of vectors of labour and capital inputs requires that the payments to these two factors of production be clearly specified. To this end, the item "net income of unincorporated business" must be split between the return to the labour input of proprietors and to capital. This was achieved by applying the corporate ratio; if labour payments constitute 75 percent of total (labour and capital) payments in the corporate sector, it was assumed to be the same for the unincorporated sector. The sum of wages and salaries, supplementary labour income, and labour income of unincorporated business shows total payments to labour input; the sum of other operating surplus and capital income of unincorporated sector shows gross returns to the capital (and land) input.

O   Net capital stock and capital consumption allowances

Estimates of net returns by industry were obtained by subtracting the current dollar value of capital consumption allowances (CCAs) from gross returns. The net returns are thus net of depreciation but include corporate income taxes. The rate of return was obtained residually by assuming that all capital in an industry earns the same rate of return. The rate of return then equals the ratio of total net returns to the total current-dollar net capital stock; this is defined as the sum of the current-dollar net fixed capital stocks and inventories.

The data on CCA and net capital stock was obtained from the Science, Technology and Capital Stock Division of Statistics Canada.[8] The perpetual inventory method is used to construct net capital stock estimates starting with the year 1926. This net capital stock time series for industries is an accumulation of net fixed capital investment over time. Thus

$$K_i^f = \sum_t (I_i^f - D_i^f)$$

where K_i^f is the net capital stock of the ith industry at time t, I_i^f its gross capital formulation, and D_i^f the rate of capital consumption allowances. The latter are calculated by assuming an average economic life, say, L, for the commodity composition of the capital stock by industry and taking $1/L$ of its value every year; that is, a straight-line depreciation method is used. Net fixed capital stocks and CCA are subdivided into two categories – machinery and equipment (M&E) and construction – along with a residual entry called capital items charged to operating expenses. The perpetual inventory method is used for each of the categories.

The capital stock series are in historical (original) cost dollars, constant 1971 dollars, and current dollars. The current-dollar and constant-dollar series were used for this study. The capital stock data have not been adjusted for the degree of capital utilization in the industries. Similarly, no adjustment was made to the CCA data for the possibility of changing rates of depreciation over time. The capital stock of the housing sector is part of the capital stock in finance, insurance, and real estate because owner-occupied housing is, as indicated, included in that industry.

P   Inventories

Inventories were considered to be part of the net capital stock of an industry for the purpose of calculating the associated rates of return. We started with inventory stock estimates for 1974 and to this we added the yearly changes in inventories shown in the I/O final demand tables.

---

[8] For a comprehensive description of the methodology see Statistics Canada 13-522, *Fixed Capital Flows and Stocks, Manufacturing, Canada, 1926–1960 – Methodology* (Ottawa: Queen's Printer, 1966).

For 1961–71, no exact industry inventories stock data exist at Statistics Canada. Hence, stock levels were put together for 1961. To this vector, the yearly changes in inventory were added to arrive at the 1971 estimates.

In the I/O tables, inventories are subdivided into two categories: inventories of finished goods and goods in process (outputs) and inventories of raw materials and of goods purchased for resale (inputs). These subdivisions were kept for this study. Inventories were revalued, to conform to I/O practices, to the prices of the year in order to show their current values. The values of revalued inventories are given commodity content on the basis of certain assumptions and the commodity balancing of I/O tables.

Q   Other inputs

Land is not included because no estimates of land in use by industry exist. This implies, of course, that the estimated rate of return to capital by industry has within it the rate of return to the land input. It has also been argued that financial assets such as real-money balances should be included when working at the industry level as part of the capital stock. Even if it should be done, which is not clear, such data are not available at this time. Input–output data are collected on an establishment basis, whereas financial data are collected on a company basis. To match these two sources of data is an enormous task. The same problem applies also to corporate income taxes, which would be required to shift our net rates of return data from a before-tax base to an after-tax rate. Statistics Canada is making continuous efforts to arrive at a solution to the tax problem.

R   Labour input

The measure of labour input in the primary input matrix is total annual hours worked, not paid. Hours worked are obtained from the reported hours paid by making corrections for statutory holidays, annual holidays, strikes, and sick leave. A vector of total annual hours worked by industry was calculated as the product of average annual hours worked times the total number of jobs. Data on average hours exist for only 20 industries; this vector was disaggregated into 37 industries by giving all industries within a group the same average hours. By contrast, the vector of total number of jobs consists of 183 industries and was aggregated to the same 37. Implicit wages were obtained by dividing the total labour earnings by total annual hours worked.

The matrix Y of primary inputs can now be specified as consisting of the following three sectors; each with the listed vectors:

External trade sector: noncompeting imports, unallocated imports and exports, competing imports.

Government sector: indirect commodity taxes, subsidies, government-produced goods and services (including postal services).

A proper primary input sector: total labour earnings, capital consumption allowances, net returns to the capital stocks machinery and equipment, construction, inventories of finished goods, inventories of raw materials.

The first two sectors are primary in the sense that their goods and/or services are not produced within the boundaries of the domestic "business" economy whose rate of MFP is to be measured. In this sense, government goods and services are equivalent to imports into the domestic economy.

S   Industry production accounts

The industry production accounts of the I/O tables for the calculation of MFP can be specified as

$$g = Vi_v = U'i_u + Y'i_y \tag{4-1}$$

where i_v, i_u, and i_y are unit vectors of the proper size used to sum rows and columns over the matrices V, U', and Y', respectively; V is the 37×586 make matrix, where 37 is the number of industries and 586 is the number of commodities. Hence, for the ith industry, that is, a row of the Y matrix, the v_{ij} element represents the output of commodity j produced by the ith industry; U is the 593×37 intermediate matrix, whose u_{ij} element represents the value of commodity i used by the jth industry; Y is the 9×37 matrix of primary inputs, whose y_{lj} element shows the value of primary input l used by the jth industry; g is a 37×1 vector of total industry outputs; the g_j element shows the total value of output of the jth industry.

These accounts, then, specify inputs to and outputs from industries in commodity space. They are sufficient to derive traditional rates of growth of MFP as commodity output and input indexes can be constructed. However, for the derivation of the new measures it will be simpler to specify inputs and outputs in industry space. This is because the new formulation corrects produced inputs for their own rate of growth of MFP. These rates can be obtained only for the industries and not for commodities since the technology pertains to industries. Therefore, a commodity's "rate" will need to be defined as a weighted combination of the rates of MFP of the industries that produce that commodity, where the weights should be the proportion of the total output of the commodity produced by each industry. These weights are called market shares. This procedure for the derivation of the new MFP rates is equivalent to that obtained by squaring the intermediate input matrix into an industry-by-industry matrix. The squaring is achieved by transferring commodity demands into industry demands via the market share matrix. The next section describes the I/O model that serves as a basis for the derivation of both the new and traditional measures.

T   Input–output model for MFP measures

So far, only the data of the I/O tables were described. In this section, we use the assumptions of the I/O model to create the MFP empirical model.

Current-dollar model

The Canadian rectangular I/O model is based on two assumptions: the market share assumption and the industry technology assumption. The market share assumption, mathematically expressed, is

$$D = V\hat{q}^{-1} \tag{4-2}$$

where $\hat{q}^{-1}$ is a diagonal matrix of the reciprocal of the vector of total commodity outputs q along its diagonal and zeros elsewhere and D is the market share matrix (its d_{ji} element shows the share of the jth industry in the total output of the ith commodity).

The industry technology assumption for intermediate and primary inputs can be mathematically expressed as

$$B = U\hat{g}^{-1} \qquad E = Y\hat{g}^{-1} \tag{4-3}$$

where $\hat{g}^{-1}$ is a diagonal matrix with the reciprocal of the vector of total industry outputs g along its diagonal and zeros elsewhere. The b_{ij} element of the B matrix shows the share of the expenditures on the ith intermediate commodity input in the value of total output of the jth industry. Similarly, the e_{lj} element of the E matrix shows the share of the expenditures on the lth primary input in the value of total output of the jth industry.

A combination of these two assumptions yields the square input–output equation used for the derivation of the MFP rates:

$$g' = i'DB\hat{g} + i'E\hat{g} \tag{4-4}$$

where

g is a 37×1 vector of industry outputs,
DB is a 37×37 matrix of intermediate input coefficients,

E is a 9×37 matrix of primary input coefficients,

i' is a unit row vector with as many columns as there are rows in the adjacent matrix.

The premultiplication of the B matrix by the D matrix of commodity market share coefficients of industries serves to transfer the commodity intermediate input structure of an industry into an industry intermediate input structure; that is, it changes the commodity expenditures of an industry into industry expenditures. For each industry, its commodity cost function becomes an industry cost function.

Letting $DB = A$, we write

$$g' = i'A\hat{g} + i'E\hat{g} \qquad (4\text{-}5)$$

where the a_{ij} element shows the inputs from ith industry per unit of output of the jth industry. However, because $A = DB$,

$$a_{ij} = \sum d_{ik}b_{kj}$$

where the a_{ij} element is a weighted linear combination of the kth commodity input into the jth industry (b_{kj}) and each commodity input is weighted by the proportion of the commodity produced by the ith industry (d_{ik}).

Constant-dollar model

All previously stated assumptions and equations can be expressed as the product of constant-dollar data times the corresponding price indexes; hence rewrite (4-5) as

$$p'\hat{g} = p'A_g + i'(W \cdot E)\hat{g} \qquad (4\text{-}6)$$

where the matrices A, E, and g are defined as before but in constant dollars and p is a 37×1 vector of implicit industry output price indexes and W a 9×37 matrix of implicit primary input price indexes.

The dot product denotes element-by-element multiplication between the two matrices. The matrix W of primary input prices is full instead of diagonal because the prices of primary inputs are industry specific. For example, the wage rate or price per hour of labour services is not the same throughout the business economy but differs from industry to industry; the price of capital input or rental price per unit of capital service is also industry specific since both the ex post rate of return and the price index of capital goods vary across industries. A similar argument holds for all other primary inputs.

The constant-dollar data consist of two Laspeyres series for output and for most inputs. The first, in 1961 prices, runs from 1961 to 1971; the second, in 1971 prices, goes from 1971 to 1980. The two series were chained in 1971. Only the capital stock and CCA data are a single Laspeyres series in 1971 prices, whereas the labour input is a "true" quantity measure – hours worked, unadjusted for quality changes.

Deflation

We now give a brief description of the deflation methodology followed in order to construct the constant-dollar I/O tables.

The current-dollar value of each commodity produced by Canadian industries in the output (or make) matrix is deflated by a domestic commodity price index of the Paasche type. For example, let $p_{ij}q_{ij}$ be the (i,j)th entry of the current-dollar output matrix. Then

$$p_{ij}q_{ij} \div p_{ij}q_{ij}/p_{ij}^0 q_{ij} = p_{ij}^0 q_{ij}$$

where the zero superscript represents base-year prices and all others are current-period prices. The current-dollar value is divided by the Paasche price index to yield a Laspeyres constant-dollar quantity, which becomes the cells of the constant-dollar matrix.

Note that price indexes are commodity specific only; the same commodity price index is used to deflate the corresponding commodity row of the make matrix or the Use matrix over all producing industries. It is not quite exact to call these indexes Paasche. Each of the 586 commodities are, in reality, commodity groups, and the weight of each commodity in the group is kept constant over the reference period. This means that the Paasche-type indexes are true Paasche only if the composition of the commodity group is unchanged over the period; that is,

$$p_i = \sum_k p_{i_k} q_{i_k}^0$$

No subscript j is needed since p_i is constant over industry space, and $q_{i_k}^0$ is assumed constant over the reference period.

Imports were deflated with a similarly constructed Paasche-type price index but based on import price changes only.

Trade margins are deflated by calculating a constant-price margin as the average of the current-dollar and base-year rates. This constant margin rate is multiplied by the constant producers' price value of the traded commodity to derive the constant-dollar trade margins.[9]

The deflation of indirect commodity taxes is straightforward. The base-year tax rate is applied to the constant-dollar value (ex tax) of the commodity in question to obtain the constant-dollar value of taxes. Hence,

---

[9] It is the special treatment of the output of trade industries in the I/O tables that requires a special deflator to be developed within the I/O system.

changes in tax rates in the reference period have no effect on the calculation of constant-dollar taxes. A very similar procedure is applied to subsidies by calculating a subsidy rate for the base year as the ratio of the subsidy to the industry's gross output. This base-year subsidy rate is multiplied by the constant-dollar gross output of the industry to obtain constant-dollar subsidies.

Property taxes are the main component of other indirect taxes. Therefore, their constant-dollar values are constructed to reflect the growth in the quantity of rental services rendered by the building industry.

The capital stocks are deflated using Paasche-type price indexes of gross capital formation by type of expenditure and industry.

All these price deflators are, when relevant and subject to data limitations, adjusted for costly quality changes in the goods and services whose quantities they are designed to measure.

U   Complete model for the estimation of MFP

The above I/O model and data base are sufficient for the estimation of traditional measures of MFP. However, the computation of the new measures needs two added modifications:

1. partition of the matrix of primary inputs between those that are produced inputs and proper primary inputs from the point of view of the domestic business economy;
2. the specification of the domestic industry of origin of the produced durable inputs. To this end, equation (4-6) of the I/O production account of industries is rewritten as

$$p'\hat{g} = p'A\hat{g} + i'(W_d \cdot E_d)\hat{g} + i'(W_k \cdot E_k)\hat{g} + i'(W_f \cdot E_f)\hat{g}$$
$$+ i'(W_r \cdot E_r)\hat{g} + i'(W_p \cdot E_p)\hat{g} \tag{4-7}$$

The primary input matrix Y and associated coefficient matrix E have been replaced by the matrices Y_d, E_d and Y_k, E_k for the produced durable inputs: CCA and net capital stocks, respectively; Y_f, E_f and Y_r, E_r for the inventories of finished goods and raw materials, respectively; and Y_p and E_p for the rest. The corresponding matrices of input price indexes are $W_d, W_k, W_f, W_r,$ and W_p.

There is, in fact, little disaggregated information on what are the goods content and the industry of origin of capital stocks, as would be required in order to correct each good for the technical change taking place in its industry of production.

The matrices Y_d and Y_k were obtained by making use of the information contained in the gross fixed capital formation submatrix of the final demand matrix.[10] The two rows of CCA in machinery and equipment and net capital stock in machinery and equipment of the Y matrix were broken down according to the industry of origin of the domestically produced gross investment for the year. Hence, the E_d and E_k matrices are both of dimension 37×37 and the E_p matrix is of dimension 10×37 because it contains the import component of the net capital stock in machinery and equipment, the import component of CCA in machinery and equipment, and the import component of the inventory of raw materials.

The matrix Y_f contains the vector of the inventory of own finished goods held by producing industries along its diagonal and has zero elements elsewhere. The matrix Y_r was obtained by assuming that an industry keeps inventories of all its inputs, including imported ones, in the proportion in which it uses them, information available from the use matrix.

The notation of equation (4-7) can be simplified by defining matrices Y_c, E_c, and W_c:

$$
Y_c = \begin{bmatrix} Y_d \\ \vdots \\ Y_k \\ \vdots \\ Y_f \\ \vdots \\ Y_r \end{bmatrix}
\qquad
E_c = \begin{bmatrix} E_d \\ \vdots \\ E_k \\ \vdots \\ E_f \\ \vdots \\ E_r \end{bmatrix}
\qquad
W_c = \begin{bmatrix} W_d \\ \vdots \\ W_k \\ \vdots \\ W_f \\ \vdots \\ W_r \end{bmatrix}
$$

and hence equation (4-8) as

$$ p'\hat{g} = p'A\hat{g} + i'(W_c \cdot E_c)\hat{g} + i'(W_p \cdot E_p)\hat{g} \qquad (4\text{-}8) $$

where the matrix E_c is the set of all domestically produced primary inputs and E_p contains all proper primary inputs, that is, all primary inputs produced outside the boundary of the domestic private business economy.

Equation (4-8) is used for the derivation of all the traditional productivity empirical results presented in this study; equation (4-7) is used for the derivation of all new results.

V   Traditional rate of MFP by industry

Applying the definition of traditional MFP as the rate of growth of the Divisia index of output minus the Divisia indexes of the weighted rate of growth of inputs and the I/O technological relations to equation (4-8),

---

[10] For a detailed description of the construction of these matrices and assumptions used, see Appendix 3.

we obtain t^*, the vector of rates of growth of the traditional measures of MFP, by industry,

$$t^* = -\text{diag}\left[\hat{p}^{-1}A'\hat{p}\frac{d\ln A}{dt} + \hat{p}^{-1}(E_c'\cdot W_c')\frac{d\ln E_c}{dt} \right.$$
$$\left. + \hat{p}^{-1}(E_p'\cdot W_p')\frac{d\ln E_p}{dt} \right]$$

Cancelling out the terms in the derivative of the logarithm against those outside, we write

$$t^* = -\left[\hat{p}^{-1}\frac{dA'}{dt}p + \hat{p}^{-1}\left(\frac{dE_c'}{dt}\cdot W_c'\right)i + \hat{p}^{-1}\left(\frac{dE_p'}{dt}\cdot W_p'\right)i \right] \quad (4\text{-}9)$$

where the rate of growth of MFP for the ith industry, t_i^* (where $t_i^* \in t^*$), is

$$t_i^* = -\frac{1}{p_i}\left[p_j\frac{d(a_{ji})}{dt} + \sum_I wc_{li}\frac{d(ec_{li})}{dt} + \sum_p wp_{pi}\frac{d(ep_{pi})}{dt} \right]$$

Necessary but not sufficient conditions for changes in the rate of growth of MFP are changes in the coefficients of either the intermediate or the primary input matrices. Changes in dA/dt can be decomposed into

$$\frac{dA}{dt} = \frac{d(DB)}{dt} = \frac{dD}{dt}B + D\frac{dB}{dt} \quad (4\text{-}10)$$

Changes in the A matrix come from either of two sources: changes in the market share matrix D or changes in the industry technology matrix B or both. Equation (4-9) is the continuous analogue of Leontief's[11] measure of structural change.

W   New measures of MFP by industry

From the point of view of the new measures, inputs can be classified into two broad groups: domestically produced inputs and primary inputs. Domestically produced inputs are those produced by the industries whose MFP we attempt to measure, whereas primary inputs are all those produced outside the boundaries of the industries composing the private domestic business economy. Hence, imports are primary inputs, since they are produced abroad; so are goods and services produced in the government sector and so is labour sometimes considered as the output of the

---

[11] Leontief, *Studies in the Structure of the American Economics*. See also E. D. Domar, "On the Measurement of Technological Change", *Economic Journal*, LXXI, December 1961, 709–29.

household sector.[12] In this sense, the new measures are closed with respect to the domestic private business economy.

Equation (4-7) is used for the derivation of the new measures because it clearly specifies and differentiates domestically produced inputs from primary inputs. Adjusting all domestically produced inputs for the rate of MFP in their industry of origin, we write

$$p'\hat{g} = p'\hat{h}\hat{h}^{-1}A\hat{g} + i'[(\hat{h}W_d)\cdot(\hat{h}^{-1}E_d)]\hat{g} + i'[(\hat{h}W_k)\cdot(\hat{h}^{-1}E_k)]\hat{g}$$
$$+ i'[(\hat{h}W_f)/(\hat{h}^{-1}E_f)]\hat{g} + i'[(\hat{h}W_r)\cdot(\hat{h}^{-1}E_r)]\hat{g} + i'(W_p\cdot E_p)\hat{g} \qquad (4\text{-}11)$$

The application of the definition of the rate of growth of MFP to equation (4-11) yields the new measure. In this form, it is easy to see the logic behind it. Under the assumption of a positive rate of growth of the MFP, h_i is greater than unity and the rate of growth of the new measures of multifactor productivity will be greater than zero.[13] The input price index expressed as $p_i h_i$ is seen to be running ahead of the output price index p_i, and this will be so in any year in which there is a positive change in the MFP. Equation (4-11) can be regarded as completing the process of deflation by adjusting the prices and quantities of produced inputs to show decreases in the quantity of inputs required to produce them in the current year. As an example, take the current-dollar value, say, c_{ij}, of the ith input into the jth industry,

$$c_{ij} = p_i g_{ij} \qquad (4\text{-}12)$$

In terms of the base-year price, p_i^0, the constant-dollar quantity and corresponding price index are

$$c_{ij} = p_i/p_i^0(p_i^0 g_{ij}) \qquad (4\text{-}13)$$

Under the assumption of a costly z increase in the quality index of good i, the adjustment to (4-13) is

---

[12] This suggests the possibility of closing the model to foreign trade, government, and the household sectors by treating them as I/O industries. In so doing, the model will be completely closed to the world economy in the input–output sense. For an attempt to deal with imports in this fashion, see Postner and Wesa, *Canadian Productivity Growth.*

[13] The Divisia index of traditional MFP is

$$t_i = \frac{\exp(d\ln g_i/dt)}{\exp(\sum_j u_{ji}\,d\ln g_{ji}/dt + \sum_l u_{li}\,d\ln n_{li}/dt)}$$

or the ratio of the Divisia index of gross output to the Divisia index of inputs. By comparison, the Divisia index of new MFP, assuming that the only produced inputs are intermediate, is

$$h_i = \frac{\exp(d\ln g_i/dt)}{\exp(\sum_j u_{ji}\,d\ln(g_{ji}/h_j)/dt + \sum_l u_{li}\,d\ln(n_{li}/dt))}$$

$$c_{ij} = (p_i/p_i^0 z)(z p_i^0 g_{ij}) \tag{4-14}$$

and the constant-dollar "quantity" of good j is seen as going up, whereas its price goes down, by z. Similarly, under the assumption of an h_i increase in efficiency in the production of good i, the new adjustment is

$$c_{ij} = (p_i h_i/p_i^0 z)(z/h_i p_i^0 g_{ij}) \tag{4-15}$$

and the quantity of good i is seen as going down by h_i in terms of the base-year quantity because of a decrease in the quantities of inputs used in its production, whereas the price index moves up by just that much.

Applying the definition of the MFP and using the I/O technological relations, we obtain, h^*, the new MFP rate:

$$
\begin{aligned}
h^* = -\mathrm{diag}\Bigg[& \hat{p}^{-1}A'\hat{p}\, \frac{d\ln(\hat{h}^{-1}A)}{dt} \\
& + \hat{p}^{-1}(E'_d \cdot W'_d)\, \frac{d\ln(\hat{h}^{-1}E_d)}{dt} \\
& + \hat{p}^{-1}(E'_k \cdot W'_k)\, \frac{d\ln(\hat{h}^{-1}E_k)}{dt} \\
& + \hat{p}^{-1}(E'_f \cdot W'_f)\, \frac{d\ln(\hat{h}^{-1}E_f)}{dt} \\
& + \hat{p}^{-1}(E'_r \cdot W'_r)\, \frac{d\ln(\hat{h}^{-1}E_r)}{dt} \\
& + \hat{p}^{-1}(E'_p \cdot W'_p)\, \frac{d\ln(E_p)}{dt} \Bigg] \\
= t^* + [& \hat{p}^{-1}A'\hat{p} + \hat{p}^{-1}(E'_d \cdot W'_d) + \hat{p}^{-1}(E'_k \cdot W'_k) \\
& + \hat{p}^{-1}(E'_f \cdot W'_f) + \hat{p}^{-1}(E'_r \cdot W'_r)]h^* \\
= t^* + & Sh^* \tag{4-16}
\end{aligned}
$$

with the obvious substitution for S, the matrix of weights. The new measures of the rate of growth of MFP in terms of the traditional measures are

$$h^* = (I - S)^{-1}t^* \tag{4-17}$$

The new rate for the ith industry is a weighted linear combination of the old measures where the weight s_{ij} represents the share of inputs from the ith industry in the total inputs of the jth industry. Hence, for the ith industry we have

$$h_i^* = -\sum_j \left(\frac{p_j}{p_i}\right) a_{ji} \left(\frac{d \ln a_{ji}}{dt} - \frac{d \ln h_j}{dt}\right)$$

$$-\sum_j \left(\frac{wd_{ji}}{p_i}\right) ed_{ji} \left(\frac{d \ln ed_{ji}}{dt} - \frac{d \ln h_j}{dt}\right)$$

$$-\sum_j \left(\frac{wk_{ji}}{p_i}\right) ek_{ji} \left(\frac{d \ln ek_{ji}}{dt} - \frac{d \ln h_j}{dt}\right)$$

$$-\left(\frac{wf_{ii}}{p_i}\right) ef_{ii} \left(\frac{d \ln ef_{ii}}{dt} - \frac{d \ln h_i}{dt}\right)$$

$$-\sum_j \left(\frac{wr_{ji}}{p_i}\right) er_{ji} \left(\frac{d \ln er_{ji}}{dt} - \frac{d \ln h_j}{dt}\right)$$

$$-\sum_p \left(\frac{wp_{pi}}{p_i}\right) ep_{pi} \frac{d \ln ep_{pi}}{dt}$$

$$= t_i^* + \sum_j \frac{1}{p_i}(p_j a_{ji} + wd_{ji} ed_{ji} + wk_{ji} ek_{ji} + wf_{ji} ef_{ji} + wr_{ji}) h_j^*$$

$$= t_i^* + \sum_j s_{ji} h_j^* \tag{4-18}$$

where s_{ji} is the sum of the shares of all the input – intermediate, CCA, and capital stocks including inventories – coming from the jth industry in the total input of the ith industry. Going back to equation (4-16), we write

$$\frac{d \ln(\hat{h}^{-1}A)}{dt} = \frac{d \ln DB}{dt} - \frac{d \ln \bar{h}}{dt} \tag{4-19}$$

where $\bar{h}$ is a 37×37 matrix whose columns are all equal to the diagonal of $\hat{h}$. Necessary conditions for change in the MFP are changes in one or the other coefficient matrices (D and B) *and/or* in the MFP of the supplying industries. This last element is missing from the traditional equation. Hence, for any industry, the traditional and new rates of MFP will diverge from each other to the extent that there are changes in the direct and indirect efficiency of the supplying industries. Furthermore, the new rate will always be at least equal to the old as long as industries undergo increases in efficiency; and it will always be at most equal to the traditional measure under conditions of widespread decreases in efficiency. Hence,

$$|t^*| \le |h^*| \tag{4-20}$$

To conclude, we stress that a necessary condition for variations in the rate of growth of an industry's traditional MFP is that there be changes in the quantity of intermediate and primary input requirements per unit of output *in that industry*. Changes in the new measures may come from the above as well as from changes in input requirements of the industries that supply that industry with intermediate and durable inputs. Thus, the new measure captures both the interdependence of industries and the produced nature of inputs including the services of the capital stocks and CCA. Even when an industry uses the same amount of a capital good (or other produced input) per unit of output, if that capital good in today's technology needs fewer inputs to be produced, the new measure says that the industry has benefitted from the technical change in the production of its capital goods, whereas the traditional measure does not. What matters is the replacement production of that capital stock, that is, the amount of resources it would take to produce the services of such capital goods with today's technology. This is the adjustment that the new formulation makes; it adjusts all domestically produced inputs for the changes in the efficiency of their industry of origin.[14]

[14] The same adjustment could be made in principle to imported goods if an equivalent set of information was available, but the new measures would no longer represent the productivity, as traditionally conceived, of the domestic economy.

CHAPTER 5

Estimation of the rates of growth of MFP by industry

Traditional and new measures of the rate of growth of MFP were obtained using time series of the previously described rearranged I/O tables from 1961 to 1980. Based on them, year-to-year rates of growth of MFP were obtained. These yearly data were then averaged into periods for decomposition analysis. The discrete index number formula used to approximate the continuous Divisia indexes of outputs and inputs in equation (4-9) were Törnquist indexes.[1] For example, the proportionate rate of growth of the ith industry's output, g_i, between two adjacent years $t-1$ and t is defined as

$$\frac{d \ln g_i}{dt} \approx \ln\left(\frac{g_i^t}{g_i^{t-1}}\right)$$

where the g_i are from the constant-dollar tables. With respect to the Törnquist indexes of inputs, the changing weights are the average shares of the current-dollar total expenditure on the jth input in the value of the total input of the ith industry, and the weight for the jth input in the ith industry is defined as

$$\bar{u}_{ji} = \frac{u_{ji}^t + u_{ji}^{t-1}}{2} \quad \text{where} \quad u_{ji} = \frac{p_j a_{ji} g_i}{p_i g_i} = \frac{p_j}{p_i} a_{ji}$$

As an illustration of the weights used, Table 5-1 gives the weights for the agriculture and fishing and machinery industries. For instance, in agriculture and fishing, the share in total inputs of the net capital construction stock was 5 percent in 1961.

Tables 5-2 and 5-3 present the results of the year-to-year computation of the traditional and new rates of MFP for the period 1961–80. The discrete version of equation (4-9) was used to estimate the traditional measures; equation (4-18) was used to estimate the new ones.

[1] The Törnquist indexes have two advantages. First, they are discrete approximations to the Divisia indexes; second, Diewert has shown that they are exact indexes for the homogeneous translogarithmic production function; i.e., they measure the same change as would be measured by that kind of function. See W. E. Diewert, "Exact and Superlative Index Numbers", *Journal of Econometrics,* IV, May 1976, 115–45.

Table 5-1. *Input weights, 1961*

	01 Agriculture and fishing	17 Machinery
Intermediate inputs		
Agriculture and fishing	0.04	0.00
Food and beverages	0.08	—
Rubber and plastic products	—	0.01
Printing	—	0.01
Primary metals	0.01	0.09
Metal fabricating	—	0.04
Machinery	—	0.04
Transportation equipment	—	0.01
Electrical products	—	0.03
Petroleum and coal products	0.04	—
Chemical and chemical products	0.03	0.01
Construction	0.02	—
Railway transportation and telegraph	0.01	0.01
Motor transport	0.01	0.01
Telephones	—	0.01
Trade	0.04	0.03
Finance	0.03	0.02
Commercial services	—	0.01
Imports	0.04	0.13
Total intermediate inputs	0.35	0.46
Durable inputs		
Capital consumption allowances		
Construction	0.03	—
Machinery	0.01	—
Transportation equipment	0.04	—
Trade	0.02	—
Imports	0.07	0.01
Net capital stock		
Construction	0.05	0.03
Machinery	0.01	0.01
Transportation equipment	0.02	0.01
Trade	0.01	—
Imports	0.03	0.01
Inventories		
Finished goods and in process raw materials	0.03	0.04
Primary metals	—	0.01
Food and beverages	0.01	—
Trade	0.01	—
Imports	0.01	0.01

Table 5-1 *(cont.)*

	01 Agriculture and fishing	17 Machinery
Primary inputs		
Indirect taxes less subsidies	0.04	0.02
Labour income	0.20	0.33

Notes: Totals do not add due to rounding. Printing means printing, publishing, and allied industries. Finance means finance, insurance, and real estate industries.

The most general findings are as follows:

1. The rates of growth of MFP are, on the whole, positive for most industries in most years. Both measures show the 1960s were more productive than the 1970s. Particularly bad years were 1966-7, 1969-70, 1973-4, 1974-5, and 1979-80, with 1973-4 and 1974-5 being particularly bad from the point of view of the new measures. Over the twenty years, 30 percent of all industries had a negative rate of growth of traditional MFP for at least one year and fewer (26.4 percent) had a negative new rate. (See Table 5-4.)

2. The new measures are generally greater than the traditional ones for most industries in most years, as expected under the assumption of increases in efficiency. However, there are exceptions, notably in the 1970s. Table 5-5 shows, by industry, the number of years in the decades 1961-70 and 1971-80 in which the traditional rate exceeds the new rate, that is, the exceptional or odd years.

3. The traditional measures exceed the new ones for only 7.9 percent of the observations in the years 1961-71. For the years 1971-80, the traditional rates exceed the new rates for 35.7 percent of the observations. The implication is that the industries undergoing decreases in efficiency in the latter period are important intermediate input producers. In fact, when important intermediate input producers undergo changes in efficiency, the new measure rates compound the traditional result; that is, good traditional years are very good new years and vice-versa. The new rates accentuate the cyclical variations in the traditional rates. The result is rates whose trend values are higher than the traditional ones and whose fluctuations around the trend are wider.

Table 5-2. *Annual rate of growth of traditional MFP by industry and year, 1961–80*

		1961–2	1962–3	1963–4	1964–5	1965–6	1966–7	1967–8
01	Agriculture and fishing	14.78	6.69	−4.12	2.42	8.02	−15.13	6.13
02	Forestry	4.14	2.36	0.68	−0.25	1.51	−0.60	1.73
03	Mines, quarries, and oil wells	−1.69	1.24	5.83	−3.44	−1.95	1.03	0.17
04	Food and beverage	1.20	−0.11	0.92	0.89	0.23	1.14	0.28
05	Tobacco products	1.69	1.81	3.80	0.53	−4.73	−0.67	−0.95
06	Rubber and plastic products	8.46	0.43	2.94	2.72	2.54	2.40	4.48
07	Leather	1.86	3.12	2.50	−1.46	−2.48	3.41	1.30
08	Textiles	5.84	2.51	1.17	0.11	0.51	2.06	4.70
09	Knitting mills	5.24	1.84	1.74	2.05	1.69	−0.29	5.21
10	Clothing	1.51	0.01	−0.66	0.79	0.24	−0.40	1.94
11	Woods	0.82	0.24	0.41	−0.59	1.80	0.62	−0.96
12	Furniture and fixtures	1.67	1.64	0.50	2.83	1.42	0.44	1.73
13	Paper and allied industries	0.73	1.03	1.54	−1.16	−0.15	−2.75	1.95
14	Printing, publishing, and allied industries	1.00	−0.25	0.10	0.71	0.99	−0.30	1.23
15	Primary metals	2.19	1.85	1.01	0.91	−2.30	−0.87	2.63
16	Metal fabricating	4.66	1.38	2.90	2.34	1.44	0.23	2.63
17	Machinery	4.94	−0.75	4.70	0.40	1.82	−0.48	1.38
18	Transportation equipment	2.92	3.01	0.31	4.25	−1.82	3.77	2.28
19	Electrical products	6.74	0.18	3.19	1.25	−1.51	−2.35	5.09
20	Nonmetallic mineral products	7.04	−0.30	2.82	1.49	0.60	−6.05	4.02
21	Petroleum and coal products	3.20	1.75	0.77	2.62	0.69	−0.50	2.33
22	Chemical and chemical products	3.66	1.56	2.56	−0.12	1.12	−1.00	1.13
23	Miscellaneous manufacturing	1.81	−1.57	2.40	−1.03	1.85	−1.08	5.57
24	Construction	1.58	−0.22	0.53	0.23	0.37	2.46	1.77
25	Air transportation and other utilities and transportation	5.84	1.80	5.80	1.95	3.99	1.46	1.44
26	Railway transportation and telegraph	6.92	11.07	8.65	7.26	6.62	10.88	7.45
27	Water transport	2.81	5.18	1.21	2.95	8.61	−4.28	−0.15
28	Motor transport	3.20	1.79	0.29	2.71	0.71	0.31	1.78
29	Urban and suburban transportation	1.31	−4.17	4.79	−3.59	4.11	−4.41	−0.07
30	Storage	−7.70	8.82	5.60	−2.18	4.00	−0.62	−3.36
31	Broadcasting	6.08	8.99	12.89	−3.53	2.39	−11.27	4.44
32	Telephones	3.26	0.28	2.88	5.85	3.58	4.56	5.52
33	Electric power	0.86	0.94	2.84	3.94	1.52	−4.83	−2.39
34	Gas distribution	7.64	1.50	5.63	11.75	−0.58	5.78	4.73
35	Trade	6.28	2.37	3.00	1.45	3.53	2.02	2.71
36	Finance, insurance, and real estate	0.20	−0.73	1.04	1.50	−0.03	−2.21	0.37
37	Commercial services	−0.46	0.25	−0.28	−1.07	−0.63	−1.72	0.57

For the subperiods 1961–71, 1971–80, 1961–73, and 1973–80, average annual rates are presented in Tables 5-6 and 5-7. The change of year end from 1971 to 1973 shows the extent to which the choice of year end can affect the results. The year 1973 was chosen as the one in which it would appear that a cyclical decline occurred. We briefly discuss these results:

4. For the whole period 1961–80 and the two subperiods 1961–71 and 1971–80, the new measures are always greater than the traditional ones except for two industries: primary metals and petroleum

1968-9	1969-70	1970-1	1971-2	1972-3	1973-4	1974-5	1975-6	1976-7	1977-8	1978-9	1979-80
1.61	-5.96	8.64	-4.87	3.41	-5.31	3.40	3.47	-1.13	-1.40	-6.83	2.47
3.30	4.43	-3.11	4.04	-3.54	1.51	-2.35	4.45	1.79	-0.66	-3.80	3.13
0.71	0.03	-4.98	3.60	7.71	-14.80	-15.31	-3.43	-4.65	-6.25	3.81	-5.57
0.14	1.51	0.07	-0.30	0.66	1.04	-2.30	3.29	0.86	-1.17	0.41	0.33
4.65	1.83	2.76	4.82	4.99	11.33	-9.43	-2.15	4.62	-1.34	4.36	2.60
3.37	-0.84	1.58	2.70	3.42	-7.23	-3.86	5.26	3.98	1.14	2.75	-4.29
-0.36	1.73	0.57	-5.32	1.93	3.23	3.02	1.69	0.60	2.29	-4.19	4.74
4.12	0.38	4.36	4.66	0.83	-1.11	1.31	1.30	3.86	3.22	1.66	-0.87
2.72	0.15	3.61	4.95	0.94	0.71	5.12	4.55	4.76	6.04	1.76	2.66
-0.53	0.70	2.48	0.08	2.33	0.46	2.52	2.00	1.40	3.67	1.38	-0.05
-1.70	1.91	0.46	-4.15	-0.67	1.85	1.53	2.46	2.84	-3.42	-2.75	5.08
1.47	-1.89	0.34	3.63	2.14	-7.00	-0.69	3.81	0.80	2.54	-2.96	-0.05
3.56	-0.92	-1.63	3.58	3.89	-1.06	-13.07	6.51	1.00	4.01	2.21	-3.95
1.09	-0.47	0.72	3.24	3.45	-0.34	0.55	5.60	2.67	1.03	0.41	0.52
1.24	-3.30	2.55	1.35	0.41	1.76	2.82	-0.44	4.24	1.14	-7.31	-0.24
1.33	-0.91	0.79	0.79	2.49	0.46	-3.95	2.18	0.89	0.64	1.70	2.32
2.53	-0.03	-6.40	0.52	2.69	2.46	-2.59	1.67	2.33	2.78	3.91	0.19
3.60	-4.47	4.63	2.52	3.18	-0.01	2.32	1.47	0.49	0.63	-0.81	-5.01
2.29	-1.46	4.76	4.92	3.57	-1.32	-1.16	4.27	3.51	-1.02	2.63	1.23
0.64	-1.05	5.34	3.71	3.13	-0.02	-3.47	0.79	-1.39	2.04	1.21	-4.03
1.66	3.41	-4.79	1.61	-0.87	-2.10	-0.89	0.30	4.07	-3.19	7.27	2.04
2.13	-0.62	1.21	2.10	3.90	-2.76	-6.51	2.59	1.25	1.86	-0.87	-2.96
0.57	2.97	-0.49	2.99	0.29	0.29	-1.05	3.83	0.94	-0.32	-1.32	-4.23
0.87	0.70	0.52	-0.64	1.33	0.19	3.26	-1.08	-1.05	-1.34	0.01	2.81
3.58	-0.03	-1.30	6.59	4.73	-1.82	-5.01	-1.16	3.58	1.68	5.01	-10.28
-1.12	5.26	1.38	4.09	4.52	4.18	5.24	1.75	0.78	4.77	6.17	-1.76
3.39	3.24	3.58	-2.08	-1.49	0.32	-1.22	6.25	-0.97	-0.40	2.26	3.18
-2.26	-1.19	-0.23	1.28	0.69	-2.11	4.61	-1.49	-2.25	3.93	6.59	-5.05
-3.94	-3.58	-1.33	2.76	-7.88	-8.89	4.00	-0.11	-3.39	0.02	-7.00	9.95
10.65	8.03	-13.89	2.95	-1.58	0.93	0.57	3.03	-0.18	3.17	1.91	2.52
-2.48	1.93	0.92	5.09	1.18	5.33	9.13	1.83	-5.78	1.18	2.40	4.24
2.70	4.38	0.68	2.81	3.62	5.56	9.55	0.33	4.02	6.40	6.78	6.90
1.82	-0.37	-3.64	6.94	5.84	2.02	-10.09	3.87	-0.73	0.75	1.40	-0.89
1.84	8.26	0.40	4.01	-0.29	1.64	-5.09	2.38	9.22	-9.09	2.64	2.71
1.97	2.23	0.70	4.01	2.16	0.38	-0.97	3.95	-2.15	-0.90	1.03	-1.38
-1.28	0.14	0.52	-0.41	-1.54	-0.42	-0.05	0.35	-0.72	0.89	1.01	0.03
-0.73	-1.99	2.30	-0.38	0.65	-0.36	-1.69	2.40	-1.09	0.83	-0.67	1.40

and coal products in the period 1971-80. A surprising result is that four industries have an almost consistently negative rate of traditional MFP over the periods: mines, quarries, and oil wells; urban and suburban transport; finance insurance and real estate; and commercial services. For urban and suburban transport, even the new measures are consistently negative.

5. For the subperiods 1961-73 and 1973-80, a different picture emerges. The year 1973 is regarded as the start of a substantial

Table 5-3. *Annual rate of growth of new MFP by industry and year,*
1961–80

		1961–2	1962–3	1963–4	1964–5	1965–6	1966–7	1967–8
01	Agriculture and fishing	20.26	8.99	−2.26	4.24	10.07	−16.22	9.32
02	Forestry	7.57	3.77	2.29	1.06	2.52	−0.45	3.67
03	Mines, quarries, and oil wells	1.94	2.45	8.46	−2.32	−1.13	1.74	2.67
04	Food and beverages	10.81	4.18	1.67	3.29	4.60	−4.36	5.02
05	Tobacco products	12.15	6.87	5.61	2.73	−2.13	−7.74	3.93
06	Rubber and plastic products	12.39	2.05	5.21	3.69	3.66	2.66	6.86
07	Leather	5.43	4.91	4.56	−0.83	−1.92	4.17	3.23
08	Textiles	9.77	4.22	2.98	0.91	1.48	2.73	7.62
09	Knitting mills	10.13	3.90	3.64	2.91	2.73	0.68	8.98
10	Clothing	5.47	1.64	0.91	1.58	1.26	0.18	5.16
11	Woods	5.35	2.39	2.29	0.45	3.47	0.72	1.23
12	Furniture and fixtures	5.46	3.22	2.62	3.99	2.62	0.82	4.11
13	Paper and allied industries	5.03	3.05	3.99	−0.14	1.22	−3.02	4.38
14	Printing, publishing, and allied industries	3.63	0.94	1.86	1.35	1.83	−0.71	3.21
15	Primary metals	5.24	3.78	4.86	1.30	−2.28	−0.28	5.07
16	Metal fabricating	8.41	3.25	5.66	3.65	1.67	0.39	5.29
17	Machinery	8.42	0.49	7.19	1.58	2.37	−0.36	3.66
18	Transportation equipment	6.24	4.75	2.18	6.07	−1.70	4.52	4.43
19	Electrical products	10.64	1.53	5.73	2.47	−1.32	−2.58	7.92
20	Nonmettalic mineral products	11.11	1.22	5.63	2.77	1.53	−6.38	6.57
21	Petroleum and coal products	5.72	3.16	4.84	2.41	0.91	0.35	4.25
22	Chemical and chemical products	7.74	3.31	5.32	0.99	2.38	−1.15	3.53
23	Miscellaneous manufacturing	4.98	−0.28	4.59	−0.22	2.66	−1.08	7.90
24	Construction	5.66	1.30	3.11	1.42	1.19	2.27	4.14
25	Air transportation and other utilities and transportation	9.78	3.00	8.18	3.27	4.80	2.18	3.93
26	Railway transportation and telegraph	9.85	12.23	10.47	8.34	7.40	11.79	9.52
27	Water transport	6.04	7.61	2.86	4.93	11.42	−4.86	1.37
28	Motor transport	6.23	3.32	2.05	4.28	1.46	1.21	3.78
29	Urban and suburban transportation	2.94	−3.51	5.66	−2.89	4.37	−4.16	0.65
30	Storage	−4.89	10.18	7.48	−1.04	4.96	0.18	−1.49
31	Broadcasting	9.97	10.35	15.58	−2.14	3.69	−11.76	7.44
32	Telephones	6.93	1.02	4.70	6.86	3.95	4.94	7.91
33	Electric power	5.07	1.97	5.16	5.06	2.23	−3.88	0.25
34	Gas distribution	11.25	2.44	7.72	12.86	0.18	7.09	7.39
35	Trade	9.23	3.61	4.40	2.48	4.40	1.50	4.44
36	Finance, insurance, and real estate	3.51	0.05	2.94	2.49	0.72	−1.21	2.76
37	Commercial services	2.63	1.40	1.01	−0.08	0.28	−1.89	2.33

and continuous decline in productivity. Both the traditional and new measures reflect this decline with twelve industries showing negative annual average rates of growth of traditional MFP for the subperiod 1973–80. Moreover, twelve industries have average new rates that are below the traditional ones, a different picture from that of 1961–73.

To analyze these results, we present, in the next section, the decomposition of both the traditional and new rates of growth of MFP into their component parts.

1968-9	1969-70	1970-1	1971-2	1972-3	1973-4	1974-5	1975-6	1976-7	1977-8	1978-9	1979-80
3.37	-6.15	9.96	-3.72	6.17	-6.62	2.60	5.69	-1.15	-2.02	-6.20	2.49
4.40	5.10	-2.92	5.68	-2.77	1.05	-2.86	6.08	1.78	-0.58	-2.58	3.26
2.04	0.23	-4.63	5.14	10.28	-16.10	-16.04	-2.58	-5.25	-6.95	5.10	-4.95
2.24	-0.16	3.75	-0.41	4.28	-1.44	-2.72	7.16	0.67	-1.90	-1.07	1.06
8.64	0.14	7.50	6.83	10.23	12.58	-12.94	0.93	5.91	-1.73	4.53	3.71
5.11	-0.77	2.41	4.77	5.65	-8.41	-6.18	7.23	4.59	1.73	3.70	-5.43
0.58	2.14	1.22	-4.63	3.69	2.77	2.23	3.58	1.07	2.85	-4.02	4.93
6.33	0.65	5.81	7.19	2.49	-1.83	0.47	2.97	4.88	4.20	2.79	-1.57
5.54	0.52	5.88	8.12	2.56	0.05	5.02	6.32	6.31	7.62	3.09	2.18
1.56	1.06	4.46	2.59	3.79	0.10	2.92	3.86	2.72	5.24	2.41	-0.29
0.09	3.93	-0.10	-2.00	-0.55	2.17	0.39	5.39	3.72	-3.92	-3.27	6.45
2.93	-1.69	1.12	5.44	3.93	-7.80	-1.93	5.84	1.73	2.83	-2.66	-0.02
5.70	0.06	-2.13	6.30	5.69	-1.54	-16.59	9.59	1.71	4.10	3.21	-4.16
2.75	-0.39	0.67	5.45	5.69	-0.86	-2.94	8.55	3.19	2.07	1.67	-0.40
2.73	-3.63	1.82	4.03	4.51	-2.77	-1.61	-0.34	3.57	-0.20	-6.50	-1.77
2.76	-1.73	1.59	2.76	4.91	-0.35	-5.28	3.17	1.94	0.75	0.81	2.03
3.87	-0.45	-6.09	2.08	4.56	2.06	-3.55	2.78	3.04	3.07	4.21	-0.03
5.06	-5.28	5.79	4.12	4.97	-0.50	1.80	2.54	0.95	0.85	-0.74	-5.64
3.79	-2.13	6.04	7.18	5.92	-2.15	-2.31	5.92	4.58	-0.94	2.82	1.00
1.95	-0.98	6.12	6.15	5.91	-1.40	-6.13	2.07	-1.78	1.88	2.93	-5.43
3.09	3.55	-6.24	4.21	3.43	-8.05	-7.46	-0.44	1.85	-6.67	10.35	-0.72
3.70	-0.47	1.59	4.33	6.69	-4.20	-9.48	4.51	1.50	1.71	0.85	-4.07
1.69	3.12	0.16	4.82	2.12	-0.36	-2.38	5.55	1.45	-0.06	-1.04	-4.84
2.01	0.60	1.40	1.07	3.34	-0.60	1.68	0.45	-0.76	-1.53	0.85	2.47
4.95	0.11	-0.78	8.39	7.15	-2.82	-6.01	-0.41	3.82	0.98	7.27	-11.01
-0.21	5.64	1.88	5.18	6.03	3.80	5.26	2.47	0.87	4.39	7.65	-1.45
5.62	4.19	5.30	-1.55	-0.67	-0.33	-2.34	9.17	-1.01	-0.83	4.36	3.40
-1.35	-1.19	0.38	2.96	2.27	-2.86	4.60	-0.71	-2.32	4.08	8.83	-6.04
-3.50	-3.64	-1.13	3.49	-7.40	-9.13	2.51	0.25	-3.01	0.59	-6.24	8.51
11.68	8.44	-13.55	3.91	-0.33	0.71	0.57	3.85	-0.30	3.17	2.85	2.84
-1.37	2.06	1.93	6.92	3.53	5.52	9.25	3.68	-5.85	1.77	3.69	5.32
3.87	4.41	2.04	4.55	5.47	5.34	9.89	1.36	4.52	6.30	7.74	7.87
3.15	-0.11	-2.80	8.34	8.21	1.07	-10.23	4.49	-0.92	-0.34	2.60	-0.10
3.19	8.56	1.30	5.04	2.01	1.19	-4.34	3.05	8.87	-9.91	3.53	3.89
2.88	2.32	1.16	5.05	3.49	0.02	-1.30	5.00	-2.16	-0.84	1.88	-1.19
-0.21	0.47	1.33	0.38	0.30	-0.76	0.67	0.92	-1.11	0.25	1.78	1.37
0.11	-1.92	3.02	0.52	2.04	-0.71	-2.08	3.74	-1.10	0.79	-0.10	1.54

A Components of the traditional measures of multifactor productivity

In the previous section, two measures of MFP for thirty-seven industries were presented and compared. In this section we aim at some understanding of their determinants and of the contribution of the included
variables to the recorded changes in MFP. Undoubtedly, the final value
of any MFP is the result of many excluded or ignored variables, such as

Table 5-4. *Number of industries with negative MFP growth*

	Traditional	New
1961–2	3	1
1962–3	8	2
1963–4	3	1
1964–5	11	8
1965–6	10	6
1966–7	21	18
1967–8	6	1
1968–9	9	5
1969–70	17	16
1970–1	11	10
1971–2	8	5
1972–3	8	5
1973–4	17	23
1974–5	21	22
1975–6	7	5
1976–7	13	13
1977–8	13	15
1978–9	11	11
1979–80	16	19
Total	213 (703)	186 (703)

Note: Number in parentheses is the sum total of MFP rates over years and industries, i.e., $37 \times 19 = 703$.

returns to scale, quality of labour, land, aggregation, and measurement errors, which are not discussed here.

The decomposition analysis is presented for the subperiods 1961–71, 1971–80, 1961–73, and 1973–80 and the full period 1961–80. The rate of growth of the MFP is expressed as the rate of growth of output minus the weighted rate of growth of inputs. Inputs have been grouped into six categories: intermediate, imported, government, labour, CCA, and net capital stocks. Törnquist indexes for each input were obtained before aggregation. For example, the Törnquist index of intermediate inputs in the jth industry is

$$I_j = \sum_{i=1}^{37} \frac{1}{2} \left(\frac{p_i^t a_{ij}^t}{p_j^t} + \frac{p_i^{t-1} a_{ij}^{t-1}}{p_j^{t-1}} \right) \ln \frac{g_{ij}^t}{g_{ij}^{t-1}} \qquad (5\text{-}1)$$

so that it is a sum of the individual Törnquist indexes of the inputs in that group.

Table 5-5. *Number of years in which traditional measures exceed the new*

		1961–71	1971–80
01	Agriculture and fishing	2	4
02	Forestry	–	3
03	Mines, quarries, and oil wells	–	4
04	Food and beverages	2	6
05	Tobacco products	2	2
06	Rubber and plastic products	–	3
07	Leather	–	2
08	Textiles	–	3
09	Knitting mills	–	3
10	Clothing	–	2
11	Woods	1	3
12	Furniture and fixtures	–	2
13	Paper and allied industries	2	3
14	Printing, publishing, and allied industries	2	3
15	Primary metals	2	5
16	Metal fabricating	1	4
17	Machinery	1	3
18	Transportation equipment	1	3
19	Electrical products	2	3
20	Nonmetallic mineral products	1	5
21	Petroleum and coal products	1	6
22	Chemical and chemical products	1	4
23	Miscellaneous manufacturing	1	3
24	Construction	2	4
25	Air transportation and other utilities and transportation	–	3
26	Railway transportation and telegraph	–	2
27	Water transport	1	4
28	Motor transport	–	3
29	Urban and suburban transportation	1	3
30	Storage	–	2
31	Broadcasting	1	1
32	Telephones	–	2
33	Electric power	–	3
34	Gas distribution	–	3
35	Trade	1	3
36	Finance, insurance, and real estate	–	3
37	Commercial services	1	4
	Total	29 (370)	119 (333)

Note: Numbers in parentheses are the total number of industry MFP rates in the period; i.e., $37 \times 10 = 370$ and $37 \times 9 = 333$.

Table 5-6. *Average of annual rates of growth of traditional MFP by periods*

		1961-71	1971-80	1961-80	1961-73	1973-80
01	Agriculture and fishing	2.31	-0.75	0.86	1.80	-0.76
02	Forestry	1.42	0.51	0.99	1.23	0.58
03	Mines, quarries, and oil wells	-0.30	-3.88	-2.00	0.69	-6.60
04	Food and beverages	0.63	0.31	0.48	0.55	0.35
05	Tobacco products	1.07	2.20	1.61	1.71	1.43
06	Rubber and plastic products	2.81	0.43	1.68	2.85	-0.32
07	Leather	1.02	0.89	0.96	0.57	1.63
08	Textiles	2.57	1.65	2.14	2.60	1.34
09	Knitting mills	2.40	3.50	2.92	2.49	3.66
10	Clothing	0.61	1.53	1.05	0.71	1.63
11	Woods	0.30	0.31	0.30	-0.15	1.08
12	Furniture and fixtures	1.01	0.26	0.66	1.33	-0.49
13	Paper and allied industries	0.22	0.35	0.28	0.81	-0.62
14	Printing, publishing, and allied industries	0.48	1.90	1.15	0.96	1.49
15	Primary metals	0.59	0.41	0.51	0.64	0.28
16	Metal fabricating	1.68	0.84	1.28	1.67	0.61
17	Machinery	0.81	1.55	1.16	0.94	1.54
18	Transportation equipment	1.85	0.53	1.22	2.01	-0.13
19	Electrical products	1.82	1.85	1.83	2.22	1.16
20	Nonmetallic mineral products	1.45	0.22	0.87	1.78	-0.70
21	Petroleum and coal products	1.11	0.92	1.02	0.99	1.07
22	Chemical and chemical products	1.16	-0.16	0.54	1.47	-1.06
23	Miscellaneous manufacturing	1.10	0.16	0.65	1.19	-0.27
24	Construction	0.88	0.39	0.65	0.79	0.40
25	Air transportation and other utilities and transportation	2.45	0.37	1.47	2.99	-1.14
26	Railway transportation and telegraph	6.44	3.31	4.95	6.08	3.02
27	Water transport	2.65	0.65	1.71	1.91	1.35
28	Motor transport	0.71	0.69	0.70	0.76	0.60
29	Urban and suburban transportation	-1.09	-1.17	-1.13	-1.33	-0.77
30	Storage	0.94	1.48	1.19	0.89	1.71
31	Broadcasting	2.04	2.73	2.37	2.22	2.62
32	Telephones	3.37	5.11	4.19	3.34	5.65
33	Electric power	0.07	1.01	0.52	1.12	-0.53
34	Gas distribution	4.69	0.91	2.90	4.22	0.63
35	Trade	2.61	0.68	1.69	2.69	-
36	Finance, insurance, and real estate	-0.05	-0.10	-0.07	-0.20	0.16
37	Commercial services	-0.38	0.12	-0.14	-0.29	0.12

Tables 5-8 to 5-12 show, for each column, the rate of growth of output minus the weighted rate of growth of inputs, which by definition equals the rate of growth of MFP, the last column in the tables. Take, for instance, the first industry in Table 5-8, agriculture and fishing. The first column, output, shows that the rate of growth of output was 3.73. The intermediate inputs column is the sum of the weighted rate of growth of

Table 5-7. *Average of annual rates of growth of new MFP by periods*

		1961–71	1971–80	1961–80	1961–73	1973–80
01	Agriculture and fishing	4.16	−0.31	2.04	3.67	−0.74
02	Forestry	2.70	1.01	1.90	2.49	0.88
03	Mines, quarries, and oil wells	1.14	−3.48	−1.05	2.24	−6.68
04	Food and beverages	3.10	0.63	1.93	2.91	0.25
05	Tobacco products	3.77	3.34	3.57	4.56	1.86
06	Rubber and plastic products	4.33	0.85	2.68	4.47	−0.40
07	Leather	2.35	1.38	1.89	1.88	1.91
08	Textiles	4.25	2.40	3.37	4.35	1.70
09	Knitting mills	4.49	4.58	4.53	4.63	4.37
10	Clothing	2.33	2.59	2.45	2.47	2.42
11	Woods	1.98	0.93	1.48	1.44	1.56
12	Furniture and fixtures	2.52	0.82	1.71	2.88	−0.29
13	Paper and allied industries	1.81	0.92	1.39	2.51	−0.53
14	Printing, publishing, and allied industries	1.51	2.49	1.98	2.19	1.61
15	Primary metals	1.86	−0.12	0.92	2.26	−1.37
16	Metal fabricating	3.09	1.19	2.19	3.22	0.44
17	Machinery	2.07	2.03	2.05	2.28	1.65
18	Transportation equipment	3.21	0.93	2.13	3.43	−0.11
19	Electrical products	3.21	2.45	2.85	3.77	1.28
20	Nonmetallic mineral products	2.95	0.47	1.78	3.47	−1.12
21	Petroleum and coal products	2.20	−0.39	0.98	2.47	−1.59
22	Chemical and chemical products	2.69	0.20	1.51	3.16	−1.31
23	Miscellaneous manufacturing	2.35	0.58	1.52	2.54	−0.24
24	Construction	2.31	0.77	1.58	2.29	0.37
25	Air transportation and other utilities and transportation	3.94	0.82	2.46	4.58	−1.17
26	Railway transportation and telegraph	7.69	3.80	5.85	7.34	3.29
27	Water transport	4.45	1.13	2.88	3.52	1.78
28	Motor transport	2.02	1.20	1.63	2.12	0.80
29	Urban and suburban transportation	−0.52	−1.16	−0.82	−0.76	−0.93
30	Storage	2.19	1.92	2.06	2.13	1.96
31	Broadcasting	3.58	3.76	3.66	3.85	3.34
32	Telephones	4.66	5.89	5.25	4.72	6.15
33	Electric power	1.61	1.46	1.54	2.72	−0.49
34	Gas distribution	6.20	1.48	3.96	5.75	0.90
35	Trade	3.64	1.10	2.44	3.75	0.20
36	Finance, insurance, and real estate	1.28	0.42	0.88	1.13	0.45
37	Commercial services	0.69	0.51	0.61	0.79	0.30

each intermediate input; they add up to 1.13. The imports column is the sum of the weighted rate of growth of all the imported inputs: intermediate, capital consumption allowances on the stock of imported capital goods, and the net stock of imported capital goods; they grew by 0.19. Government is the sum of the weighted rate of growth of purchases of government foods and services, indirect taxes, and subsidies; they grew by 0.04. Labour shows the negative rate of growth of hours worked into

Table 5-8. *Breakdown of the average of annual rates of growth of traditional MFP, 1961–71*

	Output	Inter-mediate input	Imports	Govern-ment	Labour	CCA	Capital	MFP rate
01 Agriculture and fishing	3.73	-1.13	-0.19	-0.04	0.60	-0.22	-0.44	2.31
02 Forestry	1.87	-1.15	-0.23	-0.02	1.30	-0.22	-0.13	1.42
03 Mines, quarries, and oil wells	6.33	-2.47	-0.38	-0.19	-0.37	-0.90	-2.33	-0.30
04 Food and beverages	3.73	-2.47	-0.22	—	-0.03	-0.09	-0.29	0.63
05 Tobacco products	2.88	-1.86	-0.09	-0.02	0.22	-0.09	0.03	1.07
06 Rubber and plastic products	9.77	-3.15	-1.61	-0.09	-1.24	-0.24	-0.63	2.81
07 Leather	1.13	-0.01	-0.67	-0.02	0.62	-0.03	—	1.02
08 Textiles	7.10	-2.64	-1.27	-0.06	-0.17	-0.14	-0.25	2.57
09 Knitting mills	6.78	-2.64	-1.32	-0.02	-0.16	-0.08	-0.16	2.40
10 Clothing	3.80	-2.33	-0.55	-0.02	-0.18	-0.01	-0.10	0.61
11 Woods	4.40	-2.83	-0.35	-0.11	-0.34	-0.18	-0.30	0.30
12 Furniture and fixtures	5.73	-2.61	-0.68	-0.07	-0.78	-0.07	-0.50	1.01
13 Paper and allied industries	4.32	-2.36	-0.32	-0.07	-0.38	-0.43	-0.54	0.22
14 Printing, publishing, and allied industries	3.30	-1.66	-0.17	-0.06	-0.43	-0.11	-0.38	0.48
15 Primary metals	5.02	-2.77	-0.67	-0.05	-0.42	-0.25	-0.27	0.59
16 Metal fabricating	6.66	-2.75	-0.65	-0.05	-0.96	-0.08	-0.48	1.68
17 Machinery	7.31	-2.95	-1.54	-0.06	-1.08	-0.11	-0.76	0.81
18 Transportation equipment	11.72	-4.21	-4.06	-0.04	-0.99	-0.11	-0.46	1.85
19 Electrical products	6.94	-2.64	-0.96	-0.05	-0.94	-0.12	-0.41	1.82
20 Nonmetallic mineral products	5.57	-2.35	-0.30	-0.10	-0.45	-0.29	-0.62	1.45
21 Petroleum and coal products	5.34	-2.41	-1.50	-0.03	-0.11	-0.14	-0.04	1.11

22	Chemical and chemical products	5.84	−2.49	−0.67	−0.07	−0.43	−0.31	−0.71	1.16
23	Miscellaneous manufacturing	5.84	−2.28	−1.06	−0.09	−0.62	−0.17	−0.51	1.10
24	Construction	4.46	−2.42	−0.31	−0.30	−0.41	−0.03	−0.10	0.88
25	Air transportation and other utilities and transportation	9.35	−2.65	−0.42	−0.52	−0.90	−1.25	−1.16	2.45
26	Railway transportation and telegraph	5.45	−0.60	−0.19	0.26	1.41	0.12	−0.01	6.44
27	Water transport	5.24	−2.12	−0.24	−0.07	0.28	−0.36	−0.08	2.65
28	Motor transport	7.06	−3.29	−0.43	−0.49	−1.17	−0.17	−0.80	0.71
29	Urban and suburban transportation	0.63	−0.49	−0.09	0.03	−0.76	−0.86	0.44	−1.09
30	Storage	2.20	−0.03	0.01	−0.21	−0.07	−0.26	−0.71	0.94
31	Broadcasting	7.01	−3.73	−0.80	3.40	−1.73	−0.64	−1.47	2.04
32	Telephones	8.20	−0.50	−0.05	−0.28	−0.86	−1.20	−1.94	3.37
33	Electric power	6.12	−0.89	−0.54	−0.14	−0.94	−1.62	−1.92	0.07
34	Gas distribution	9.33	−0.34	0.05	−0.25	0.01	−0.78	−3.34	4.69
35	Trade	5.21	−1.00	−0.11	−0.06	−1.15	−0.12	−0.16	2.61
36	Finance, insurance, and real estate	4.45	−1.08	−0.07	−0.78	−0.90	−0.39	−1.28	−0.05
37	Commercial services	5.46	−1.75	−0.34	−0.16	−2.15	−0.29	−1.14	−0.38

Table 5-9. *Breakdown of the average of annual rates of growth of traditional MFP, 1971–80*

	Output	Inter-mediate input	Imports	Govern-ment	Labour	CCA	Capital	MFP rate
01 Agriculture and fishing	1.90	−1.39	−0.22	0.01	0.10	−0.91	−0.24	−0.75
02 Forestry	3.43	−2.46	−0.18	−0.12	0.12	−0.25	−0.03	0.51
03 Mines, quarries, and oil wells	3.30	−3.89	−0.33	−0.20	−0.44	−0.74	−1.57	−3.88
04 Food and beverages	2.45	−1.54	−0.31	–	−0.04	−0.03	−0.22	0.31
05 Tobacco products	0.79	1.35	−0.35	0.01	0.34	−0.02	0.08	2.20
06 Rubber and plastic products	5.15	−2.29	−0.76	−0.04	−0.91	−0.22	−0.50	0.43
07 Leather	0.93	−0.54	–	0.01	0.57	−0.04	−0.04	0.89
08 Textiles	2.83	−0.76	−0.44	−0.01	0.19	−0.03	−0.13	1.65
09 Knitting mills	3.16	0.08	−0.22	0.02	0.67	–	−0.21	3.50
10 Clothing	2.67	−0.73	−0.34	–	0.26	−0.01	−0.32	1.53
11 Woods	4.38	−2.43	−0.32	−0.05	−0.59	−0.19	−0.49	0.31
12 Furniture and fixtures	2.54	1.11	−0.36	−0.01	−0.48	−0.05	−0.28	0.26
13 Paper and allied industries	3.11	−1.77	−0.37	−0.01	−0.32	−0.17	−0.12	0.35
14 Printing, publishing, and allied industries	5.36	−1.75	−0.38	−0.03	−0.82	−0.08	−0.40	1.90
15 Primary metals	2.02	−0.35	−0.69	−0.03	−0.25	−0.20	−0.09	0.41
16 Metal fabricating	2.91	−0.93	−0.37	−0.02	−0.40	−0.08	−0.29	0.84
17 Machinery	7.44	−1.87	−2.07	−0.06	−1.28	−0.10	−0.51	1.55
18 Transportation equipment	2.64	−0.59	−0.89	−0.01	−0.28	−0.07	−0.27	0.53
19 Electrical products	3.57	−0.37	−1.04	−0.01	0.13	−0.07	0.37	1.85
20 Nonmetallic mineral products	2.20	−0.93	−0.32	−0.05	−0.04	−0.24	−0.41	0.22
21 Petroleum and coal products	4.55	−4.39	0.80	0.36	−0.18	−0.15	−0.07	0.92

22	Chemical and chemical products	4.98	-3.08	-0.77	-0.06	-0.17	-0.48	-0.57	-0.16
23	Miscellaneous manufacturing	2.73	-0.97	-1.07	-0.02	-0.30	-0.05	-0.17	0.16
24	Construction	2.94	1.12	-0.30	-0.14	-0.65	-0.08	-0.27	0.39
25	Air transportation and other utilities and transportation	6.31	-2.52	-0.19	-0.21	-1.52	-1.00	-0.50	0.37
26	Railway transportation and telegraph	3.30	-1.88	—	1.27	0.73	-0.15	0.02	3.31
27	Water transport	1.93	-1.32	-0.02	-0.12	0.17	-0.01	0.01	0.65
28	Motor transport	5.15	-1.68	-0.21	-0.25	-1.36	-0.19	-0.78	0.69
29	Urban and suburban transportation	3.10	-2.37	-0.46	-0.29	-4.10	-1.86	4.79	-1.17
30	Storage	3.08	-0.89	-0.02	0.04	0.12	-0.53	-0.32	1.48
31	Broadcasting	8.16	-3.36	-0.61	3.33	-2.22	-0.78	-1.80	2.73
32	Telephones	10.42	-0.75	-0.10	-0.38	-1.31	-1.18	-1.59	5.11
33	Electric power	6.56	-0.64	-0.39	-0.05	-0.87	-1.96	-1.63	1.01
34	Gas distribution	4.65	-0.58	-0.02	0.16	-0.76	-0.67	-1.88	0.91
35	Trade	3.78	-1.07	-0.06	-0.12	-1.53	-0.10	-0.21	0.68
36	Finance, insurance, and real estate	5.33	-1.31	-0.16	-0.77	-1.04	-0.53	-1.62	-0.10
37	Commercial services	6.46	-1.46	-0.19	-0.11	-2.70	-0.49	-1.40	0.12

Table 5-10. *Breakdown of the average of annual rates of growth of traditional MFP, 1961–80*

		Output	Inter-mediate input	Imports	Govern-ment	Labour	CCA	Capital	MFP rate
01	Agriculture and fishing	2.86	−1.25	−0.20	−0.02	0.36	−0.55	−0.34	0.86
02	Forestry	2.61	−1.77	−0.21	−0.07	0.74	−0.24	−0.08	0.99
03	Mines, quarries, and oil wells	4.89	−3.15	−0.36	−0.20	−0.40	−0.82	−1.97	−2.00
04	Food and beverages	3.13	−2.03	−0.26	—	−0.03	−0.06	−0.26	0.48
05	Tobacco products	1.89	−0.34	−0.21	−0.01	0.28	−0.06	0.05	1.61
06	Rubber and plastic products	7.58	−2.74	−1.21	−0.07	−1.08	−0.23	−0.57	1.68
07	Leather	1.04	−0.26	−0.35	−0.01	0.59	−0.04	−0.02	0.96
08	Textiles	5.08	−1.75	−0.88	−0.04	—	−0.09	−0.19	2.14
09	Knitting mills	5.06	−1.35	−0.80	—	0.23	−0.04	−0.18	2.92
10	Clothing	3.27	−1.57	−0.45	−0.01	0.03	−0.01	−0.20	1.05
11	Woods	4.39	−2.64	−0.34	−0.08	−0.46	−0.18	−0.39	0.30
12	Furniture and fixtures	4.22	−1.90	−0.53	−0.04	−0.64	−0.06	−0.40	0.66
13	Paper and allied industries	3.74	−2.08	−0.34	−0.04	−0.35	−0.31	−0.34	0.28
14	Printing, publishing, and allied industries	4.28	−1.70	−0.27	−0.05	−0.62	−0.10	−0.39	1.15
15	Primary metals	3.60	−1.62	−0.68	−0.04	−0.34	−0.23	−0.18	0.51
16	Metal fabricating	4.88	−1.89	−0.52	−0.04	−0.69	−0.08	−0.39	1.28
17	Machinery	7.37	−2.44	−1.79	−0.06	−1.18	−0.11	−0.64	1.16
18	Transportation equipment	7.42	−2.50	−2.56	−0.03	−0.65	−0.09	−0.37	1.22
19	Electrical products	5.35	−1.57	−1.00	−0.03	−0.44	−0.10	−0.39	1.83
20	Nonmetallic mineral products	3.97	−1.68	−0.31	−0.08	−0.25	−0.26	−0.52	0.87
21	Petroleum and coal products	4.97	−3.35	−0.41	0.16	−0.14	−0.14	−0.06	1.02

22	Chemical and chemical products	5.44	-2.77	-0.72	-0.07	-0.31	-0.39	-0.64	0.54
23	Miscellaneous manufacturing	4.37	-1.66	-1.07	-0.06	-0.47	-0.11	-0.35	0.65
24	Construction	3.74	-1.81	-0.31	-0.22	-0.52	-0.06	-0.18	0.65
25	Air transportation and other utilities and transportation	7.91	-2.59	-0.31	-0.37	-1.19	-1.13	-0.85	1.47
26	Railway transportation and telegraph	4.43	-1.21	-0.10	0.74	1.09	-0.01	0.01	4.95
27	Water transport	3.67	-1.74	-0.13	-0.09	0.23	-0.19	-0.04	1.71
28	Motor transport	6.16	-2.53	-0.33	-0.38	-1.76	-0.18	0.79	0.70
29	Urban and suburban transportation	1.80	-1.38	-0.27	-0.12	-2.34	-1.33	2.50	-1.13
30	Storage	2.62	-0.44	-0.01	-0.09	0.02	-0.38	-0.53	1.19
31	Broadcasting	7.55	-3.55	-0.71	3.37	-1.96	0.71	1.62	2.37
32	Telephones	9.25	-0.62	-0.07	-0.33	-1.07	-1.19	-1.77	4.19
33	Electric power	6.33	-0.77	-0.47	-0.10	-0.91	-1.78	-1.78	0.52
34	Gas distribution	7.11	-0.45	0.02	-0.06	-0.35	-0.72	2.65	2.90
35	Trade	4.53	-1.03	-0.09	-0.09	-1.33	-0.11	-0.19	-1.69
36	Finance, insurance, and real estate	4.86	1.19	-0.11	-0.77	-0.97	-0.46	-1.44	-0.07
37	Commercial services	5.93	-1.61	-0.27	-0.14	-2.41	-0.39	-1.26	-0.14

Table 5-11. *Breakdown of the average of annual rates of growth of traditional MFP, 1961–73*

		Output	Inter-mediate input	Imports	Govern-ment	Labour	CCA	Capital	MFP rate
01	Agriculture and fishing	3.36	-1.45	-0.24	-0.03	0.60	-0.28	-0.16	1.80
02	Forestry	3.71	-2.63	-0.31	-0.15	0.93	-0.24	-0.09	1.23
03	Mines, quarries, and oil wells	7.34	-2.58	-0.40	-0.24	-0.37	-0.90	-2.16	0.69
04	Food and beverages	3.59	-2.30	-0.32	—	-0.03	-0.09	-0.29	0.55
05	Tobacco products	2.39	-0.76	-0.17	-0.01	0.25	-0.07	0.08	1.71
06	Rubber and plastic products	10.48	-3.37	-1.66	-0.09	-1.50	-0.27	-0.74	2.85
07	Leather	0.92	-0.37	-0.54	-0.02	0.62	-0.04	-0.01	0.57
08	Textiles	7.35	-2.58	-1.37	-0.06	-0.36	-0.13	-0.26	2.60
09	Knitting mills	6.84	-2.31	-1.37	-0.02	-0.29	-0.08	-0.28	2.49
10	Clothing	4.27	-2.36	-0.73	-0.02	-0.27	-0.01	-0.17	0.71
11	Woods	5.22	-3.62	-0.43	-0.10	-0.68	-0.19	-0.36	-0.15
12	Furniture and fixtures	6.74	-2.95	-0.79	-0.07	-1.01	-0.07	-0.52	1.33
13	Paper and allied industries	4.74	-2.31	-0.33	-0.07	-0.37	-0.40	-0.47	0.81
14	Printing, publishing, and allied industries	4.11	-1.75	-0.26	-0.05	-0.57	-0.11	-0.41	0.96
15	Primary metals	5.32	-2.94	-0.77	-0.05	-0.41	-0.25	-0.24	0.64
16	Metal fabricating	6.86	-2.98	-0.67	-0.05	-0.94	-0.09	-0.46	1.67
17	Machinery	7.91	-3.04	-1.82	-0.06	-1.26	-0.11	-0.67	0.94
18	Transportation equipment	11.75	-3.89	-4.16	-0.04	-1.10	-0.10	-0.44	2.01
19	Electrical products	7.51	-2.70	-1.08	-0.04	-0.90	-0.12	-0.45	2.22
20	Nonmetallic mineral products	6.13	-2.44	-0.36	-0.11	-0.55	-0.28	-0.60	1.78
21	Petroleum and coal products	6.12	-2.81	-2.00	-0.03	-0.09	-0.16	-0.05	0.99

22	Chemical and chemical products	6.14	-2.57	-0.77	-0.07	-0.36	-0.29	-0.62	1.47
23	Miscellaneous manufacturing	6.12	-2.34	-1.17	-0.09	-0.69	-0.15	-0.49	1.19
24	Construction	4.43	-2.26	-0.33	-0.29	-0.62	-0.05	-0.09	0.79
25	Air transportation and other utilities and transportation	10.42	-3.02	-0.46	-0.51	-1.04	-1.25	-1.14	2.99
26	Railway transportation and telegraph	5.20	-0.68	-0.17	0.20	1.47	0.07	-0.01	6.08
27	Water transport	5.98	-3.38	-0.48	-0.18	0.37	-0.35	-0.05	1.91
28	Motor transport	6.91	-2.94	-0.44	-0.50	-1.23	-0.18	-0.87	0.76
29	Urban and suburban transportation	1.59	-1.04	-0.28	-0.05	-1.17	-0.87	0.48	-1.33
30	Storage	1.96	0.01	0.05	-0.10	-0.20	-0.26	-0.57	0.89
31	Broadcasting	7.65	-3.89	-0.98	3.59	-1.74	-0.71	-1.70	2.22
32	Telephones	8.46	-0.54	-0.06	-0.31	-1.05	-1.22	-1.94	3.34
33	Electric power	6.77	-0.79	-0.44	-0.09	-0.81	-1.64	-1.88	1.12
34	Gas distribution	8.81	-0.28	0.03	-0.22	-0.17	-0.77	-3.18	4.22
35	Trade	5.56	-1.06	-0.12	-0.07	-1.40	-0.12	-0.11	2.69
36	Finance, insurance, and real estate	4.67	-1.19	-0.11	-0.80	-1.00	-0.42	-1.36	-0.20
37	Commercial services	5.77	-1.75	-0.34	-0.16	-2.29	-0.31	-1.21	-0.29

Table 5-12. *Breakdown of the average of annual rates of growth of traditional MFP, 1973–80*

		Output	Inter-mediate input	Imports	Govern-ment	Labour	CCA	Capital	MFP rate
01	Agriculture and fishing	2.00	-0.92	-0.15	0.01	-0.04	-1.00	-0.66	-0.76
02	Forestry	0.71	-0.29	-0.04	0.07	0.43	-0.24	-0.06	0.58
03	Mines, quarries, and oil wells	0.71	-4.12	-0.29	-0.12	-0.45	-0.69	-1.64	-6.60
04	Food and beverages	2.33	-1.56	-0.16	—	-0.04	-0.02	-0.20	0.35
05	Tobacco products	1.03	0.38	-0.29	—	0.32	-0.02	—	1.43
06	Rubber and plastic products	2.61	-1.67	-0.43	-0.03	-0.36	-0.17	-0.28	-0.32
07	Leather	1.24	-0.07	-0.03	0.01	0.55	-0.04	-0.04	1.63
08	Textiles	1.17	-0.32	-0.03	—	0.61	-0.02	-0.08	1.34
09	Knitting mills	2.02	0.29	0.19	0.03	1.13	0.03	-0.02	3.66
10	Clothing	1.54	-0.23	0.03	0.01	0.53	-0.01	-0.26	1.63
11	Woods	2.96	-0.96	-0.18	-0.04	-0.08	-0.17	-0.43	1.08
12	Furniture and fixtures	-0.10	-0.10	-0.07	—	0.01	-0.05	-0.19	-0.49
13	Paper and allied industries	2.03	-1.70	-0.36	—	-0.31	-0.15	-0.13	-0.62
14	Printing, publishing, and allied industries	4.56	-1.62	-0.29	-0.03	-0.68	-0.08	-0.36	1.49
15	Primary metals	0.65	0.64	-0.51	-0.02	-0.22	-0.18	-0.08	0.28
16	Metal fabricating	1.49	-0.01	-0.26	-0.01	-0.27	-0.07	-0.27	0.61
17	Machinery	6.45	-1.41	-1.74	-0.05	-1.03	-0.10	-0.58	1.54
18	Transportation equipment	—	-0.11	0.19	—	0.12	-0.08	-0.26	-0.13
19	Electrical products	1.63	0.37	-0.85	—	0.37	-0.06	-0.29	1.16
20	Nonmetallic mineral products	0.28	-0.37	-0.23	-0.02	0.26	-0.24	-0.37	-0.70
21	Petroleum and coal products	2.99	-4.27	2.31	0.47	-0.23	-0.13	-0.06	1.07

142

#									
22	Chemical and chemical products	4.22	−3.12	−0.62	−0.07	−0.22	−0.57	−0.68	−1.06
23	Miscellaneous manufacturing	1.36	−0.49	−0.89	—	−0.09	−0.05	−0.11	−0.27
24	Construction	2.55	−1.02	−0.26	−0.11	−0.36	−0.08	−0.33	0.40
25	Air transportation and other utilities and transportation	3.61	−1.85	−0.05	−0.15	−1.44	−0.93	−0.35	−1.14
26	Railway transportation and telegraph	3.11	−2.11	0.02	1.66	0.45	−0.13	0.03	3.02
27	Water transport	−0.28	1.06	0.46	0.05	−0.02	0.08	−0.01	1.35
28	Motor transport	4.86	−1.81	−0.13	−0.17	−1.32	−0.17	−0.66	0.60
29	Urban and suburban transportation	2.16	−1.96	−0.25	−0.24	−4.34	−2.12	5.97	−0.77
30	Storage	3.74	−1.21	−0.11	−0.06	0.40	−0.60	−0.45	1.71
31	Broadcasting	7.39	−2.97	−0.25	2.99	−2.33	−0.71	−1.49	2.62
32	Telephones	10.61	−0.76	−0.09	−0.35	−1.12	−1.14	−1.49	5.65
33	Electric power	5.57	−0.74	−0.52	−0.11	−1.07	−2.03	−1.63	−0.53
34	Gas distribution	4.20	−0.74	—	0.22	−0.67	−0.65	−1.73	0.63
35	Trade	2.77	−0.98	−0.04	−0.12	−1.22	−0.10	−0.32	—
36	Finance, insurance, and real estate	5.19	−1.19	−0.11	−0.73	−0.91	−0.52	−1.57	0.16
37	Commercial services	6.21	−1.37	−0.15	−0.09	−2.62	−0.51	−1.36	0.12

the industry; overall, hours worked diminished, which is why the weighted rate of growth is −0.60. The CCA and capital columns show a positive weighted rate of growth of these inputs of 0.22 and 0.44, respectively. The sum of all these input rates of growth is 1.42, which when substracted from the rate of growth of output yields a MFP rate of 2.31. That is, the rate of growth of all inputs together accounts for 1.42 of the 3.73 output growth rate; the rest, 2.31, is due to increases in efficiency in the use of these inputs.

For the period 1961–80, four industries, as noted, have a negative rate of growth of MFP: mines, quarries, and oil wells; urban and suburban transport; finance, insurance, and real estate; and commercial services. Of these four industries, the second consistently has a negative rate in every subperiod, the first and third in four of the five, and the fourth in three of them. Such results prompted a closer look at the underlying data. The following findings may help explain the persistent measured decline in efficiency for these industries:

   i. *Mines, quarries, and oil wells:* Annual average rate of growth of MFP for this industry deteriorates sharply for the period 1973–80. However, it has a very large rate of growth of weighted capital input. Relative to both its own output growth rate and the weighted rate of growth of capital of the other industries, this industry ranks first. It has apparently been a capital-intensive industry and is becoming more so.[2] A look at its profit data also shows a relatively large rate of return, which gives capital a larger weight in the MFP rate. Government policies, such as subsidies, taxation, and generous depreciation allowances, may help to explain the possible overcapitalization of this industry. Yet it does not explain the high measured rate of profits. Many companies have interests in both the mines and the petroleum and coal products industries. The I/O tables are establishment based, and therefore an attempt is made in these tables to allocate the outputs and inputs of the establishment to the corresponding industry. In the data section, we discussed problems related to the construction of I/O tables for mines, quarries, and oil wells and the refining of petroleum and coal products due to the high degree of vertical integration exhibited by parts by these two industries. It is probably here that the explanation lies. The internal flow of goods and services among such parts is not considered a market transaction and therefore is not valued as it moves from establishments

---

[2] Its unweighted capital–output ratio (excluding inventories) has increased from 2.47 in 1961 to 3.14 in 1980; the rank was 10 in 1961 and was up to 6 in 1980.

in one industry to those in the other. The I/O tables attempt to estimate these flows. However, although the I/O procedure is conceptually correct, if the estimates are biased, measurement errors can distort the MFP measurement. If the gross output of mines and oil wells is overestimated, then that of petroleum refineries will be underestimated; to make matters worse, the intermediate inputs into the latter could, as a result, also be overestimated. These two errors together will cause, in addition to the obvious bias in the growth rate of outputs and inputs, a very low level of profit for the refining industry, for this is calculated residually in the balancing of the tables. Hence, it is possible that the profits of mines, quarries, and oil wells are overstated and those of the petroleum industry understated. In fact, in many years the petroleum industry shows a very small, sometimes zero, rate of return, even after 1973. In the face of large relative price changes favouring the oil industry, it is difficult to explain such zero profits. Mines and quarries and the petroleum industries should possibly be aggregated into one category in future studies of this kind. However, one could also consider the hypothesis that these are industries with increasing costs. Increases in output are obtained at increasing cost as mines and deposits of lower quality and accessibility come into production.

ii. *Urban and suburban transport:* This is a heavily subsidized industry whose output may be considered to be largely a public good. The industry does not operate according to the principles of market economics, and thus its MFP rate is to some extent meaningless. There are two main problems: subsidies and the rate of return on the capital stock. The MFP measures could be improved by a different treatment of subsidies (to be discussed). With respect to the capital input, for the period 1961–80, the contribution of capital is a large +2.50. Output increased by an average of 1.8 percent annually during the period, whereas the weighted rate of growth of the capital input declines by 2.50; that is, it would appear as if less capital was required to produce more output. A closer look at the data shows that this illusion is caused by negative rates of profit. After subtracting capital consumption allowance from the operating surplus of this industry, a negative amount is left. Thus, if we were to impose the restriction that the rate of profit should at least be zero, the average of annual rates of MFP for this industry will stand even lower – at 3.56 for the period 1961–80.

iii. *Finance, insurance, and real estate and commercial services:* These two industries are known to have output measurement problems. (In the data section we described the special procedures to value the output of the finance, insurance, and real estate industry.) The measured rate of growth of output for the two industries may well be understated, thus resulting in a negative rate of growth of MFP. They both show their best MFP performance in the last subperiod, 1973–80, which may partly reflect continuing efforts by Statistics Canada to improve the measurement of the output of these industries. It is hard to believe that in the wake of the computer revolution, affecting especially these two industries, only negligible gains in efficiency have been made, especially when there was no major quality adjustment on these goods.[3]

Paradoxically, the highest industry rate of MFP for the period 1961–80 and the subperiods 1961–71 and 1961–73 may also be partly the result of data anomalies. Railway transport shows an annual average growth of MFP of 4.95 percent. A look at the decomposition of the rate shows a problem similar to that for urban and suburban transport. Whereas output grew at the rate of 4.4 percent per annum, the weighted capital input suffered a marginal decrease of 0.01 percent. This was caused by a rate of return that was zero or very close to zero, from the negative side, in many years; hence, capital input received a small weight, and the contribution of capital to output growth is negligible. The (weighted) labour input declines by 1.09 percent, thus suggesting that there were considerable gains in labour productivity that, ceteris paribus, would tend to increase MFP in this industry. However, it must be remembered that railways is also a highly subsidized, government-controlled industry (particularly passenger railways), and the pricing of its output and of some of its factor inputs may be so far removed from the assumptions and economic theory behind our MFP measure as to invalidate the results of this study for this particular industry.

The highest rate of MFP for the period (excluding railways) goes first to telephones followed by knitting mills and gas distribution. For telephones and gas distribution, these results are not surprising. Both are regulated utilities, probably subject to increasing returns to scale. The telephone industry is a well-known case of an industry continuously undergoing technical change. The average annual rate of growth of output of telephones is 9.25 percent, the highest for the period and also among the

---

[3] For an account and the effect of quality adjustment on computers on MFP see Denison, *Estimates of Productivity Change in Industry.* Statistics Canada is *now* applying deflation procedures that resemble those of the BEA discussed by Denison. However, our data were not affected.

highest in every subperiod. The situation is similar for gas distribution, except in the last subperiod, 1973–80, when its average annual growth of output declined to 4.20 percent from 8.81 percent in 1961–73 and its MFP declined to 0.63 percent per annum. The knitting mills seems to be a different case; it maintained a good rate of growth of MFP even with moderate rates of output growth. This is perhaps more a case of an industry rationalizing its production and removing inefficiencies.

B   Treatment of taxes and subsidies

Some of the MFP results that have been discussed so far call for a revision of the government input item in the MFP calculations. It consists of the sum of the rates of growth of the Törnquist indexes of two items: purchases of government goods and services and net indirect taxes. Subsidies are treated as negative taxes and substracted from indirect taxes to yield net indirect taxes; as a result, the average annual rate of growth of government input in the calculation of MFP is positive in industries where subsidies are greater than the two other components. This is consistently the case for railway transport and telegraph (item 26) and broadcasting (item 31), as shown in Tables 5-8 to 5-12; it is also the case for all other industries that have a positive entry in the government column in the tables. This positive entry adds to the rate of growth of output and has, therefore, the effect of raising that rate of growth and yielding a higher MFP rate.

A different treatment of subsidies and indirect commodity taxes is possible, and this would improve measures by bringing payments to the factor inputs and outputs closer to those they actually face, and therefore react to in markets, and so will change the shares of the Törnquist indexes. Two kinds of subsidies are possible, input subsidies and output subsidies. Output subsidies should be transferred to the output side and added to the value of output.[4] This adjustment will have a double impact on output: The price deflator for output will change, but the constant-dollar output series will stay the same; sectoral value added increases for industries receiving subsidies, and hence aggregation weights based on value added will change and so will the corresponding economy's measure of MFP based on the sectoral measures.[5]

---

[4] See, e.g., Jorgenson et al., *Productivity and US Economic Growth*. They call it producer's value, but it is different from the so-called producer's value in the I/O tables.

[5] This change will have no effect on our measures as they are based on constant-dollar gross output. However, if we had calculated the rate of growth of output as a weighted index of commodity outputs of an industry, gross output would also change because of the changing weights.

In the case of input subsidies the treatment should be the same if it is the establishment that receives them. It helps pay for the cost of production and keeps product prices lower than would otherwise be the case as well as keeps profits higher. Input subsidies paid directly to the owners of labour services or capital will not show up in the industry production account; they have no effect on the MFP measures.

The proper treatment of commodity indirect taxes is conceptually similar. Commodity tax payments should be added to the cost of intermediate purchases to reflect purchasers' price. The Canadian I/O system has information on commodity tax rates for every year, and it is possible to build 37×37 commodity tax matrices for each of the twelve types of commodity taxes. These matrices, when added to the current-dollar matrix of intermediate inputs, will value them at purchasers' price. As a result of these adjustments, the constant-dollar interindustry matrices do not change; only the intermediate input deflators do.

The output price deflator and the intermediate input deflator will differ as a result of the proposed adjustments by the ratio of rate of subsidies (producers' price deflator) to commodity tax rates (purchasers' price deflator).[6] A further adjustment could be made by netting out other indirect taxes and adding them to other operating surplus or residual profits, which are gross of corporate income taxes; for other indirect taxes it consists largely of property taxes on land. As a result of these suggested adjustments, the item "government input" will become almost negligible. Only the purchases of government produced foods and services will remain.

The two industries most affected by subsidies, resulting in negative net taxes, are railway transport and broadcasting. The latter has the highest level of subsidies. However, the level of subsidies to petroleum and coal products and gas distribution have increased after 1973 as a result of government policy. For example, it resulted in a 0.47 percent annual average of the weighted rate of growth of government input for 1973–80, up from −0.03 for the period 1961–73, for the petroleum industry (see Tables 5-11 and 5-12).

C   Components of new measures of multifactor productivity

With the use of equation (14) in Appendix 5 for any industry, the new measures are expressed as the sum of the traditional rates of growth of MFP plus contributions from changes in the new MFP rates of the supplying industries. The traditional component plus the contribution from

---

[6] Such matrices were constructed at a late stage of this study. They were used to calculate the MFP rates for comparisons purposes. The results did not change for most industries and changed slightly for those with higher net indirect taxes less subsidies.

the use of its own output is called the own effect because it is endogenous to the industry; the rest will be called the input effect.[7] The method allows us to separate changes that are *purely* internal to the industry, or own effect, from those that originate in other industries, the so-called input effect. For any industry, the sum of all its contributions to the new rates of MFP of other industries is called its output effect, whereas the sum of the contributions of other industries to an industry's new MFP rate is called its input effect. The input effect, then, sums all benefits accruing to an industry from the changes in efficiency in its supplying industries. The output effect indicates how much an industry's changes in efficiency affect all industries that use its output.

We have the following definitions for the jth industry:

$$\text{New MFP} = \text{own effect} + \text{input effect}$$

where

$$\text{Input effect} = \sum_{i \neq j} s_{ij} h_i^*$$

$$\text{Own effect} = h_j^* + s_{jj} h_j^*$$

and for the ith industry we define

$$\text{Total contribution} = \text{own effect} + \text{output effect}$$

where

$$\text{Output effect} = \sum_{j \neq i} s_{ij} h_i^*$$

where s_{ij} is the sum of the shares of the current value of intermediate inputs, capital consumption allowances, and the returns to the net capital stock of the ith industry in the value of the total inputs of the jth industry. Intuitively, the input effect is defined over the rows of the share matrix for any column, whereas the output effect is defined over the columns of the share matrix for any row.

Tables 5-13 to 5-17 present the results. The first column in Table 5-13, labeled 01, refers to the first industry in the MFP list, agriculture and fishing. Column 01 shows the new MFP of agriculture and fishing decomposed into the sums of the own effect, which in turn is the sum of the traditional MFP of that industry plus the contribution to MFP from the use of its own agriculture output as an input; this is why the intersection of the column labeled agriculture and fishing with the row labeled agriculture and fishing is empty; its value has been added to own effect. All other rows under column 01 show the contribution to the new MFP of

---

[7] The terminology is taken from the 1983 Economic Council of Canada study [Postner and Wesa, *Canadian Productivity Growth – An Alternative (Input–Output) Analysis*] because it resembles what they define as own and input effect.

Table 5-13.　*Breakdown of the average of annual rates of growth of new MFP as the sum of own and input effects, 1961–71*

	01	02	03	04	05	06	07
New MFP =	4.16	2.70	1.14	3.10	3.77	4.33	2.35
Own effect +	2.61	1.68	−0.25	1.10	2.08	2.97	1.40
01 Agriculture and fishing	–	0.01	–	1.26	1.12	–	0.01
02 Forestry	–	–	–	–	–	–	–
03 Mines, quarries, and oil wells	–	–	–	–	–	–	–
04 Food and beverages	0.30	0.06	0.01	–	0.02	0.01	0.09
05 Tobacco products	–	–	–	–	–	–	–
06 Rubber and plastic products	0.02	0.02	0.02	0.01	–	–	0.18
07 Leather	–	–	–	–	–	0.01	–
08 Textiles	0.02	0.01	0.01	0.01	0.02	0.29	0.07
09 Knitting mills	–	–	–	–	–	–	–
10 Clothing	–	–	–	–	–	–	0.01
11 Woods	–	–	–	–	0.01	–	0.01
12 Furniture and fixtures	–	–	–	–	–	–	–
13 Paper and allied industries	–	–	0.01	0.06	0.11	0.05	0.03
14 Printing, publishing, and allied industries	–	–	–	0.02	0.04	0.02	0.01
15 Primary metals	–	–	0.01	–	–	–	–
16 Metal fabricating	0.03	0.04	0.04	0.07	0.02	0.04	0.03
17 Machinery	0.06	0.02	0.05	0.01	0.02	0.03	0.01
18 Transportation equipment	0.16	0.06	0.06	0.03	0.02	0.04	0.01
19 Electrical products	0.01	0.02	0.02	0.01	–	0.01	0.01
20 Nonmetallic mineral products	–	–	–	0.03	–	0.01	–
21 Petroleum and coal products	0.08	0.04	0.02	0.01	–	0.01	0.01
22 Chemical and chemical products	0.09	0.02	0.05	0.02	0.01	0.36	0.03
23 Miscellaneous manufacturing	–	0.01	0.01	–	0.01	0.01	0.03
24 Construction	0.28	0.15	0.68	0.07	0.05	0.08	0.04
25 Air transportation and other utilities and transportation	–	–	0.02	0.02	0.01	0.02	0.02
26 Railway transportation and telegraph	0.07	0.04	0.05	0.10	0.04	0.08	0.07
27 Water transport	0.01	0.06	0.01	0.01	0.01	0.01	0.01
28 Motor transport	0.02	0.15	0.01	0.02	0.01	0.02	0.02
29 Urban and suburban transportation	–	–	–	–	–	–	–
30 Storage	0.01	–	–	0.01	–	–	–
31 Broadcasting	–	–	–	0.01	0.03	0.01	0.01
32 Telephones	0.02	0.01	0.01	0.02	0.02	0.03	0.02
33 Electric power	0.02	–	0.03	0.01	–	0.01	0.01
34 Gas distribution	–	–	–	–	–	–	–
35 Trade	0.29	0.15	0.16	0.16	0.08	0.16	0.19
36 Finance, insurance, and real estate	0.04	0.11	0.10	0.01	0.02	0.02	0.02
37 Commercial services	–	0.01	0.02	0.01	0.01	0.01	0.01
Input effect	1.55	1.02	1.39	2.01	1.69	1.36	0.95

agriculture and fishing from the use of inputs produced in industries undergoing increases in MFP. Because of this, the entries are positive. If we now take the row 01, agriculture and fishing, in the same table and sum over all columns, we get the output effect (the last column), which

08	09	10	11	12	13	14	15	16	17	18	19
4.25	4.49	2.33	1.98	2.52	1.81	1.51	1.86	3.09	2.07	3.21	3.21
3.50	2.59	0.73	0.53	1.12	0.46	0.59	0.88	2.05	1.80	2.36	2.26
0.01	–	0.03	0.02	–	0.01	–	–	–	–	–	–
–	–	–	0.78	0.01	0.38	–	–	–	–	–	–
–	–	–	–	–	0.01	–	0.27	–	–	–	–
0.01	–	0.01	–	0.01	0.01	0.01	0.01	0.01	0.01	–	0.01
–	–	–	–	–	–	–	–	–	–	–	–
0.04	0.02	0.03	0.01	0.13	0.02	0.01	0.01	0.01	0.04	0.08	0.06
–	0.01	0.01	–	–	–	–	–	–	–	–	–
–	1.38	0.86	0.01	0.23	0.03	0.01	–	–	–	0.04	0.01
0.01	–	0.23	–	–	–	–	–	–	–	–	–
0.02	0.05	–	–	–	–	–	–	–	–	–	–
–	–	–	–	0.15	0.06	–	–	0.01	0.01	0.01	–
0.01	0.01	–	0.02	–	–	0.01	–	–	0.01	0.01	0.01
0.03	0.03	0.01	0.01	0.04	–	0.31	0.01	0.01	0.01	0.01	0.02
0.01	0.01	0.01	–	0.01	0.01	–	–	0.01	0.01	0.01	0.01
–	–	–	–	0.05	0.01	0.01	–	0.40	0.17	0.10	0.19
0.02	0.01	0.01	0.03	0.17	0.05	0.01	0.05	–	0.17	0.13	0.11
0.03	0.02	0.01	0.02	0.01	0.05	0.03	0.04	0.03	–	0.03	0.03
0.02	0.01	0.01	0.04	0.03	0.02	0.02	0.02	0.04	0.06	–	0.03
0.02	0.01	0.01	0.01	0.02	0.02	0.01	0.02	0.04	0.12	0.06	–
–	–	–	0.01	0.02	0.01	–	0.02	0.01	–	0.03	0.01
0.01	–	–	0.01	0.01	0.02	0.01	0.01	0.01	0.01	–	0.01
0.10	0.02	0.01	0.03	0.05	0.08	0.04	0.02	0.03	0.02	0.02	0.04
0.02	0.01	0.04	–	0.03	0.01	0.01	0.01	0.01	0.01	0.01	0.01
0.05	0.03	0.03	0.06	0.06	0.11	0.08	0.09	0.08	0.08	0.06	0.05
0.01	0.01	0.01	0.01	0.01	0.01	0.03	0.01	0.01	0.01	0.01	0.01
0.07	0.04	0.03	0.10	0.07	0.14	0.07	0.12	0.07	0.06	0.07	0.06
0.01	–	–	0.01	0.01	0.02	0.01	0.01	0.01	0.01	0.01	0.01
0.02	0.01	0.01	0.02	0.02	0.03	0.02	0.03	0.02	0.02	0.02	0.02
–	–	–	–	–	–	–	–	–	–	–	–
–	–	–	–	–	–	–	–	–	–	–	–
–	0.01	0.01	–	0.01	–	0.01	–	–	0.01	0.01	0.01
0.02	0.02	0.02	0.02	0.02	0.01	0.05	0.01	0.03	0.03	0.02	0.04
0.01	0.01	–	0.02	0.01	0.04	0.01	0.02	0.01	–	0.01	0.01
–	–	–	–	–	0.01	–	0.01	–	–	–	–
0.17	0.13	0.17	0.17	0.19	0.15	0.11	0.18	0.16	0.15	0.11	0.14
0.01	0.03	0.03	0.02	0.02	0.01	0.03	0.01	0.01	0.03	0.01	0.02
0.01	0.01	0.01	0.01	0.01	0.01	0.02	0.01	0.01	0.01	0.01	0.01
0.75	1.90	1.59	1.45	1.39	1.35	0.92	0.98	1.05	1.07	0.85	0.95

Continued

shows the contribution that agriculture and fishing has made to the new MFP of all industries that use their output as an input; this output effect is positive because the new MFP rate of agriculture is increasing. Other columns and rows in the tables are similarly read.

Table 5-13 *Continued*

		20	21	22	23	24	25	26
	New MFP =	2.95	2.20	2.69	2.35	2.31	3.94	7.69
	Own effect +	1.80	1.14	1.55	1.24	0.90	2.58	6.65
01	Agriculture and fishing	–	–	–	–	–	–	–
02	Forestry	–	–	–	–	–	–	–
03	Mines, quarries, and oil wells	0.06	0.37	0.02	0.01	0.03	–	–
04	Food and beverages	0.01	–	0.05	0.01	0.01	–	0.01
05	Tobacco products	–	–	–	–	–	–	–
06	Rubber and plastic products	0.02	–	0.04	0.05	0.03	0.02	0.01
07	Leather	–	–	–	0.01	–	–	–
08	Textiles	0.01	–	0.01	0.06	0.01	–	0.01
09	Knitting mills	–	–	–	0.01	–	–	–
10	Clothing	–	–	–	–	–	–	–
11	Woods	–	–	–	0.04	0.10	–	–
12	Furniture and fixtures	0.01	–	–	–	0.01	–	–
13	Paper and allied industries	0.04	–	0.05	0.04	0.02	–	–
14	Printing, publishing, and allied industries	0.01	0.01	0.04	0.03	–	0.02	0.01
15	Primary metals	0.02	–	0.02	0.11	0.07	–	0.01
16	Metal fabricating	0.06	0.02	0.08	0.08	0.30	0.02	0.06
17	Machinery	0.03	0.01	0.03	0.02	0.03	0.03	0.02
18	Transportation equipment	0.07	0.02	0.02	0.03	0.04	0.08	0.05
19	Electrical products	0.03	–	0.01	0.03	0.12	0.13	0.04
20	Nonmetallic mineral products	–	–	0.03	0.03	0.18	–	–
21	Petroleum and coal products	0.03	–	0.05	0.01	0.02	0.07	0.05
22	Chemical and chemical products	0.05	0.06	–	0.09	0.04	0.01	0.01
23	Miscellaneous manufacturing	0.01	0.01	0.02	–	0.02	0.01	0.02
24	Construction	0.14	0.17	0.14	0.07	–	0.63	0.51
25	Air transportation and other utilities and transportation	0.03	0.27	0.04	0.02	0.01	–	–
26	Railway transportation and telegraph	0.15	0.02	0.11	0.07	0.09	0.03	–
27	Water transport	0.02	–	0.01	0.01	0.01	–	–
28	Motor transport	0.03	0.01	0.03	0.02	0.03	0.03	0.01
29	Urban and suburban transportation	–	–	–	–	–	–	–
30	Storage	–	–	–	–	–	–	–
31	Broadcasting	–	0.01	0.02	0.01	–	0.01	–
32	Telephones	0.02	0.01	0.03	0.03	0.01	0.06	0.07
33	Electric power	0.03	0.01	0.02	0.01	–	0.02	–
34	Gas distribution	0.02	–	0.01	–	–	–	–
35	Trade	0.22	0.05	0.18	0.17	0.21	0.11	0.09
36	Finance, insurance, and real estate	0.02	0.02	0.02	0.03	0.01	0.03	0.02
37	Commercial services	0.01	–	0.02	0.02	0.02	0.02	0.01
	Input effect	1.15	1.06	1.14	1.11	1.41	1.36	1.04

For any period, the last column represents the output effect of the corresponding industry. It is interesting to note that the highest output effect (6.06) over the period 1961–80 holds for the construction industry (see Table 5-15). By itself, it has a relatively small annual percentage of average rate of growth of MFP (1.58, top row in Table 5-15) with a rank of 16 in our thirty-seven industries. However, it ranks first as an intermediate and capital goods producer, whose output is purchased by all other

27	28	29	30	31	32	33	34	35	36	37	Output effect
4.45	2.02	−0.52	2.19	3.58	4.66	1.61	6.20	3.64	1.28	0.69	—
3.67	0.81	−1.09	0.98	2.15	3.53	0.10	4.69	2.72	0.03	−0.35	—
—	—	—	—	—	—	—	—	0.13	—	0.04	2.66
—	—	—	—	—	—	—	—	—	—	—	1.18
—	—	—	—	—	—	0.01	—	—	—	—	0.82
0.01	—	—	—	—	—	0.01	—	0.02	—	0.22	0.93
—	—	—	—	—	—	—	—	—	—	—	
0.01	0.07	0.03	0.02	0.03	—	—	0.01	0.02	0.01	0.01	1.10
—	—	—	—	—	—	—	—	—	—	—	0.04
0.01	—	—	0.02	—	—	—	—	0.01	—	0.02	3.18
—	—	—	—	—	—	—	—	—	—	—	0.28
—	—	—	—	—	—	—	—	—	—	—	0.10
—	—	—	—	—	—	—	—	—	—	0.01	0.43
—	—	—	—	—	—	0.03	—	0.01	—	0.01	0.17
—	—	—	0.02	0.01	—	—	—	0.03	—	0.01	0.99
0.01	0.01	0.02	0.01	0.04	0.02	—	0.01	0.04	0.01	0.02	0.49
—	—	—	—	—	—	—	—	—	—	—	1.20
0.03	0.02	0.01	0.01	0.03	0.01	—	0.01	0.03	0.01	0.02	1.82
0.02	0.01	—	0.01	0.08	0.01	0.01	0.01	0.01	0.01	0.01	0.87
0.23	0.25	0.13	0.07	0.01	0.01	0.01	0.07	0.04	—	0.06	1.88
0.02	0.03	0.01	0.01	0.03	0.45	0.18	0.01	0.01	0.01	0.02	1.57
—	—	—	—	—	—	—	—	—	—	—	0.42
0.07	0.12	0.05	0.03	0.01	—	0.02	—	0.03	—	0.01	0.87
0.01	0.01	—	0.01	0.01	—	—	0.01	0.01	—	0.03	1.40
—	—	—	—	0.02	—	0.01	—	0.01	—	0.02	0.39
0.13	0.10	0.11	0.48	0.17	0.53	1.10	1.22	0.15	1.08	0.18	9.05
0.01	0.04	—	0.01	0.06	—	0.01	—	0.02	0.01	0.01	0.77
0.04	0.19	0.03	0.21	0.05	0.01	0.03	0.01	0.05	0.01	0.03	2.46
—	0.01	—	0.04	—	—	—	—	0.01	—	—	0.36
0.01	—	0.01	0.02	0.01	—	0.01	—	0.02	—	0.01	0.72
—	—	—	—	—	—	—	—	0.03	—	—	0.07
—	—	—	—	—	—	—	—	0.02	—	0.01	0.22
0.03	0.05	0.02	0.04	0.45	—	0.01	0.03	0.07	0.04	0.06	1.43
—	—	0.04	0.02	0.02	—	—	0.01	0.02	—	0.01	0.44
—	—	—	—	—	—	—	0.01	—	—	0.11
0.09	0.22	0.06	0.09	0.13	0.04	0.04	0.04	—	0.03	0.15	4.93
0.02	0.04	0.02	0.07	0.07	0.02	0.03	0.03	0.09	—	0.05	1.15
0.01	0.01	—	0.01	0.18	—	—	0.01	0.02	0.01	—	0.56
0.78	1.20	0.57	1.22	1.43	1.13	1.51	1.50	0.92	1.26	1.04	—

industries. Therefore, even small increases in its MFP have a great output effect via its dispersion through all industries that use its output.

Of course, if an industry has a negative rate of new MFP, its output effect can only be negative. It will spread a negative rate of MFP to its buyers.[8] This is the case for the ten industries whose MFP rate is negative over

[8] One may question the meaning of distributing what are purely cyclical changes in MFP of the supplying industries to the using industries.

Table 5-14. *Breakdown of the average of annual rates of growth of new MFP as the sum of own and input effects, 1971-80*

	01	02	03	04	05	06
New MFP =	−0.31	1.01	−3.48	0.63	3.34	0.85
Own effect +	−0.78	0.63	−4.04	0.42	3.06	0.46
01 Agriculture and fishing	−	−	−	−0.10	−0.07	−
02 Forestry	−	−	−	−	−	−
03 Mines, quarries, and oil wells	−0.04	−	−	−0.01	−	−0.01
04 Food and beverages	0.07	−	−	−	−	−
05 Tobacco products	−	−	−	−	−	−
06 Rubber and plastic products	−	−	−	−	−	−
07 Leather	−	−	−	−	−	−
08 Textiles	−	0.01	−	−	0.01	0.11
09 Knitting mills	−	−	−	−	−	−
10 Clothing	−	−	−	−	−	−
11 Woods	−	−	−	−	−	−
12 Furniture and fixtures	−	−	−	−	−	−
13 Paper and allied industries	−	−	−	0.03	0.07	0.02
14 Printing, publishing, and allied industries	−	−	−	0.03	0.06	0.02
15 Primary metals	−	−	−	−	−	−
16 Metal fabricating	0.01	0.02	0.01	0.03	0.01	0.02
17 Machinery	0.06	0.02	0.04	0.01	0.02	0.02
18 Transportation equipment	0.03	0.01	0.01	0.01	0.01	0.01
19 Electrical equipment	0.01	0.01	0.01	−	−	0.01
20 Nonmetallic mineral products	−	−	−	0.01	−	−
21 Petroleum and coal products	−0.01	−0.02	−	−	−	−
22 Chemical and chemical products	0.01	−	0.01	−	−	−0.01
23 Miscellaneous manufacturing	−	−	−	−	−	−
24 Construction	0.12	0.05	0.25	0.02	0.03	0.03
25 Air transportation and other utilities and transportation	−	−	−	−	−	−
26 Railway transportation and telegraph	0.02	0.02	0.02	0.03	0.02	0.02
27 Water transport	−	0.02	−	−	−	−
28 Motor transport	0.01	0.10	0.01	0.02	0.01	0.01
29 Urban and suburban transportation	−	−	−	−	−	−
30 Storage	−	−	−	0.01	−	−
31 Broadcasting	−	−	−	0.01	0.03	0.01
32 Telephones	0.03	0.01	0.01	0.02	0.02	0.03
33 Electric power	0.02	−	0.03	0.01	−	0.01
34 Gas distribution	−	−	−	−	−	−
35 Trade	0.09	0.05	0.05	0.04	0.03	0.05
36 Finance, insurance, and real estate	0.01	0.04	0.07	−	0.01	0.01
37 Commercial services	−	0.01	0.01	0.01	0.01	0.01
Input effect	0.47	0.38	0.55	0.20	0.28	0.39

the period 1973–80. If these industries were also important intermediate input suppliers, the dispersion of their negative rate through other industries could yield a sizable negative output effect. A look at the results in the last column of Table 5-17 (1973–80), the output effect, shows it to be the

07	08	09	10	11	12	13	14	15	16	17	18	19
1.38	2.40	4.58	2.59	0.93	0.82	0.92	2.49	−0.12	1.19	2.03	0.93	2.45
1.04	2.09	3.65	1.70	0.41	0.29	0.44	2.09	0.39	0.96	1.70	0.64	2.16
—	—	—	—	—	—	—	—	—	—	—	—	—
—	—	—	—	0.27	—	0.11	—	—	—	—	—	—
−0.01	−0.01	—	—	−0.01	−0.01	−0.03	—	−0.80	—	−0.01	—	−0.01
0.02	—	—	—	—	—	—	—	—	—	—	—	—
—	—	—	—	—	—	—	—	—	—	—	—	—
0.04	0.01	0.01	0.01	—	0.02	0.01	—	—	—	0.01	0.02	0.01
—	—	—	0.02	—	—	—	—	—	—	—	—	—
0.04	—	0.66	0.36	—	0.12	0.01	—	—	—	—	0.02	—
—	0.02	—	0.34	—	—	—	—	—	—	—	—	—
0.01	0.03	0.07	—	—	—	—	—	—	—	—	—	—
—	—	—	—	—	0.06	0.06	—	—	—	—	—	—
—	—	—	—	—	—	—	—	—	—	—	—	—
0.01	0.01	0.01	—	—	0.02	—	0.14	—	0.01	—	—	0.01
0.02	0.02	0.02	0.02	0.01	0.02	0.01	—	—	0.01	0.02	0.01	0.02
—	—	—	—	—	−0.01	—	—	—	−0.03	−0.01	−0.01	−0.02
0.01	0.01	0.01	—	0.02	0.07	0.01	0.01	0.02	—	0.07	0.04	0.03
0.02	0.02	0.02	0.01	0.02	0.01	0.04	0.02	0.03	0.03	—	0.03	0.03
0.01	0.01	0.01	—	0.01	0.01	0.01	0.01	0.01	0.01	0.01	—	0.01
0.01	0.01	0.01	—	0.01	0.02	0.02	—	0.02	0.02	0.06	0.04	—
—	—	—	—	—	—	—	—	—	—	—	0.01	—
—	—	—	—	—	−0.01	—	—	—	—	—	—	—
—	0.01	—	—	—	0.01	—	—	—	—	—	—	—
0.01	0.01	—	0.01	—	0.01	—	—	—	—	—	—	—
0.01	0.02	0.01	0.01	0.02	0.02	0.03	0.03	0.02	0.03	0.02	0.02	0.02
—	—	—	—	—	—	0.01	—	—	—	—	—	—
0.02	0.02	0.01	0.01	0.03	0.02	0.05	0.03	0.04	0.03	0.02	0.03	0.02
—	—	—	—	—	0.01	—	—	—	—	—	—	—
0.01	0.01	0.01	0.01	0.01	0.01	0.02	0.01	0.02	0.01	0.01	0.01	0.01
—	—	—	—	—	—	—	—	—	—	—	—	—
0.01	0.01	0.01	0.01	—	0.01	—	0.01	—	—	0.01	—	0.01
0.02	0.02	0.02	0.02	0.02	0.02	0.01	0.05	0.01	0.03	0.03	0.02	0.06
0.01	0.01	0.01	—	0.01	0.01	0.05	0.01	0.03	0.01	0.01	—	0.01
—	—	—	—	—	—	—	—	—	—	—	—	—
0.05	0.05	0.05	0.04	0.06	0.06	0.05	0.04	0.05	0.05	0.04	0.03	0.04
0.01	0.01	0.01	0.01	0.01	0.01	—	0.01	—	0.01	0.01	—	0.01
0.01	0.01	0.01	0.01	0.01	0.01	0.01	0.01	—	0.01	0.01	0.02	0.01
0.34	0.31	0.94	0.89	0.52	0.53	0.48	0.40	−0.51	0.23	0.33	0.29	0.29

Continued

case. The mines, quarries, and oil wells industry suffered a large decline in its average annual rate of MFP of −6.68. Moreover, being an important intermediate supplier, its total output effect was −5.59. It is responsible for the negative average of annual rates of new MFP of the primary

Table 5-14 *Continued*

	20	21	22	23	24	25
New MFP =	0.47	−0.39	0.20	0.58	0.77	0.82
Own effect +	0.28	0.90	−0.16	0.20	0.40	0.39
01 Agriculture and fishing	−	−	−	−	−	−
02 Forestry	−	−	−	−	−	−
03 Mines, quarries, and oil wells	−0.21	−1.49	−0.10	−0.01	−0.09	−0.06
04 Food and beverages	−	−	−0.01	−	−	−
05 Tobacco products	−	−	−	−	−	−
06 Rubber and plastic products	−	−	0.01	0.01	0.01	−
07 Leather	−	−	−	−	−	−
08 Textiles	−	−	−	0.03	0.01	−
09 Knitting mills	−	−	−	0.02	−	−
10 Clothing	−	−	−	−	−	−
11 Woods	−	−	−	0.01	0.04	−
12 Furniture and fixtures	−	−	−	−	−	−
13 Paper and allied industries	0.01	−	0.02	0.02	0.01	−
14 Printing, publishing, and allied industries	0.01	0.01	0.05	0.04	−	0.02
15 Primary metals	−	−	−	−	−	−
16 Metal fabricating	0.02	0.01	0.03	0.02	0.10	0.01
17 Machinery	0.04	−	0.02	0.01	0.03	0.02
18 Transportation equipment	0.02	−	0.01	0.01	0.01	0.02
19 Electric products	0.02	−	0.01	0.02	0.07	0.07
20 Nonmetallic mineral products	−	−	0.01	−	0.03	−
21 Petroleum and coal products	−0.01	−	−0.01	−	−	−0.03
22 Chemical and chemical products	−	0.01	−	−	−	−
23 Miscellaneous manufacturing	−	−	−	−	−	−
24 Construction	0.05	0.04	0.04	0.02	−	0.17
25 Air transportation and other utilities and transportation	0.01	0.06	0.01	0.01	−	−
26 Railway transportation and telegraph	0.05	0.01	0.04	0.02	0.03	0.01
27 Water transport	0.01	−	−	−	−	−
28 Motor transport	0.02	−	0.02	0.01	0.02	0.03
29 Urban and suburban transportation	−	−	−	−	−	−
30 Storage	−	−	−	−	−	−
31 Broadcasting	−	0.01	0.03	0.02	−	0.01
32 Telephones	0.03	0.01	0.04	0.04	0.01	0.06
33 Electric power	0.03	0.01	0.03	0.01	−	0.02
34 Gas distribution	0.01	−	−	−	−	−
35 Trade	0.07	0.01	0.06	0.04	0.06	0.03
36 Finance, insurance, and real estate	0.01	−	0.01	0.01	0.01	0.01
37 Commercial services	0.01	−	0.02	0.02	0.02	0.02
Input effect	0.19	−1.29	0.36	0.39	0.38	0.43

metal industry and petroleum and coal products. They had a positive own effect, but their new rate is negative due to a large negative input effect coming from mines, quarries, and oil wells. By contrast, miscellaneous manufacturing suffered declines in its new MFP, but these contribute little

26	27	28	29	30	31	32	33	34	35	36	37	Output effect
3.80	1.13	1.20	−1.16	1.92	3.76	5.89	1.46	1.48	1.10	0.42	0.51	−
3.41	0.86	0.82	−1.17	1.50	2.89	5.36	1.03	0.91	0.71	−0.07	0.14	−
−	−	−	−	−	−	−	−	−	−	−	−	−0.18
−	−	−	−	−	−	−	−	−	−	−	−	0.38
−0.01	−0.01	−0.01	−0.01	−0.01	−	−	−0.10	−0.03	−0.01	−	−	−3.11
−	−	−	−	−	−	−	−	−	−	−	0.04	0.18
−	−	−	−	−	−	−	−	−	−	−	−	−
−	−	0.01	−	−	−	−	−	−	−	−	−	0.22
−	−	−	−	−	−	−	−	−	−	−	−	0.04
−	0.01	−	−	0.01	−	−	−	−	−	−	0.01	1.42
−	−	−	−	−	−	−	−	−	−	−	−	0.39
−	−	−	−	−	−	−	−	−	−	−	−	0.14
−	−	−	−	−	−	−	−	−	−	−	−	0.20
−	−	−	−	−	−	−	0.01	−	−	−	−	0.05
−	−	−	−	0.01	−	−	−	−	0.01	−	−	0.44
0.01	0.02	0.01	0.03	0.01	0.05	0.02	0.01	0.01	0.05	0.02	0.03	0.67
−	−	−	−	−	−	−	−	−	−	−	−	−0.10
0.02	−	−	−	−	0.01	−	−	−	0.01	−	0.01	0.63
0.01	0.02	0.01	−	0.01	0.09	−	−	0.01	0.01	−	0.01	0.75
0.02	0.05	0.06	0.04	0.01	−	−	−	0.02	0.01	−	0.01	0.46
0.02	0.01	0.01	0.01	−	0.03	0.30	0.12	0.02	0.01	−	0.01	0.99
−	−	−	−	−	−	−	−	−	−	−	−	0.07
−0.02	−0.03	−0.03	−0.01	−	−	−	−	−	−	−	−	−0.22
−	−	−	−	−	−	−	−	−	−	−	−	0.05
0.01	−	−	−	−	0.01	−	−	−	−	−	−	0.11
0.14	0.03	0.03	−0.19	0.13	0.10	0.17	0.34	0.42	0.06	0.35	0.05	2.75
−	−	0.01	−	−	0.01	−	0.01	0.01	−	−	−	0.17
−	0.03	0.08	0.01	0.08	0.01	−	0.01	−	0.02	−	0.01	0.90
−	−	−	−	0.01	−	−	−	−	−	−	−	0.11
0.01	0.01	−	0.02	0.01	0.01	−	−	−	0.01	−	0.01	0.50
−	−	−	−	−	−	−	−	−	−	−	−	−
−	−	0.01	−	−	−	−	−	−	0.01	−	−	0.04
−	−	−	−	−	−	−	−	0.01	0.02	0.01	0.01	0.26
0.13	0.07	0.07	0.03	0.06	0.35	−	0.01	0.06	0.09	0.07	0.08	1.65
−	−	0.01	0.03	0.02	0.01	−	−	0.01	0.03	0.01	0.01	0.45
−	−	−	−	−	−	−	−	−	−	−	−	0.04
0.03	0.03	0.06	0.03	0.02	0.04	0.01	0.01	0.01	−	0.01	0.05	1.52
0.01	0.01	0.01	0.01	0.03	0.02	−	0.01	0.01	0.03	−	0.02	0.47
0.01	0.01	0.01	0.01	0.01	0.12	−	−	0.01	0.02	0.01	−	0.46
0.39	0.27	0.39	0.01	0.42	0.87	0.54	0.43	0.58	0.39	0.49	0.37	−

to the decline of other industries because this industry is largely a final demand producer.

For any industry, the difference between its new and own effect is its total input effect (the last row in the tables). With few exceptions, it serves

Table 5-15. *Breakdown of the average of annual rates of growth of new MFP as the sum of own and input effects, 1961–80*

	01	02	03	04	05	06	07
New MFP =	2.04	1.90	−1.05	1.93	3.57	2.68	1.89
Own effect +	1.00	1.18	−2.04	0.78	2.55	1.78	1.23
01 Agriculture and fishing	−	0.01	−	0.62	0.55	−	−
02 Forestry	−	−	−	−	−	−	−
03 Mines, quarries, and oil wells	−0.02	−	−	−	−	−	−
04 Food and beverages	0.19	0.03	−	−	0.01	−	0.06
05 Tobacco products	−	−	−	−	−	−	−
06 Rubber and plastic products	0.01	0.01	0.01	−	−	0.12	0.03
07 Leather	−	−	−	−	−	−	−
08 Textiles	0.01	0.01	−	0.01	0.02	0.21	0.06
09 Knitting mills	−	−	−	−	−	−	−
10 Clothing	−	−	−	−	−	−	0.01
11 Woods	−	−	−	−	−	−	−
12 Furniture and fixtures	−	−	−	−	−	−	−
13 Paper and allied industries	−	−	−	0.04	0.09	0.03	0.02
14 Printing, publishing, and allied industries	−	−	−	0.03	0.05	0.02	0.01
15 Primary metals	−	−	0.01	−	−	−	−
16 Metal fabricating	0.02	0.03	0.02	0.05	0.01	0.03	0.02
17 Machinery	0.06	0.02	0.05	0.01	0.02	0.02	0.01
18 Transportation equipment	0.10	0.04	0.04	0.02	0.02	0.03	0.01
19 Electrical products	0.01	0.02	0.02	0.01	−	0.01	0.01
20 Nonmetallic mineral products	−	−	−	0.02	−	−	−
21 Petroleum and coal products	0.04	0.01	0.01	0.01	−	−	−
22 Chemical and chemical products	0.05	0.01	0.03	0.01	0.01	0.19	0.02
23 Miscellaneous manufacturing	−	0.01	−	−	0.01	0.01	0.02
24 Construction	0.20	0.10	0.48	0.05	0.04	0.06	0.03
25 Air transportation and other utilities and transportation	−	−	0.01	0.01	−	0.01	0.01
26 Railway transportation and telegraph	0.05	0.03	0.03	0.07	0.03	0.05	0.05
27 Water transport	0.01	0.04	0.01	0.01	−	0.01	−
28 Motor transport	0.01	0.12	0.01	0.02	0.01	0.02	0.01
29 Urban and suburban transportation	−	−	−	−	−	−	−
30 Storage	−	−	−	0.01	−	−	−
31 Broadcasting	−	−	−	0.01	0.03	0.01	0.01
32 Telephones	0.02	0.01	0.01	0.02	0.02	0.03	0.02
33 Electric power	0.02	−	0.03	0.01	−	0.01	0.01
34 Gas distribution	−	−	−	−	−	−	−
35 Trade	0.19	0.10	0.10	0.10	0.06	0.11	0.12
36 Finance, insurance, and real estate	0.03	0.08	0.09	0.01	0.01	0.02	0.02
37 Commercial services	−	0.01	0.02	0.01	0.01	0.01	0.01
Input effect	1.04	0.72	0.99	1.15	1.02	0.90	0.66

to increase the new rate of MFP for industries above their various traditional rates.

Tables 5-18 to 5-22 present a similar set of results to Tables 5-8 to 5-12 but for the new MFP measures. A comparison of these two sets shows

08	09	10	11	12	13	14	15	16	17	18	19	20
3.37	4.53	2.45	1.48	1.71	1.39	1.98	0.92	2.19	2.05	2.13	2.85	1.78
2.83	3.09	1.19	0.47	0.73	0.45	1.30	0.65	1.53	1.33	1.54	2.21	1.08
—	—	0.01	0.01	—	0.01	—	—	—	—	—	—	—
—	—	—	0.54	—	0.25	—	—	—	—	—	—	—
—	—	—	—	—	−0.01	—	−0.24	—	—	—	—	−0.07
0.01	—	—	—	0.01	0.01	—	—	—	—	—	—	—
—	—	—	—	—	—	—	—	—	—	—	—	—
0.02	0.02	—	0.01	0.07	0.01	—	—	0.01	0.03	0.05	0.04	0.01
—	—	0.02	—	—	—	—	—	—	—	—	—	—
—	1.04	0.62	—	0.17	0.02	0.01	—	—	—	0.03	0.01	0.01
0.01	—	0.28	—	—	—	—	—	—	—	—	—	—
0.03	0.06	—	—	—	—	—	—	—	—	—	—	—
—	—	—	—	0.11	0.06	—	—	—	—	—	—	—
—	—	—	0.01	—	—	0.01	—	—	0.01	—	0.01	0.01
0.02	0.02	0.01	0.01	0.03	—	0.23	—	0.01	—	—	0.01	0.01
0.01	0.02	0.01	—	0.02	0.01	—	—	0.01	0.01	0.01	0.02	0.01
—	—	—	—	0.02	0.01	—	—	0.20	0.08	0.05	0.09	0.01
0.02	0.01	0.01	0.03	0.12	0.03	0.01	0.04	—	0.12	0.09	0.07	0.04
0.02	0.02	0.01	0.02	0.01	0.04	0.03	0.03	0.03	—	0.03	0.03	0.03
0.01	0.01	0.01	0.03	0.02	0.01	0.02	0.02	0.02	0.04	—	0.02	0.05
0.01	0.01	0.01	0.01	0.02	0.02	0.01	0.02	0.03	0.09	0.05	—	0.02
—	—	—	0.01	0.01	0.01	—	0.01	0.01	—	0.02	0.01	—
—	—	—	0.01	—	0.01	—	0.01	—	—	—	—	0.01
0.05	0.01	—	0.01	0.03	0.05	0.02	0.01	0.02	0.01	0.01	0.02	0.03
0.01	0.01	0.03	—	0.02	0.01	0.01	—	0.01	0.01	0.01	0.01	0.01
0.04	0.02	0.02	0.04	0.04	0.07	0.06	0.06	0.05	0.05	0.04	0.04	0.10
0.01	—	0.01	—	0.01	0.01	0.02	0.01	0.01	0.01	0.01	0.01	0.02
0.05	0.03	0.02	0.07	0.05	0.10	0.05	0.08	0.05	0.04	0.05	0.04	0.11
0.01	—	—	0.01	0.01	0.01	0.01	0.01	0.01	—	—	—	0.01
0.01	0.01	0.01	0.02	0.01	0.03	0.02	0.02	0.02	0.01	0.01	0.02	0.03
—	—	—	—	—	—	—	—	—	—	—	—	—
0.01	0.01	0.01	—	0.01	—	0.01	—	—	0.01	—	0.01	—
0.02	0.02	0.02	0.02	0.02	0.01	0.05	0.01	0.03	0.03	0.02	0.05	0.02
0.01	0.01	—	0.01	0.01	0.04	0.01	0.02	0.01	0.01	0.01	0.01	0.03
—	—	—	—	0.01	—	0.01	—	—	—	—	—	0.01
0.11	0.09	0.11	0.12	0.13	0.10	0.08	0.12	0.11	0.10	0.07	0.10	0.15
0.01	0.02	0.02	0.02	0.02	0.01	0.02	0.01	0.01	0.02	0.01	0.02	0.01
0.01	0.01	0.01	0.01	0.01	0.01	0.02	—	0.01	0.01	0.02	0.01	0.01
0.54	1.44	1.26	1.01	0.98	0.94	0.67	0.28	0.66	0.72	0.58	0.64	0.70

Continued

that their only difference rests with the values in the intermediate input, capital consumption allowance, and capital columns and, as a result, with their respective MFP rates. The contribution of the (weighted) rates of growth of the intermediate input, CCA, and capital input to the new

Table 5-15 *Continued*

	21	22	23	24	25	26
New MFP =	0.98	1.51	1.52	1.58	2.46	5.85
Own effect +	1.03	0.74	0.74	0.66	1.54	5.12
01 Agriculture and fishing	−	−	−	−	−	−
02 Forestry	−	−	−	−	−	−
03 Mines, quarries, and oil wells	−0.51	−0.04	−	−0.03	−0.02	−0.01
04 Food and beverages	−	0.03	0.01	−	−	0.01
05 Tobacco products	−	−	−	−	−	−
06 Rubber and plastic products	−	0.02	0.03	0.02	0.01	0.01
07 Leather	−	−	0.01	−	−	−
08 Textiles	−	0.01	0.05	0.01	−	−
09 Knitting mills	−	−	0.02	−	−	−
10 Clothing	−	−	−	−	−	−
11 Woods	−	−	0.02	0.07	−	−
12 Furniture and fixtures	−	−	−	−	−	−
13 Paper and allied industries	−	0.04	0.03	0.01	−	−
14 Printing, publishing, and allied industries	0.01	0.04	0.03	−	0.02	0.01
15 Primary metals	−	0.01	0.05	0.04	−	−
16 Metal fabricating	0.02	0.06	0.05	0.20	0.01	0.04
17 Machinery	−	0.03	0.01	0.03	0.03	0.02
18 Transportation equipment	0.01	0.01	0.02	0.03	0.05	0.04
19 Electrical products	−	0.01	0.03	0.10	0.10	0.03
20 Nonmetallic mineral products	−	0.02	0.02	0.11	−	−
21 Petroleum and coal products	−	0.02	−	0.01	0.02	0.02
22 Chemical and chemical products	0.04	−	0.05	0.02	0.01	−
23 Miscellaneous manufacturing	−	0.01	−	0.01	0.01	0.01
24 Construction	0.11	0.09	0.05	−	0.41	0.33
25 Air transportation and other utilities and transportation	0.17	0.02	0.02	−	−	−
26 Railway transportation and telegraph	0.01	0.08	0.04	0.06	0.02	−
27 Water transport	−	0.01	−	0.01	−	−
28 Motor transport	−	0.03	0.02	0.02	0.03	0.01
29 Urban and suburban transportation	−	−	−	−	−	−
30 Storage	−	−	−	−	−	−
31 Broadcasting	0.01	0.02	0.02	−	0.01	−
32 Telephones	0.01	0.03	0.04	0.01	0.06	0.10
33 Electric power	0.01	0.03	0.01	−	0.02	−
34 Gas distribution	−	0.01	−	−	−	−
35 Trade	0.03	0.12	0.11	0.14	0.07	0.06
36 Finance, insurance, and real estate	0.01	0.02	0.02	0.01	0.02	0.02
37 Commercial services	−	0.02	0.02	0.02	0.02	0.01
Input effect	−0.05	0.77	0.77	0.92	0.92	0.73

MFP rate is smaller when these inputs come from industries with a positive rate of MFP. As was shown previously, this is the result of adjusting all produced inputs for the rate of MFP in their industry of origin.

For comparison purpose, consider the breakdown of both the traditional and the new rate of MFP for industry 21, petroleum and coal products,

27	28	29	30	31	32	33	34	35	36	37	Output effect
2.88	1.63	-0.82	2.06	3.66	5.25	1.54	3.96	2.44	0.88	0.61	—
2.34	0.81	-1.13	1.22	2.50	4.40	0.54	2.90	1.77	-0.02	-0.11	—
—	—	—	—	—	—	—	—	0.07	—	0.02	1.31
—	—	—	—	—	—	—	—	—	—	—	0.80
—	—	-0.01	—	—	—	-0.04	-0.01	—	—	—	-1.04
0.01	—	—	—	—	—	—	—	0.01	—	0.13	0.57
—	—	—	—	—	—	—	—	—	—	—	—
0.01	0.04	0.02	0.01	0.02	—	—	0.01	0.01	—	0.01	0.68
—	—	—	—	—	—	—	—	—	—	—	0.04
0.01	—	—	0.01	—	—	—	—	0.01	—	0.01	2.35
—	—	—	—	—	—	—	—	—	—	—	0.33
—	—	—	—	—	—	—	—	—	—	—	0.12
—	—	—	—	—	—	—	—	—	—	—	0.32
—	—	—	—	—	—	0.02	—	—	—	0.01	0.12
—	—	—	0.01	—	—	—	—	0.02	—	0.01	0.73
0.01	0.01	0.02	0.01	0.04	0.02	—	0.01	0.04	0.02	0.02	0.58
—	—	—	—	—	—	—	—	—	—	—	0.58
0.02	0.01	—	0.01	0.02	—	—	0.01	0.02	—	0.01	1.26
0.02	0.01	—	0.01	0.09	0.01	—	0.01	0.01	0.01	0.01	0.81
0.14	0.16	0.09	0.04	0.01	0.01	0.01	0.04	0.03	—	0.03	1.20
0.02	0.02	0.01	0.01	0.03	0.38	0.15	0.01	0.01	0.01	0.02	1.30
—	—	—	—	—	—	—	—	—	—	—	0.26
0.02	0.05	0.02	0.01	0.01	—	0.01	—	0.01	—	0.01	0.35
0.01	0.01	—	—	0.01	—	—	—	0.01	—	0.02	0.76
—	—	—	—	0.01	—	—	—	0.01	—	0.01	0.26
0.08	0.07	-0.03	0.32	0.14	0.36	0.74	0.84	0.11	0.74	0.12	6.06
—	0.02	—	0.01	0.04	—	0.01	—	0.01	—	0.01	0.48
0.03	0.14	0.02	0.15	0.03	0.01	0.02	0.01	0.03	0.01	0.02	1.72
—	—	—	0.03	—	—	—	—	0.01	—	—	0.24
0.01	—	0.01	0.01	0.01	—	—	—	0.02	—	0.01	0.62
—	—	—	—	—	—	—	—	—	—	—	—
—	0.01	—	—	—	—	—	—	0.02	—	—	0.05
—	—	—	—	—	—	—	0.01	0.02	—	0.01	0.24
0.05	0.06	0.02	0.05	0.40	—	0.01	0.05	0.08	0.05	0.07	1.54
—	—	0.04	0.02	0.02	—	—	0.01	0.02	—	0.01	0.44
—	—	—	—	—	—	—	—	0.01	—	—	0.08
0.06	0.14	0.05	0.06	0.09	0.03	0.03	0.03	—	0.02	0.10	3.32
0.02	0.03	0.02	0.05	0.05	0.01	0.02	0.02	0.06	—	0.04	0.82
0.01	0.01	0.01	0.01	0.15	—	—	0.01	0.02	0.01	—	0.51
0.54	0.82	0.30	0.84	1.16	0.85	1.00	1.06	0.67	0.89	0.72	—

from Tables 5-12 and 5-22 for the period 1973–80 (Table 5-23, p. 180). It is an interesting case.

For the two measures of MFP, the weighted rates of growth of the inputs produced outside the domestic private business economy – imports, government, and labour – do not change, nor does the rate of growth of

Table 5-16. *Breakdown of the average of annual rates of growth of new MFP as the sum of own and input effects, 1961–73*

	01	02	03	04	05	06	07
New MFP =	3.67	2.49	2.24	2.91	4.56	4.47	1.88
Own effect +	2.07	1.47	0.81	1.00	2.93	3.02	0.87
01 Agriculture and fishing	–	0.01	–	1.12	0.98	–	0.01
02 Forestry	–	–	–	–	–	–	–
03 Mines, quarries, and oil wells	0.01	–	–	–	–	–	–
04 Food and beverages	0.29	0.05	0.01	–	0.01	0.01	0.09
05 Tobacco products	–	–	–	–	–	–	–
06 Rubber and plastic products	0.02	0.02	0.02	0.01	0.01	–	0.20
07 Leather	–	–	–	–	–	0.01	–
08 Textiles	0.01	0.01	0.01	0.01	0.02	0.29	0.08
09 Knitting mills	–	–	–	–	–	–	–
10 Clothing	–	–	–	–	–	–	0.01
11 Woods	–	–	–	–	–	–	–
12 Furniture and fixtures	–	–	–	–	0.01	–	–
13 Paper and allied industries	–	–	0.01	0.08	0.15	0.06	0.04
14 Printing, publishing, and allied industries	–	–	–	0.03	0.06	0.02	0.02
15 Primary metals	–	–	0.02	–	–	–	–
16 Metal fabricating	0.03	0.04	0.04	0.07	0.02	0.04	0.03
17 Machinery	0.06	0.02	0.06	0.01	0.02	0.03	0.01
18 Transportation equipment	0.16	0.06	0.06	0.03	0.02	0.04	0.01
19 Electrical products	4.02	0.03	0.02	0.01	–	0.01	0.01
20 Nonmetallic mineral products	–	–	0.01	0.04	–	0.01	–
21 Petroleum and coal products	0.09	0.04	0.02	0.01	–	0.01	0.01
22 Chemical and chemical products	0.10	0.02	0.05	0.02	0.02	0.41	0.04
23 Miscellaneous manufacturing	–	0.01	0.01	0.01	0.01	0.01	0.03
24 Construction	0.29	0.15	0.68	0.07	0.05	0.09	0.04
25 Air transportation and other utilities and transportation	0.01	–	0.02	0.02	0.01	0.03	0.02
26 Railway transportation and telegraph	0.06	0.04	0.05	0.09	0.04	0.08	0.06
27 Water transport	0.01	0.05	0.01	0.01	–	0.01	0.01
28 Motor transport	0.02	0.16	0.01	0.03	0.01	0.02	0.02
29 Urban and suburban transportation	–	–	–	–	–	–	–
30 Storage	0.01	–	–	0.01	–	–	–
31 Broadcasting	–	–	–	0.01	0.03	0.01	0.01
32 Telephones	0.02	0.01	0.01	0.02	0.01	0.03	0.02
33 Electric power	0.04	0.01	0.05	0.01	0.01	0.02	0.01
34 Gas distribution	–	–	–	–	–	–	–
35 Trade	0.30	0.16	0.16	0.16	0.09	0.17	0.19
36 Finance, insurance, and real estate	0.03	0.09	0.09	0.01	0.01	0.02	0.02
37 Commercial services	–	0.01	0.02	0.01	0.01	0.02	0.02
Input effect	1.60	1.03	1.43	1.91	1.63	1.46	1.01

output. However, the rate of growth of intermediate inputs increases substantially because intermediate inputs originated in industries whose MFP rate must have been decreasing. To check on this, we go to Table 5-17, column 21, which is repeated in column 3 in Table 5-23. We see that

08	09	10	11	12	13	14	15	16	17	18	19	20
4.35	4.63	2.47	1.44	2.88	2.51	2.19	2.26	3.22	2.28	3.43	3.77	3.47
3.53	2.68	0.85	0.01	1.46	1.14	1.12	0.98	2.05	1.14	2.52	2.73	2.19
0.01	—	0.02	0.02	—	0.01	—	—	—	—	—	—	—
—	—	—	0.72	0.01	0.34	—	—	—	—	—	—	—
—	—	—	—	—	0.02	—	0.54	—	—	—	—	0.11
0.01	—	0.01	—	0.01	0.01	—	0.01	0.01	0.01	—	0.01	0.01
—	—	—	—	—	—	—	—	—	—	—	—	—
0.05	0.02	0.02	0.01	0.13	0.02	0.01	0.01	0.01	0.04	0.08	0.06	0.02
—	—	0.01	—	—	—	—	—	—	—	—	—	—
—	1.39	0.84	0.01	0.23	0.03	0.01	—	—	—	0.04	0.01	0.01
0.01	—	0.28	—	—	—	—	—	—	—	—	—	—
0.02	0.06	—	—	—	—	—	—	—	—	—	—	—
—	—	—	—	0.11	0.04	—	—	—	—	—	—	—
0.01	0.01	—	0.02	—	—	0.02	—	—	0.01	0.01	0.01	0.01
0.05	0.04	0.02	0.01	0.06	—	0.43	0.01	0.02	0.01	0.01	0.02	0.05
0.01	0.02	0.02	—	0.02	0.01	—	—	0.01	0.02	0.01	0.02	0.01
—	—	—	0.01	0.06	0.01	0.01	—	0.49	0.20	0.13	0.23	0.02
0.03	0.01	0.01	0.04	0.18	0.05	0.01	0.05	—	0.18	0.13	0.11	0.06
0.03	0.02	0.01	0.02	0.01	0.05	0.03	0.04	0.04	—	0.03	0.04	0.04
0.02	0.02	0.01	0.04	0.03	0.02	0.02	0.02	0.04	0.06	—	0.04	0.07
0.02	0.01	0.01	0.01	0.02	0.03	0.01	0.03	0.04	0.13	0.06	—	0.03
—	—	—	0.01	0.02	0.01	—	0.02	0.02	0.01	0.03	0.02	—
0.01	0.01	—	0.01	0.01	0.03	0.01	0.02	0.01	0.01	—	0.01	0.03
0.11	0.02	0.01	0.03	0.05	0.10	0.04	0.03	0.04	0.02	0.02	0.05	0.06
0.03	0.01	0.04	—	0.03	0.01	0.01	0.01	0.01	0.01	0.01	0.01	0.01
0.06	0.03	0.02	0.06	0.06	0.10	0.09	0.08	0.08	0.08	0.06	0.05	0.14
0.01	0.01	0.01	0.01	0.02	0.02	0.03	0.01	0.02	0.02	0.01	0.42	0.03
0.06	0.04	0.02	0.09	0.06	0.13	0.07	0.11	0.07	0.06	0.06	0.05	0.14
0.01	—	—	0.01	0.01	0.02	0.01	0.01	0.01	0.01	0.01	—	0.01
0.02	0.01	0.01	0.02	0.02	0.03	0.02	0.03	0.02	0.02	0.02	0.02	0.04
—	—	—	—	—	—	—	—	—	—	—	—	—
0.01	0.01	0.01	—	0.01	—	0.01	—	—	0.01	0.01	0.01	—
0.02	0.02	0.02	0.02	0.02	0.01	0.05	0.01	0.03	0.03	0.02	0.04	0.02
0.02	0.01	0.01	0.03	0.01	0.07	0.01	0.04	0.01	0.01	0.01	0.01	0.05
—	—	—	—	—	0.01	—	0.01	—	—	—	—	0.02
0.17	0.14	0.17	0.18	0.20	0.15	0.12	0.18	0.16	0.15	0.11	0.15	0.23
0.01	0.02	0.02	0.02	0.02	0.01	0.02	0.01	0.01	0.03	0.01	0.02	0.02
0.01	0.01	0.01	0.01	0.01	0.01	0.02	0.01	0.01	0.01	0.02	0.01	0.01
0.81	1.95	1.62	1.43	1.42	1.37	1.07	1.29	1.17	1.13	0.91	1.04	1.27

Continued

the MFP is, indeed, the sum of the own effect and the input effect. The input effect is negative mainly because of the inputs that the petroleum and coal industry bought from industry 03, which has a negative rate of new MFP of -6.68. Note also that the own effect is less than the

Table 5-16 *Continued*

	21	22	23	24	25	26	27
New MFP =	2.47	3.16	2.54	2.29	4.58	7.34	3.52
Own effect +	1.03	1.91	1.34	0.81	3.16	6.29	2.71
01 Agriculture and fishing	–	–	–	–	–	–	–
02 Forestry	–	–	–	–	–	–	–
03 Mines, quarries, and oil wells	0.71	0.04	0.01	0.02	0.01	–	–
04 Food and beverages	–	0.05	0.01	0.01	–	0.01	0.01
05 Tobacco products	–	–	–	–	–	–	–
06 Rubber and plastic products	–	0.04	0.05	0.04	0.02	0.01	0.02
07 Leather	–	–	0.01	–	–	–	–
08 Textiles	–	0.01	0.06	0.01	–	0.01	0.01
09 Knitting mills	–	–	0.02	–	–	–	–
10 Clothing	–	–	–	–	–	–	–
11 Woods	–	–	0.03	0.08	–	–	–
12 Furniture and fixtures	–	0.01	–	0.01	–	–	–
13 Paper and allied industry	–	0.07	0.06	0.02	–	–	0.01
14 Printing, publishing, and allied industries	0.01	0.05	0.04	–	0.02	0.01	0.01
15 Primary metals	–	0.02	0.13	0.08	–	0.01	–
16 Metal fabricating	0.02	0.09	0.08	0.03	0.02	0.06	0.02
17 Machinery	0.01	0.03	0.02	0.04	0.04	0.02	0.02
18 Transportation equipment	0.02	0.02	0.03	0.04	0.09	0.06	0.24
19 Electrical products	–	0.02	0.04	0.13	0.14	0.05	0.02
20 Nonmetallic mineral products	–	0.03	0.03	0.20	–	–	–
21 Petroleum and coal products	–	0.06	0.01	0.03	0.08	0.06	0.08
22 Chemical and chemical products	0.07	–	0.10	0.04	0.02	0.01	0.01
23 Miscellaneous manufacturing	0.01	0.02	–	0.02	0.01	0.02	–
24 Construction	0.16	0.14	0.07	–	0.62	0.49	0.12
25 Air transportation and other utilities and transportation	0.29	0.05	0.05	0.01	–	0.01	0.01
26 Railway transportation and telegraph	0.02	0.10	0.06	0.08	0.03	–	0.04
27 Water transport	–	0.01	0.01	0.01	–	–	–
28 Motor transport	0.01	0.03	0.02	0.03	0.04	0.01	0.01
29 Urban and suburban transportation	–	–	–	–	–	–	–
30 Storage	–	–	–	–	–	–	–
31 Broadcasting	0.01	0.03	0.02	–	0.01	–	–
32 Telephones	0.01	0.03	0.03	0.01	0.06	0.07	0.03
33 Electric power	0.02	0.05	0.01	–	0.03	–	–
34 Gas distribution	–	0.01	–	–	–	–	–
35 Trade	0.05	0.19	0.17	0.21	0.11	0.10	0.09
36 Finance, insurance, and real estate	0.01	0.02	0.03	0.01	0.03	0.02	0.02
37 Commercial services	0.01	0.3	0.02	0.02	0.03	0.01	0.01
Input effect	1.45	1.25	1.20	1.48	1.42	1.05	0.81

traditional MFP rate for this industry because its own new MFP rate is negative.[9]

[9] Numbers in the example do not necessarily add up to the input effect due to rounding. Industries with an absolute value of less than 0.01 are excluded. The own new MFP measure for petroleum and coal products is 1.04. However, it has been using intermediate inputs with a combined MFP of -2.63 so that the total new MFP for the industry is $1.04 - 2.63 = -1.59$.

28	29	30	31	32	33	34	35	36	37	Output effect
2.12	−0.76	2.13	3.85	4.72	2.72	5.75	3.75	1.13	0.79	—
0.89	−1.33	0.93	2.35	3.51	1.16	4.22	2.80	−0.14	−0.26	—
—	—	—	—	—	—	—	0.12	—	0.03	2.34
—	—	—	—	—	—	—	—	—	—	1.08
—	—	—	—	—	0.04	0.01	—	—	—	1.61
—	—	—	—	—	0.01	—	0.02	—	0.20	0.87
—	—	—	—	—	—	—	—	—	—	—
0.07	0.04	0.02	0.03	—	—	0.01	0.02	0.01	0.01	1.16
—	—	—	—	—	—	—	—	—	—	0.04
—	—	0.02	—	—	—	—	0.01	—	0.02	3.17
—	—	—	—	—	—	—	—	—	—	0.32
—	—	—	—	—	—	—	—	—	—	0.11
—	—	—	—	—	—	—	—	—	—	0.32
—	—	—	—	0.01	0.03	—	0.01	—	0.01	0.20
—	—	0.03	0.01	—	—	—	0.04	—	0.02	1.35
0.01	0.02	0.02	0.05	0.02	0.01	0.01	0.05	0.02	0.02	0.68
—	—	—	—	—	—	—	—	—	—	1.46
0.02	0.01	0.01	0.03	0.01	—	0.01	0.03	0.01	0.02	1.87
0.01	0.01	0.01	0.10	0.01	0.01	0.01	0.01	0.01	0.02	0.93
0.26	0.13	0.07	0.01	0.01	0.01	0.07	0.05	—	0.06	1.97
0.03	0.02	0.01	0.04	0.52	0.20	0.01	0.01	0.01	0.03	1.78
—	—	—	—	—	—	—	—	—	—	0.49
0.12	0.06	0.03	0.01	0.01	0.02	—	0.03	—	0.02	0.97
0.01	0.01	0.01	0.01	—	—	0.01	0.01	—	0.03	1.59
—	—	—	0.02	—	0.01	—	0.01	—	0.02	0.42
0.10	0.06	0.46	0.19	0.53	1.09	1.21	0.15	1.06	0.18	8.92
0.04	—	0.01	0.07	—	0.01	0.01	0.02	0.01	0.01	0.90
0.18	0.02	0.19	0.04	0.01	0.03	0.01	0.05	0.01	0.03	2.29
—	—	0.03	—	—	—	—	0.01	—	—	0.28
—	0.01	0.02	0.01	—	0.01	—	0.03	—	0.01	0.79
—	—	—	—	—	—	—	—	—	—	—
—	—	—	—	—	—	—	0.02	—	—	0.06
—	—	—	—	—	—	0.01	0.02	—	0.01	0.25
0.05	0.02	0.05	0.43	—	0.01	0.04	0.07	0.04	0.06	1.43
0.01	0.06	0.03	0.03	0.01	—	0.01	0.04	0.01	0.01	0.76
—	—	—	—	—	—	—	0.01	—	—	0.11
0.22	0.07	0.09	0.13	0.04	0.04	0.04	—	0.03	0.16	5.09
0.03	0.02	0.06	0.06	0.02	0.03	0.03	0.08	—	0.05	1.01
0.01	0.01	0.01	0.19	—	—	0.01	0.02	0.02	—	0.65
1.23	0.57	1.19	1.50	1.21	1.56	1.53	0.95	1.26	1.05	—

Tables 5-13 to 5-17 and 5-18 to 5-22 are therefore two ways of classifying the components of the same rate of growth of the new MFP. The former does it in terms of the own effect plus the benefits emanating from the MFP rates of the supplying industries (input effect of industry flows), the latter in terms of the rate of growth of the inputs in which these effects are embedded.

Table 5-17. *Breakdown of the average of annual rates of growth of new MFP as the sum of own and input effects, 1973–80*

	01	02	03	04	05	06	07
New MFP =	−0.74	0.88	−6.68	0.25	1.86	−0.40	1.91
Own effect +	−0.82	0.70	−6.93	0.40	1.89	−0.35	1.84
01 Agriculture and fishing	−	−	−	−0.24	−0.17	−	−
02 Forestry	−	−	−	−	−	−	−
03 Mines, quarries, and oil wells	0.07	0.01	−	0.01	−	0.02	0.01
04 Food and beverages	0.02	−	−	−	−	−	−
05 Tobacco products	−	−	−	−	−	−	−
06 Rubber and plastic products	−	−	−	−	−	−	0.03
07 Leather	−	−	−	−	−	−	−
08 Textiles	−	−	−	−	0.01	0.07	0.02
09 Knitting mills	−	−	−	−	−	−	−
10 Clothing	−	−	−	−	−	−	0.01
11 Woods	−	−	−	−	−	−	−
12 Furniture and fixtures	−	−	−	−	−	−	−
13 Paper and allied industries	−	−	−	−0.01	−0.02	−0.01	−0.01
14 Printing, publishing, and allied industries	−	−	−	0.02	0.04	0.01	0.01
15 Primary metals	−	−	0.01	−	−	−	−
16 Metal fabricating	−	0.01	−	0.01	−	0.01	−
17 Machinery	0.06	0.02	0.03	0.01	0.02	0.02	0.01
18 Transportation equipment	−0.01	−	−0.01	−	−	−	−
19 Electrical products	−	0.01	0.01	−	−	−	−
20 Nonmetallic mineral products	−	−	−	−0.01	−	−	−
21 Petroleum and coal products	−0.05	−0.04	−0.02	−0.01	−	−0.01	−
22 Chemical and chemical products	−0.03	−0.01	−0.01	−0.01	−0.01	−0.20	−0.02
23 Miscellaneous manufacturing	−	−	−	−	−	−	−
24 Construction	0.06	0.02	0.13	0.01	0.01	0.01	0.01
25 Air transportation and other utilities and transportation	−	−	−	−	−	−0.01	−0.01
26 Railway transportation and telegraph	0.02	0.01	0.01	0.03	0.01	0.02	0.02
27 Water transport	0.01	0.03	−	0.01	−	−	−
28 Motor transport	0.01	0.06	−	0.01	0.01	0.01	0.01
29 Urban and suburban transportation	−	−	−	−	−	−	−
30 Storage	−	−	−	0.01	−	−	−
31 Broadcasting	−	−	−	0.01	0.03	0.01	0.01
32 Telephones	0.03	0.01	0.01	0.02	0.02	0.03	0.02
33 Electric power	−	−	−0.01	−	−	−	−
34 Gas distribution	−	−	−	−	−	−	−
35 Trade	0.02	0.01	0.01	0.01	0.01	0.01	0.01
36 Finance, insurance, and real estate	0.02	0.05	0.09	−	0.01	0.01	0.01
37 Commercial services	−	−	0.01	−	0.01	0.01	0.01
Input effect	0.08	0.18	0.25	−0.15	−0.04	−0.05	0.07

08	09	10	11	12	13	14	15	16	17	18	19
1.70	4.37	2.42	1.56	−0.29	−0.53	1.61	−1.37	0.44	1.65	−0.11	1.28
1.63	3.79	1.78	1.26	−0.52	−0.73	1.61	0.09	0.65	1.66	−0.13	1.32
−	−	−	−	−	−	−	−	−	−	−	−
−	−	−	0.23	−	0.09	−	−	−	−	−	−
0.02	0.01	−	−0.01	−0.01	−0.05	−0.01	−1.56	−0.01	−0.02	−0.01	−0.01
−	−	−	−	−	−	−	−	−	−	−	−
−	−	−	−	−0.01	−	−	−	−	−	−0.01	−0.01
−	−	0.03	−	0.01	−	−	−	−	−	−	−
−	0.44	0.25	−	0.08	0.01	−	−	−	−	0.01	−
0.02	−	0.30	−	−	−	−	−	−	−	−	−
0.03	0.06	−	−	−	−	−	−	−	−	−	−
−	−	−	−	0.11	0.09	−	−	−	−	0.01	−
−	−	−	−	−	−	−	−	−	−	−	−
−0.01	−0.01	−0.01	−0.01	−0.02	−	−0.11	−	−	−	−	−0.01
0.01	0.01	0.01	−	0.01	0.01	−	−	0.01	0.01	−	−0.01
−	−	−	−	−0.04	−0.01	−	−	−0.31	−0.12	−0.09	−0.16
−	−	−	0.01	0.03	−	−	0.01	−	0.02	0.01	0.01
0.02	0.01	0.01	0.02	0.01	0.03	0.02	0.03	0.02	−	0.02	0.03
−	−	−	0.01	0.01	0.01	−	0.01	0.01	0.02	0.02	−
−	−	−	−	−0.01	−	−	−0.01	−0.01	−	−0.01	−0.01
−0.01	−	−	−0.01	−	−0.03	−	−0.01	−	−	−	−
−0.05	−0.01	−	−0.01	−0.02	−0.04	−0.02	−0.02	−0.01	−0.01	−0.01	−0.02
−	−	−	−	−	−	−	−	−	−	−	−
0.01	−	−	0.01	0.01	0.02	0.01	0.01	0.01	0.01	−	0.01
−	−	−	−	−	−0.01	−0.01	−	−	−	−	−0.01
0.02	0.01	0.01	0.03	0.02	0.04	0.02	0.03	0.02	0.02	0.02	0.02
−	−	−	0.01	−	0.01	−	0.01	−	−	−	−
0.01	−	−	0.01	0.01	0.01	0.01	0.01	0.01	0.01	0.01	0.01
−	−	−	−	−	−	−	−	−	−	−	−
−	−	−	−	−	−	−	−	−	−	−	−
0.01	0.01	0.01	−	0.01	−	0.01	−	−	0.01	−	0.01
0.02	0.02	0.02	0.02	0.02	0.02	0.05	0.01	0.03	0.03	0.02	0.06
−	−	−	−	−	−0.01	−	−0.01	−	−	−	−
−	−	−	−	−	−	−	−	−	−	−	−
0.01	0.01	0.01	0.01	0.01	0.01	0.01	0.01	0.01	0.01	0.01	0.01
0.01	0.01	0.01	0.01	0.01	−	0.01	−	0.01	0.01	−	0.01
−	−	−	−	−	−	0.01	−	−	0.01	0.01	0.01
0.07	0.57	0.64	0.30	0.23	0.20	−	−1.46	−0.21	−	0.03	−0.05

Continued

Table 5-17 *Continued*

	20	21	22	23	24	25	26
New MFP =	−1.12	−1.59	−1.31	−0.24	0.37	−1.17	3.29
Own effect +	0.83	1.04	−1.27	−0.27	0.41	−1.23	3.11
01 Agriculture and fishing	—	—	—	—	—	—	—
02 Forestry	—	—	—	—	—	—	—
03 Mines, quarries, and oil wells	−0.38	−2.62	−0.16	−0.01	−0.17	−0.09	−0.02
04 Food and beverages	—	—	—	—	—	—	—
05 Tobacco products	—	—	—	—	—	—	—
06 Rubber and plastic products	—	—	—	−0.01	—	—	—
07 Leather	—	—	—	0.01	—	—	—
08 Textiles	—	—	—	0.01	0.01	—	—
09 Knitting mills	—	—	—	0.01	—	—	—
10 Clothing	—	—	—	—	—	—	—
11 Woods	0.01	—	—	0.01	0.07	—	—
12 Furniture and fixtures	—	—	—	—	—	—	—
13 Paper and allied industries	−0.02	—	−0.02	−0.02	—	—	—
14 Printing, publishing, and allied industries	0.01	0.01	0.03	0.02	—	0.01	—
15 Primary metals	−0.01	—	−0.02	−0.07	−0.03	—	−0.01
16 Metal fabricating	0.01	—	0.01	0.01	0.04	—	0.01
17 Machinery	0.03	—	0.02	0.01	0.02	0.02	0.01
18 Transportation equipment	—	—	—	—	—	—	—
19 Electrical products	0.01	—	—	0.01	0.03	0.03	0.01
20 Nonmetallic mineral products	—	—	−0.01	−0.01	−0.06	—	—
21 Petroleum and coal products	−0.03	—	−0.04	−0.01	−0.02	−0.07	−0.05
22 Chemical and chemical products	−0.03	−0.03	—	−0.05	−0.01	−0.01	—
23 Miscellaneous manufacturing	—	—	—	—	—	—	—
24 Construction	0.02	0.02	0.02	0.01	—	0.06	0.06
25 Air transportation and other utilities and transportation	−0.01	−0.03	−0.02	−0.01	—	—	—
26 Railway transportation and telegraph	0.04	0.01	0.03	0.01	0.02	0.01	—
27 Water transport	0.01	—	0.01	—	0.01	—	—
28 Motor transport	0.01	—	0.01	0.01	0.01	0.02	0.01
29 Urban and suburban transportation	—	—	—	—	—	—	—
30 Storage	—	—	—	—	—	—	—
31 Broadcasting	—	0.01	0.02	0.01	—	0.01	—
32 Telephones	0.03	0.01	0.04	0.04	0.01	0.06	0.14
33 Electric power	−0.01	—	−0.01	—	—	—	—
34 Gas distribution	—	—	—	—	—	—	—
35 Trade	0.01	—	0.01	0.01	0.01	0.01	0.01
36 Finance, insurance, and real estate	0.01	—	0.01	0.02	0.01	0.01	0.01
37 Commercial services	—	—	0.01	0.01	0.01	0.01	0.01
Input effect	−0.29	−2.63	−0.04	0.03	−0.04	0.06	0.18

27	28	29	30	31	32	33	34	35	36	37	Output effect
1.78	0.80	-0.93	1.96	3.34	6.15	-0.49	0.90	0.20	0.45	0.30	–
1.71	0.68	-0.77	1.73	2.75	5.91	-0.53	0.63	–	0.18	0.13	–
–	–	–	–	–	–	–	–	-0.01	–	–	-0.44
–	–	–	–	–	–	–	–	–	–	–	0.33
-0.01	-0.01	-0.02	-0.01	–	–	-0.18	-0.05	-0.01	-0.01	-0.01	-5.59
–	–	–	–	–	–	–	–	–	–	0.01	0.07
–	-0.01	-0.01	–	–	–	–	–	–	–	–	0.12
–	–	–	–	–	–	–	–	–	–	–	0.06
–	–	–	–	–	–	–	–	–	–	0.01	0.95
–	–	–	–	–	–	–	–	–	–	–	0.34
–	–	–	–	–	–	–	–	–	–	–	0.13
–	–	–	–	–	–	–	–	–	–	–	0.33
–	–	–	–	–	–	-0.01	–	–	–	–	-0.03
–	–	–	-0.01	–	–	–	–	-0.01	–	–	-0.33
0.01	0.01	0.02	0.01	0.03	0.01	–	0.01	0.03	0.01	0.02	0.41
–	–	–	–	–	–	–	–	–	–	–	-0.91
–	–	–	–	–	–	–	–	–	–	–	0.21
0.01	–	–	–	0.07	–	–	0.01	0.01	–	0.01	0.60
-0.03	-0.01	0.01	-0.01	–	–	–	–	-0.01	–	–	-0.11
–	–	–	–	0.02	0.14	0.07	0.01	–	–	–	0.46
–	–	–	–	–	–	–	–	–	–	–	-0.14
-0.09	-0.07	-0.04	-0.01	-0.01	–	-0.02	–	-0.02	–	-0.01	-0.71
-0.01	–	-0.01	–	-0.01	–	–	–	–	–	-0.01	-0.67
–	–	–	–	–	–	–	–	–	–	–	-0.02
0.02	0.02	-0.19	0.07	0.05	0.07	0.15	0.21	0.03	0.17	0.02	1.16
–	-0.01	–	–	-0.01	–	-0.01	-0.01	-0.01	–	-0.01	-0.23
0.03	0.07	0.01	0.07	0.01	–	0.01	–	0.01	–	0.01	0.73
–	0.01	–	0.01	–	–	–	–	–	–	–	0.17
0.01	–	0.02	0.01	0.01	–	–	–	0.01	–	0.01	0.33
–	–	–	–	–	–	–	–	–	–	–	–
–	0.01	–	–	–	–	–	–	0.01	–	–	0.04
–	–	–	–	–	–	–	0.01	0.02	0.01	0.01	0.23
0.08	0.08	0.03	0.07	0.35	–	0.01	0.07	0.10	0.07	0.08	1.72
–	–	-0.01	–	–	–	–	–	-0.01	–	–	-0.10
–	–	–	–	–	–	–	–	–	–	–	0.03
–	0.01	0.01	–	0.01	–	–	–	–	–	0.01	0.29
0.01	0.02	0.01	0.04	0.02	0.01	0.01	0.01	0.03	–	0.02	0.51
0.01	0.01	0.01	–	0.07	–	–	0.01	0.01	0.01	–	0.27
0.07	0.11	-0.16	0.23	0.59	0.23	0.04	0.27	0.20	0.26	0.12	–

Table 5-18. *Breakdown of the average of annual rates of growth of new MFP, 1961-71*

	Output	Inter-mediate input	Imports	Govern-ment	Labour	CCA	Capital	MFP rate
01 Agriculture and fishing	3.73	-0.12	-0.19	-0.04	0.60	0.07	0.11	4.16
02 Forestry	1.87	-0.08	-0.23	-0.02	1.30	-0.12	-0.02	2.70
03 Mines, quarries, and oil wells	6.33	-1.86	-0.38	-0.19	-0.37	-0.69	-1.70	1.14
04 Food and beverages	3.73	-0.22	-0.22	–	-0.03	-0.06	-0.10	3.10
05 Tobacco products	2.88	0.46	-0.09	-0.02	0.22	-0.06	0.37	3.77
06 Rubber and plastic products	9.77	-1.93	-1.61	-0.09	-1.24	-0.18	-0.39	4.33
07 Leather	1.13	1.23	-0.67	-0.02	0.62	-0.01	0.07	2.35
08 Textiles	7.10	-1.19	-1.27	-0.06	-0.17	-0.08	-0.09	4.25
09 Knitting mills	6.78	-0.76	-1.32	-0.02	-0.16	-0.03	0.01	4.49
10 Clothing	3.80	-0.75	-0.55	-0.02	-0.18	–	0.03	2.33
11 Woods	4.40	-1.30	-0.35	-0.11	-0.34	-0.12	-0.19	1.98
12 Furniture and fixtures	5.73	1.29	-0.68	-0.07	-0.78	-0.04	-0.34	2.52
13 Paper and allied industries	4.32	-1.06	-0.32	-0.07	-0.38	-0.32	-0.36	1.81
14 Printing, publishing, and allied industries	3.30	-0.84	-0.17	-0.06	-0.43	-0.06	-0.21	1.51
15 Primary metals	5.02	-1.70	-0.67	-0.05	-0.42	-0.17	-0.15	1.86
16 Metal fabricating	6.66	-1.59	-0.65	-0.05	-0.96	-0.04	-0.27	3.09
17 Machinery	7.31	-2.00	-1.54	-0.06	-1.08	-0.08	-0.48	2.07
18 Transportation equipment	11.72	-3.02	-4.06	-0.04	-0.99	-0.08	-0.32	3.21
19 Electrical products	6.94	-1.50	-0.96	-0.05	-0.94	-0.09	-0.20	3.21
20 Nonmetallic mineral products	5.57	-1.21	-0.30	-0.10	-0.45	-0.19	-0.37	2.95
21 Petroleum and coal products	5.34	-1.48	-1.50	-0.03	-0.11	-0.07	0.05	2.20

22	Chemical and chemical products	5.84	−1.29	−0.67	−0.07	−0.43	−0.23	−0.46	2.69
23	Miscellaneous manufacturing	5.84	−1.26	−1.06	−0.09	−0.62	−0.12	−0.33	2.35
24	Construction	4.46	−1.09	−0.31	−0.30	−0.41	—	−0.04	2.31
25	Air transportation and other utilities and transportation	9.35	−1.96	−0.42	−0.52	−0.90	−0.90	−0.72	3.94
26	Railway transportation and telegraph	5.45	0.24	−0.19	0.26	1.41	0.52	—	7.69
27	Water transport	5.24	−0.62	−0.24	−0.07	0.28	−0.14	−0.01	4.45
28	Motor transport	7.06	−2.32	−0.43	−0.49	−1.17	−0.11	−0.52	2.02
29	Urban and suburban transportation	0.63	−0.09	−0.09	0.03	−0.76	−0.55	0.31	−0.52
30	Storage	2.20	0.64	0.01	−0.21	−0.07	−0.15	−0.23	2.19
31	Broadcasting	7.01	−2.51	−0.80	3.40	−1.73	−0.54	−1.25	3.58
32	Telephones	8.20	−0.19	−0.05	−0.28	−0.86	−0.86	−1.30	4.66
33	Electric power	6.12	−0.61	−0.54	−0.14	−0.94	−1.08	−1.20	1.61
34	Gas distribution	9.33	−0.08	0.05	−0.25	0.01	−0.56	−2.31	6.20
35	Trade	5.21	−0.32	−0.11	−0.06	−1.15	−0.07	0.14	3.64
36	Finance, insurance, and real estate	4.45	−0.65	−0.07	−0.78	−0.90	0.19	−0.57	1.28
37	Commercial services	5.46	−0.98	−0.34	−0.16	−2.15	−0.24	−0.90	0.69

Table 5-19. *Breakdown of the average of annual rates of growth of new MFP, 1971–80*

	Output	Inter-mediate input	Imports	Govern-ment	Labour	CCA	Capital	MFP rate
01 Agriculture and fishing	1.90	−1.19	−0.22	0.01	0.10	−0.80	−0.10	−0.31
02 Forestry	3.43	−2.02	−0.18	−0.12	0.12	−0.21	−0.01	1.01
03 Mines, quarries, and oil wells	3.30	−3.74	−0.33	−0.20	−0.44	−0.66	−1.41	−3.48
04 Food and beverages	2.45	−1.30	−0.31	—	−0.04	−0.02	−0.17	0.63
05 Tobacco products	0.79	2.23	−0.35	0.01	0.34	−0.01	0.32	3.34
06 Rubber and plastic products	5.15	−1.96	−0.76	−0.04	−0.91	−0.19	−0.43	0.85
07 Leather	0.93	−0.08	—	0.01	0.57	−0.03	−0.01	1.38
08 Textiles	2.83	−0.10	−0.44	−0.01	0.19	—	−0.07	2.40
09 Knitting mills	3.16	1.02	−0.22	0.02	0.67	0.01	−0.08	4.58
10 Clothing	2.67	0.20	−0.34	—	0.26	—	−0.28	2.59
11 Woods	4.38	−1.87	−0.32	−0.05	−0.59	−0.17	0.44	0.93
12 Furniture and fixtures	2.54	−0.62	−0.36	−0.01	−0.48	−0.04	−0.22	0.82
13 Paper and allied industries	3.11	−1.28	−0.37	0.01	−0.32	−0.11	−0.09	0.92
14 Printing, publishing, and allied industries	5.36	−1.28	−0.38	−0.03	−0.82	−0.07	−0.30	2.49
15 Primary metals	2.02	−0.94	−0.69	−0.03	−0.25	−0.16	−0.07	−0.12
16 Metal fabricating	2.91	−0.66	−0.37	−0.02	−0.40	−0.06	−0.22	1.19
17 Machinery	7.44	−1.49	−2.07	−0.06	−1.28	−0.08	−0.43	2.03
18 Transportation equipment	2.64	−0.26	−0.89	−0.01	−0.28	−0.06	−0.21	0.93
19 Electrical products	3.57	0.09	−1.04	−0.01	0.13	−0.05	−0.24	2.45
20 Nonmetallic mineral products	2.20	−0.81	−0.32	−0.05	−0.04	−0.20	−0.31	0.47
21 Petroleum and coal products	4.55	−5.72	0.80	0.36	−0.18	−0.13	−0.06	−0.39

22	Chemical and chemical products	4.98	−2.81	−0.77	−0.06	−0.17	−0.43	−0.52	0.20
23	Miscellaneous manufacturing	2.73	−0.62	−1.07	−0.02	−0.30	−0.04	−0.10	0.58
24	Construction	2.94	−0.78	−0.30	0.14	−0.65	−0.08	−0.23	0.77
25	Air transportation and other utilities and transportation	6.31	−2.33	−0.19	−0.21	−1.52	−0.87	−0.38	0.82
26	Railway transportation and telegraph	3.30	−1.49	—	1.27	0.73	−0.02	—	3.80
27	Water transport	1.93	−0.89	−0.02	−0.12	0.17	0.06	−0.01	1.13
28	Motor transport	5.15	−1.25	−0.21	−0.25	−1.36	−0.18	−0.70	1.20
29	Urban and suburban transportation	3.10	−2.17	−0.46	−0.29	−4.10	−1.77	4.51	−1.16
30	Storage	3.08	0.61	−0.02	0.04	0.12	−0.48	−0.21	1.92
31	Broadcasting	8.16	−2.55	−0.61	3.33	−2.22	−0.72	−1.64	3.76
32	Telephones	10.42	−0.54	−0.10	−0.38	−1.31	−0.94	−1.26	5.89
33	Electric power	6.56	−0.65	−0.39	−0.05	−0.87	−1.73	−1.41	1.46
34	Gas distribution	4.65	−0.45	−0.02	0.16	−0.76	−0.56	−1.53	1.48
35	Trade	3.78	−0.77	−0.06	−0.12	−1.53	−0.09	−0.10	1.10
36	Finance, insurance, and real estate	5.35	−1.09	−0.16	−0.77	−1.04	−0.46	−1.39	0.42
37	Commercial services	6.46	−1.16	−0.19	−0.11	−2.70	−0.47	−1.32	0.51

Table 5-20. Breakdown of the average of annual rates of growth of new MFP, 1961–80

		Output	Inter-mediate input	Imports	Govern-ment	Labour	CCA	Capital	MFP rate
01	Agriculture and fishing	2.86	-0.62	-0.20	-0.02	0.36	-0.34	0.01	2.04
02	Forestry	2.61	-1.00	-0.21	-0.07	0.74	-0.16	-0.01	1.90
03	Mines, quarries, and oil wells	4.89	-2.76	-0.36	-0.20	-0.40	-0.67	-1.56	-1.05
04	Food and beverages	3.13	-0.73	-0.26	—	-0.03	-0.04	-0.13	1.93
05	Tobacco products	1.89	1.30	-0.21	-0.01	0.28	-0.03	0.35	3.57
06	Rubber and plastic products	7.58	-1.95	-1.21	-0.07	-1.08	-0.19	-0.41	2.68
07	Leather	1.04	0.61	-0.35	-0.01	0.59	-0.02	0.03	1.89
08	Textiles	5.08	-0.68	-0.88	-0.04	—	-0.04	-0.08	3.37
09	Knitting mills	5.06	0.08	-0.80	—	0.23	-0.01	-0.03	4.53
10	Clothing	3.27	-0.30	-0.45	-0.01	0.03	—	-0.08	2.45
11	Woods	4.39	-1.57	-0.34	-0.08	-0.46	-0.15	-0.31	1.48
12	Furniture and fixtures	4.22	-0.97	-0.53	-0.04	-0.64	-0.04	-0.28	1.71
13	Paper and allied industries	3.74	-1.17	-0.34	-0.04	-0.35	-0.22	-0.23	1.39
14	Printing, publishing, and allied industries	4.28	-1.05	-0.27	-0.05	-0.62	-0.07	-0.25	1.98
15	Primary metals	3.60	-1.34	-0.68	-0.04	-0.34	-0.16	-0.11	0.92
16	Metal fabricating	4.88	-1.15	-0.52	-0.04	-0.69	-0.05	-0.25	2.19
17	Machinery	7.37	-1.76	-1.79	-0.06	-1.18	-0.08	-0.46	2.05
18	Transportation equipment	7.42	-1.71	-2.56	-0.03	-0.65	-0.07	-0.27	2.13
19	Electrical products	5.35	-0.75	-1.00	-0.03	-0.44	-0.07	-0.22	2.85
20	Nonmetallic mineral products	3.97	-1.02	-0.31	-0.08	-0.25	-0.19	-0.34	1.78
21	Petroleum and coal products	4.97	-3.49	-0.41	0.16	-0.14	-0.10	—	0.98

174

22	Chemical and chemical products	5.44	−2.01	−0.72	−0.07	−0.31	−0.32	−0.49	1.51
23	Miscellaneous manufacturing	4.37	−0.95	−1.07	−0.06	−0.47	−0.08	−0.22	1.52
24	Construction	3.74	−0.94	−0.31	−0.22	−0.52	−0.04	−0.13	1.58
25	Air transportation and other utilities and transportation	7.91	−2.14	−0.31	−0.37	−1.19	−0.88	−0.56	2.46
26	Railway transportation and telegraph	4.43	−0.58	−0.10	0.74	1.09	0.27	—	5.85
27	Water transport	3.67	−0.74	−0.13	−0.09	0.23	−0.05	−0.01	2.88
28	Motor transport	6.16	−1.81	−0.33	−0.38	−1.26	−0.14	−0.61	1.63
29	Urban and suburban transportation	1.80	−1.08	−0.27	−0.12	−2.34	−1.13	2.30	−0.82
30	Storage	2.62	0.05	−0.01	−0.09	0.02	−0.31	−0.22	2.06
31	Broadcasting	7.55	−2.35	−0.71	3.37	−1.96	−0.63	−1.43	3.66
32	Telephones	9.25	−0.36	−0.07	−0.33	−1.07	−0.90	−1.28	5.25
33	Electric power	6.33	−0.63	−0.47	−0.10	−0.91	−1.39	−1.30	1.54
34	Gas distribution	7.11	−0.26	0.02	−0.06	−0.35	−0.56	−1.94	3.96
35	Trade	4.53	−0.54	−0.09	−0.09	−1.35	−0.08	0.03	2.44
36	Finance, insurance, and real estate	4.86	−0.86	−0.11	−0.77	−0.97	−0.32	−0.96	0.88
37	Commercial services	5.93	−1.07	−0.27	−0.14	−2.41	−0.35	−1.10	0.61

Table 5-21. *Breakdown of the average of annual rates of growth of new MFP, 1961–73*

		Output	Inter-mediate input	Imports	Govern-ment	Labour	CCA	Capital	MFP rate
01	Agriculture and fishing	3.36	−0.42	−0.24	−0.03	0.06	0.01	0.39	3.67
02	Forestry	3.71	−1.58	−0.31	−0.15	0.93	−0.13	0.01	2.49
03	Mines, quarries, and oil wells	7.34	−1.88	−0.40	−0.24	−0.37	−0.68	−1.53	2.24
04	Food and beverages	3.59	−0.17	−0.32	—	−0.03	−0.06	−0.10	2.91
05	Tobacco products	2.39	1.66	−0.17	−0.01	0.25	−0.04	0.48	4.56
06	Rubber and plastic products	10.48	−2.06	−1.66	−0.09	1.50	−0.20	−0.49	4.47
07	Leather	0.92	0.85	−0.54	−0.02	0.62	−0.01	0.05	1.88
08	Textiles	7.35	−1.07	−1.37	−0.06	−0.36	−0.06	−0.09	4.35
09	Knitting mills	6.84	−0.41	−1.37	−0.02	−0.29	−0.04	−0.08	4.63
10	Clothing	4.27	−0.75	−0.73	−0.02	−0.27	—	−0.04	2.47
11	Woods	5.22	−2.19	−0.43	−0.10	−0.68	−0.13	−0.25	1.44
12	Furniture and fixtures	6.74	−1.59	−0.79	−0.07	−1.01	−0.04	−0.34	2.88
13	Paper and allied industries	4.74	−0.89	−0.33	−0.07	−0.37	−0.28	−0.30	2.51
14	Printing, publishing, and allied industries	4.11	−0.75	−0.26	−0.05	−0.57	−0.06	−0.21	2.19
15	Primary metals	5.32	−1.53	−0.77	−0.05	−0.41	−0.16	−0.13	2.26
16	Metal fabricating	6.86	−1.70	−0.67	−0.05	−0.94	−0.04	−0.24	3.22
17	Machinery	7.91	−2.00	−1.82	−0.06	−1.26	−0.07	−0.41	2.28
18	Transportation equipment	11.75	−2.66	−4.16	−0.04	−1.10	−0.07	−0.28	3.43
19	Electrical products	7.51	−1.43	−1.08	−0.04	−0.90	−0.08	−0.20	3.77
20	Nonmetallic mineral products	6.13	−1.14	−0.36	−0.11	−0.55	−0.17	−0.33	3.47
21	Petroleum and coal products	6.12	−1.48	−2.00	−0.03	−0.09	−0.09	0.03	2.47

22	Chemical and chemical products	6.14	-1.21	-0.77	-0.07	-0.36	-0.19	-0.38	3.16
23	Miscellaneous manufacturing	6.12	-1.24	-1.17	-0.09	-0.69	-0.11	-0.29	2.54
24	Construction	4.43	-0.86	-0.33	-0.29	-0.62	-0.02	-0.02	2.29
25	Air transportation and other utilities and transportation	10.42	-2.23	-0.46	-0.51	-1.04	-0.90	-0.70	4.58
26	Railway transportation and telegraph	5.20	0.18	-0.17	0.20	1.47	0.47	—	7.34
27	Water transport	5.98	-2.04	-0.48	-0.18	0.37	-0.13	—	3.52
28	Motor transport	6.91	-1.92	-0.44	-0.50	-1.23	-0.13	-0.58	2.12
29	Urban and suburban transportation	1.59	-0.59	-0.28	-0.05	-1.17	-0.55	0.28	-0.76
30	Storage	1.96	0.67	0.05	-0.10	-0.20	-0.14	-0.12	2.13
31	Broadcasting	7.65	-2.62	-0.98	3.59	-1.74	-0.60	-1.45	3.85
32	Telephones	8.46	-0.21	-0.06	-4.31	-1.05	-0.85	-1.27	4.72
33	Electric power	6.77	-0.47	-0.44	-0.09	-0.81	-1.08	-1.16	2.72
34	Gas distribution	8.81	-0.01	0.03	-0.22	-0.17	-0.54	-2.15	5.15
35	Trade	5.56	-0.37	-0.12	-0.07	-1.40	-0.06	0.20	3.75
36	Finance, insurance, and real estate	4.67	-0.75	-0.11	-0.80	-1.00	-0.22	-0.67	1.13
37	Commercial services	5.77	-0.98	-0.34	-0.16	-2.29	-0.25	-0.96	0.79

Table 5-22. *Breakdown of the average of annual rates of growth of new MFP, 1973–80*

		Output	Inter-mediate input	Imports	Govern-ment	Labour	CCA	Capital	MFP rate
01	Agriculture and fishing	2.00	-0.97	-0.15	0.01	-0.04	-0.96	-0.63	-0.74
02	Forestry	0.71	-0.02	-0.04	0.07	0.43	-0.22	-0.05	0.88
03	Mines, quarries, and oil wells	0.71	-4.26	-0.29	-0.12	-0.45	-0.66	-1.61	-6.68
04	Food and beverages	2.33	-1.68	-0.16	—	-0.04	-0.02	-0.19	0.25
05	Tobacco products	1.03	0.68	-0.29	—	0.32	-0.02	0.13	1.86
06	Rubber and plastic products	2.61	-1.75	-0.43	-0.03	-0.36	-0.16	-0.28	-0.40
07	Leather	1.24	0.18	-0.03	0.01	0.55	-0.03	-0.01	1.91
08	Textiles	1.17	—	-0.03	—	0.61	-0.01	-0.06	1.70
09	Knitting mills	2.02	0.92	0.19	0.03	1.13	0.04	0.05	4.37
10	Clothing	1.54	0.46	0.03	0.01	0.53	-0.01	-0.15	2.42
11	Woods	2.96	-0.51	-0.18	-0.04	-0.08	-0.17	-0.41	1.56
12	Furniture and fixtures	-0.10	0.10	-0.07	—	0.01	-0.04	-0.19	-0.29
13	Paper and allied industries	2.03	-1.64	-0.36	—	-0.31	-0.12	-0.11	-0.53
14	Printing, publishing, and allied industries	4.56	-1.55	-0.29	-0.03	-0.68	-0.07	-0.32	1.61
15	Primary metals	0.65	-1.03	-0.51	-0.02	-0.22	-0.16	-0.08	-1.37
16	Metal fabricating	1.49	-0.20	-0.26	-0.01	-0.27	-0.06	-0.25	0.44
17	Machinery	6.45	-1.34	-1.74	-0.05	-1.03	-0.10	-0.53	1.65
18	Transportation equipment	—	-0.10	0.19	—	0.12	-0.07	-0.24	-0.11
19	Electrical products	1.63	0.43	-0.85	—	0.37	-0.06	-0.24	1.28
20	Nonmetallic mineral products	0.28	-0.82	-0.23	-0.02	0.26	-0.23	-0.37	-1.12
21	Petroleum and coal products	2.99	-6.94	2.31	0.47	-0.23	-0.12	-0.06	-1.59

22	Chemical and chemical products	4.22	−3.39	−0.62	−0.07	−0.22	−0.55	−0.67	−1.31
23	Miscellaneous manufacturing	1.36	−0.47	−0.89	—	−0.09	−0.04	−0.10	−0.24
24	Construction	2.55	−1.08	−0.26	−0.11	−0.36	−0.08	−0.31	0.37
25	Air transportation and other utilities and transportation	3.61	−1.98	−0.05	−0.15	−1.44	−0.86	−0.31	−1.17
26	Railway transportation and telegraph	3.11	−1.88	0.02	1.66	0.45	−0.08	0.01	3.29
27	Water transport	−0.28	1.48	0.46	0.05	−0.02	0.09	−0.02	1.78
28	Motor transport	4.86	−1.62	−0.13	−0.17	−1.32	−0.17	−0.65	0.80
29	Urban and suburban transportation	2.16	−1.91	−0.25	−0.24	−4.34	−2.12	5.76	−0.93
30	Storage	3.74	−1.02	−0.11	−0.06	0.40	−0.59	−0.40	1.96
31	Broadcasting	7.39	−2.38	−0.25	2.99	−2.33	−0.67	−1.40	3.34
32	Telephones	10.61	−0.61	−0.09	−0.35	−1.12	−0.98	−1.30	6.15
33	Electric power	5.57	−0.90	−0.52	−0.11	−1.07	−1.92	−1.54	−0.49
34	Gas distribution	4.20	−0.68	—	0.22	−0.67	−0.60	−1.57	0.90
35	Trade	2.77	−0.83	−0.04	−0.12	−1.22	−0.10	−0.27	0.20
36	Finance, insurance, and real estate	5.19	−1.04	−0.11	−0.73	−0.91	−0.49	−1.46	0.45
37	Commercial services	6.21	−1.22	−0.15	−0.09	−2.62	−0.50	−1.33	0.30

Table 5-23. *Example: Industry 21, petroleum and coal products, 1973-80*

	(1) Traditional	(2) New	(3) New Industry	Input effect
Output	2.99	2.99	03	−2.62
Intermediate input	−4.27	−6.94	14	0.01
Imports	2.31	2.31	22	−0.03
Government	0.47	0.47	24	0.02
Labour	−0.23	−0.23	25	−0.03
CCA	−0.13	−0.12	26	0.01
Capital	−0.06	−0.06	31	0.01
MFP rate	1.07	−1.59	32	0.01
			Total	−2.63
			Own effect =	1.04
			MFP =	−1.59

Multifactor productivity, measures of structural change, and the productivity of labour

A   Structural change

We saw previously that the rate of growth of multifactor productivity can be expressed as an index of structural change when the discrete terms in the original Leontief formulation are replaced by their continuous analogues. In this section we show that this result is also valid for the discrete data when Törnquist indexes are used. We formulate the Törnquist approximation to the MFP index and from it derive the index of structural change.

The Törnquist index of the traditional MFP measure for the ith industry between any two adjacent years, say, 1 and 2, is

$$t_i^* = \ln \frac{g_i^2}{g_i^1} - \sum_j \frac{u_{ji}^1 + u_{ji}^2}{2} \ln \frac{g_{ji}^2}{g_{ji}^1}$$
$$- \sum_l \frac{u_{li}^1 + u_{li}^2}{2} \ln \frac{yc_{li}^2}{yc_{li}^1} - \sum_p \frac{u_{pi}^1 + u_{pi}^2}{2} \ln \frac{yp_{pi}^2}{yp_{pi}^1} \qquad (6\text{-}1)$$

where, as before, the u_{ji}'s, u_{li}'s, and u_{pi}'s are the shares of intermediate, durable capital, and primary inputs, respectively, in total output. Substituting the I/O relationships in equation (6-1), we write

$$t_i^* = \ln \frac{g_i^2}{g_i^1} - \sum_j \bar{u}_{ji} \ln \frac{a_{ji}^2 g_i^2}{a_{ji}^1 g_i^1} - \sum_l \bar{u}_{li} \ln \frac{ec_{li}^2 g_i^2}{ec_{li}^1 g_i^1} - \sum \bar{u}_{pi} \ln \frac{ep_{pi}^2 g_i^2}{ep_{pi}^1 g_i^1}$$
$$= - \sum_j \bar{u}_{ji} \ln \frac{a_{ji}^2}{a_{ji}^1} - \sum_l u_{li} \ln \frac{ec_{li}^2}{ec_{li}^1} - \sum_p u_{pi} \ln \frac{ep_{pi}^2}{ep_{pi}^1} \qquad (6\text{-}2)$$

with the obvious substitution for the u's; equation (6-2) is the Törnquist index of structural change corresponding to the continuous Divisia index of equation (4-9).

Leontief described structural change as "a change in the structural (flow) matrix of the system".[1] However, the structural matrix of the present study is more complete because in addition to the changes in the flow structure

---

[1] Leontief, *Studies in the Structure of the American Economy,* 19.

of the economy, it reflects the changes in its capital structure.[2] The new formulation of MFP is also a departure for Leontief's analysis, which was based on the assumption that

the individual industries are structurally independent of each other in the sense that the technical possibility of substituting a new set of coefficients in any one column of [a] given structural matrix is in no way conditioned by the changes which might take place in any other column of the same matrix. This assumption should, of course, be interpreted as an empirical requirement which has to be satisfied by the industrial classification in terms of which the structural changes are actually analyzed. (p. 34)

The new formulation of structural change, starting from the Törnquist index of the new MFP, is

$$
\begin{aligned}
h_i^* = \ln \frac{g_i^2}{g_i^1} &- \sum_j \overline{ua}_{ji}\left(\ln \frac{a_{ji}^2 g_i^2}{a_{ji}^1 g_i^1} - \ln \frac{h_j^2}{h_j^1}\right) - \sum_j ud_{ji}\left(\ln \frac{ed_{ji}^2 g_i^2}{ed_{ji}^1 g_i^1} - \ln \frac{h_j^2}{h_j^1}\right) \\
&- \sum_j \overline{uk}_{ji}\left(\ln \frac{ek_{ji}^2 g_i^2}{ek_{ji}^1 g_i^1} - \ln \frac{h_j^2}{h_j^1}\right) - \overline{uf}_{ii}\left(\ln \frac{ef_{ii}^2 g_i^2}{ef_{ii}^1 g_i^1} - \ln \frac{h_i^2}{h_i^1}\right) \\
&- \sum_j \overline{ur}_{ji}\left(\ln \frac{er_{ji}^2 g_i^2}{er_{ji}^1 g_i^1} - \ln \frac{h_j^2}{h_j^1}\right) - \sum_p \overline{up}_{pi} \ln \frac{ep_{pi}^2 g_i^2}{ep_{pi}^1 g_i^1} \\
= &- \sum_j \overline{ua}_{ji}\left(\ln \frac{a_{ji}^2}{a_{ji}^1} - \ln \frac{h_j^2}{h_j^1}\right) - \sum_j \overline{ud}_{ji}\left(\ln \frac{ed_{ji}^2}{ed_{ji}^1} - \ln \frac{h_j^2}{h_j^1}\right) \\
&- \sum_j \overline{uk}_{ji}\left(\ln \frac{ek_{ji}^2}{ek_{ji}^1} - \ln \frac{h_j^2}{h_j^1}\right) - \overline{uf}_{ii} \ln \frac{ef_{ii}^2}{ef_{ii}^1} - \ln \frac{h_i^2}{h_i^1} \\
&- \sum_j \overline{ur}_{ji}\left(\ln \frac{er_{ji}^2}{er_{ji}^1} - \ln \frac{h_j^2}{h_j^1}\right) - \sum_p up_{pi} \ln \frac{ep_{pi}^2}{ep_{pi}^1}
\end{aligned} \tag{6-3}
$$

for $j = 1, \ldots, 37$ and $p = 1, \ldots, 10$. The new measures of the rate of structural change depend, indirectly, on variations in the coefficients of supplying industries.

When the rate of growth of the MFP is expressed as an index of structural change, the output variable vanishes explicitly from the decomposition analysis. There matter only changes in technical input–output coefficients or input per unit of output. Hence, a positive rate of growth of the index of structural change between two periods indicates the feasibility of producing a given bundle of industry final outputs with smaller gross outputs because of net declines in the required amounts of intermediate and/or capital inputs or other inputs. Leontief argues: "A reduction in any one or more coefficients, with the rest of the structural matrix

---

[2] Leontief, ibid., considered this omission "a very serious limitation" (p. 27) of his early study.

remaining the same, will always result in a more efficient allocation of resources" (p. 32).

Tables 6-1 to 6-5 show the input breakdown of the traditional measures of MFP. For the period 1961-80, one result is obvious. The (weighted) rate of growth of hours worked per unit of gross output has been negative in all industries (excluding urban and suburban transport). Thus, since the weights are always positive, it appears there have been widespread savings in labour input per unit of output throughout industries in the private sector. This is equivalent to increases in labour productivity. Note that, in fact, this is the case in every subperiod with the exception of the last one (1973-80), where seven industries show declines in labour productivity. However, even this is not a relatively bad performance, for the productivity of other inputs was even lower in this subperiod.

The weighted rate of growth of government input per unit of output has also been negative for all but five industries. Three of these are subsidized industries whose subsidies have apparently grown over time. It appears that for most industries, the relative importance of the government input–output coefficient has been slowly declining over the period.

The (weighted) rate of growth of the capital input–output coefficient is also negative for all but nine industries. Thus, again, in this sense there can be said to be productivity gains for capital inputs.

The situation is different regarding intermediate inputs and (intermediate) imported inputs. There have been some savings in domestic intermediate inputs. This is reflected in the weighted negative rate of growth of intermediate inputs required per unit of output. However, the part of these inputs that is imported from abroad has continued to grow. Hence, the sum of these two columns would show whether, on balance, there has been net savings on the use of intermediate input, both domestic and imported. It seems that for many industries the use of intermediate inputs has been increasing over the period.

Compared to the other periods, the period 1973-80 was considerably less efficient especially with regard to imports, capital consumption allowances, and capital inputs. This can easily be seen by the fewer positive signs in these columns. However, again it seems that the labour coefficients underwent consistent reductions throughout many industries even during this period.

B   Rate of growth of labour productivity

A very appealing by-product of the development of measures of MFP is the insights they give into the determinants of the growth of labour productivity. Under the assumption of constant returns to scale and competitive market conditions, the share of the factor inputs add to 1 and

Table 6-1. *Breakdown of the average of annual rates of growth of traditional MFP as an index of structural change, 1961–71*

		Coefficient							
		Inter-mediate input	Imports	Govern-ment	Labour	CCA	Capital	MFP rate
01	Agriculture and fishing	0.14	−0.05	0.09	1.31	0.43	0.39	2.31
02	Forestry	−0.34	−0.15	0.05	2.01	−0.13	−0.02	1.42
03	Mines, quarries, and oil wells	−0.57	−0.13	−0.04	1.09	−0.22	−0.43	−0.30
04	Food and beverages	−0.07	0.09	0.02	0.57	−0.02	0.03	0.63
05	Tobacco products	0.09	0.01	0.01	0.62	−0.03	0.37	1.07
06	Rubber and plastic products	0.83	−0.12	0.06	1.50	0.12	0.42	2.81
07	Leather	0.49	−0.51	–	1.01	−0.01	0.05	1.02
08	Textiles	0.27	0.19	0.03	1.65	0.15	0.29	2.57
09	Knitting mills	0.77	−0.54	0.06	1.68	0.11	0.31	2.40
10	Clothing	5.35	0.07	0.01	1.04	0.02	0.11	0.61
11	Woods	−0.30	−0.15	−0.05	0.92	−0.04	−0.08	0.30
12	Furniture and fixtures	0.04	−0.15	–	1.18	0.01	−0.07	1.01
13	Paper and allied industries	−0.14	−0.08	0.02	0.65	−0.13	−0.09	0.22
14	Printing, publishing, and allied industries	−0.37	−0.04	0.03	0.93	−0.02	−0.05	0.48
15	Primary metals	−0.03	−0.06	0.02	0.55	0.02	0.09	0.59
16	Metal fabricating	0.37	−0.08	0.03	1.08	0.09	0.19	1.68
17	Machinery	−0.23	−0.55	0.05	1.16	0.03	0.36	0.81
18	Transportation equipment	0.60	−1.01	0.11	1.70	0.10	0.35	1.85

19	Electrical products	0.30	−0.08	0.05	1.22	0.02	0.31	1.82
20	Nonmetallic mineral products	—	0.14	0.05	1.11	0.04	0.12	1.45
21	Petroleum and coal products	0.39	0.23	0.02	0.28	0.05	0.14	1.11
22	Chemical and chemical products	0.22	—	0.06	0.85	−0.01	0.04	1.16
23	Miscellaneous manufacturing	0.03	−0.28	0.01	1.34	−0.02	0.02	1.10
24	Construction	−0.25	−0.04	−0.06	1.12	0.05	0.06	0.88
25	Air transportation and other utilities and transportation	−0.06	−0.06	0.06	1.39	0.39	0.73	2.45
26	Railway transportation and telegraph	0.93	−0.06	0.03	4.29	1.21	0.04	6.44
27	Water transport	−0.01	0.11	−0.05	2.23	0.21	0.16	2.65
28	Motor transport	−0.92	−0.18	0.21	1.30	0.06	0.24	0.71
29	Urban and suburban transportation	−0.37	−0.08	0.07	−0.37	−0.76	0.41	−1.09
30	Storage	0.52	0.05	−0.06	0.76	−0.16	−0.18	0.94
31	Broadcasting	0.39	−0.48	0.01	2.80	−0.17	−0.51	2.04
32	Telephones	0.48	0.03	0.12	1.97	0.20	0.58	3.37
33	Electric power	−0.05	−0.33	0.03	0.37	−0.04	0.08	0.07
34	Gas distribution	0.70	0.16	0.31	2.26	0.18	1.08	4.69
35	Trade	0.42	—	0.15	1.44	0.03	0.57	2.61
36	Finance, insurance, and real estate	−0.16	−0.01	0.01	0.04	—	0.07	−0.05
37	Commercial services	−0.16	−0.14	0.01	0.48	−0.11	−0.46	−0.38

Table 6-2. Breakdown of the average of annual rates of growth of traditional MFP as an index of structural change, 1971–80

	Coefficient						MFP rate
	Intermediate input	Imports	Government	Labour	CCA	Capital	
01 Agriculture and fishing	−0.69	−0.13	−0.02	0.40	−0.60	0.28	−0.75
02 Forestry	−0.87	−0.03	0.01	1.34	−0.06	0.12	0.51
03 Mines, quarries, and oil wells	−2.73	−0.19	−0.09	0.22	−0.34	−0.75	−3.88
04 Food and beverages	0.03	−0.09	0.01	0.36	0.02	−0.02	0.31
05 Tobacco products	1.88	−0.33	0.01	0.46	—	0.18	2.20
06 Rubber and plastic products	−0.27	0.08	0.04	0.61	—	−0.02	0.43
07 Leather	−0.15	0.18	0.02	0.87	−0.02	−0.01	0.89
08 Textiles	0.38	0.16	0.03	0.94	0.09	0.04	1.65
09 Knitting mills	1.49	0.25	0.05	1.58	0.08	0.05	3.50
10 Clothing	0.37	0.12	0.02	1.15	0.01	−0.14	1.53
11 Woods	−0.01	−0.09	0.01	0.63	−0.05	−0.18	0.31
12 Furniture and fixtures	0.02	−0.10	0.03	0.37	−0.01	−0.05	0.26
13 Paper and allied industries	−0.11	−0.16	0.04	0.51	0.08	−0.05	0.35
14 Printing, publishing, and allied industries	0.34	−0.09	0.08	1.26	0.05	0.26	1.90
15 Primary metals	0.74	−0.43	—	0.17	−0.08	—	0.41
16 Metal fabricating	0.42	−0.11	0.02	0.50	—	0.01	0.84
17 Machinery	0.83	−0.49	0.03	0.99	0.05	0.14	1.55
18 Transportation equipment	0.31	—	0.02	0.25	−0.03	—	0.53

19	Electrical products	1.03	−0.51	0.03	1.23	0.01	0.05	1.85
20	Nonmetallic mineral products	−0.04	−0.18	0.02	0.58	−0.11	−0.05	0.22
21	Petroleum and coal products	−1.91	2.58	0.21	0.09	−0.01	−0.05	0.92
22	Chemical and chemical products	−0.63	−0.11	0.04	0.89	−0.15	−0.20	−0.16
23	Miscellaneous manufacturing	0.10	−0.66	0.03	0.57	0.02	0.09	0.16
24	Construction	0.20	−0.10	0.03	0.36	−0.04	−0.06	0.39
25	Air transportation and other utilities and transportation	−0.47	0.06	0.13	0.13	0.01	0.51	0.37
26	Railway transportation and telegraph	−0.79	0.09	1.19	2.44	0.45	−0.08	3.31
27	Water transport	−0.47	0.11	−0.07	0.88	0.21	–	0.65
28	Motor transport	0.20	0.01	0.11	0.62	−0.05	−0.20	0.69
29	Urban and suburban transportation	−1.50	−0.34	−0.13	−0.91	−1.07	2.78	−1.17
30	Storage	−0.17	0.02	0.32	1.49	−0.27	0.10	1.48
31	Broadcasting	0.58	−0.05	0.06	2.48	−0.14	−0.20	2.73
32	Telephones	0.40	0.01	0.17	2.50	0.76	1.26	5.11
33	Electric power	0.34	−0.03	0.06	0.64	−0.09	0.10	1.01
34	Gas distribution	0.03	0.04	0.15	0.31	0.01	0.36	0.91
35	Trade	−0.13	0.01	0.03	0.48	–	0.30	0.68
36	Finance, insurance, and real estate	−0.15	−0.07	0.05	0.07	−0.02	0.01	−0.10
37	Commercial services	0.35	0.06	0.06	0.46	−0.22	−0.58	0.12

Table 6-3. *Breakdown of the average of annual rates of growth of traditional MFP as an index of structural change, 1961–80*

	Coefficient						
	Inter-mediate input	Imports	Govern-ment	Labour	CCA	Capital	MFP rate
01 Agriculture and fishing	-0.25	-0.09	0.04	0.88	-0.06	0.34	0.86
02 Forestry	-0.59	-0.10	0.03	1.69	-0.09	0.04	0.99
03 Mines, quarries, and oil wells	-1.60	-0.16	-0.06	0.68	-0.27	-0.58	-2.00
04 Food and beverages	-0.02	0.01	0.02	0.47	–	0.01	0.48
05 Tobacco products	0.94	-0.15	0.01	0.54	-0.02	0.28	1.61
06 Rubber and plastic products	0.31	-0.03	0.05	1.08	0.06	0.21	1.68
07 Leather	0.18	-0.18	0.01	0.94	-0.02	0.02	0.96
08 Textiles	0.32	0.18	0.03	1.31	0.12	0.17	2.14
09 Knitting mills	1.11	-0.16	0.06	1.64	0.10	0.19	2.92
10 Clothing	-0.17	0.09	0.01	1.10	0.02	–	1.05
11 Woods	-0.17	-0.12	-0.02	0.79	-0.04	0.13	0.30
12 Furniture and fixtures	0.03	-0.13	0.01	0.80	–	-0.06	0.66
13 Paper and allied industries	-0.13	-0.12	0.03	0.59	-0.03	-0.06	0.28
14 Printing, publishing, and allied industries	-0.03	-0.07	0.06	1.08	0.02	0.09	1.15
15 Primary metals	0.34	-0.23	0.01	0.37	-0.03	0.05	0.51
16 Metal fabricating	0.40	-0.10	0.03	0.81	0.04	0.11	1.28
17 Machinery	0.27	-0.52	0.04	1.08	0.04	0.26	1.16
18 Transportation equipment	0.46	-0.53	0.06	1.01	0.04	0.18	1.22

19	Electrical products	0.65	−0.28	0.04	1.22	0.02	0.19	1.83
20	Nonmetallic mineral products	−0.02	−0.01	0.03	0.86	−0.03	0.04	0.87
21	Petroleum and coal products	−0.70	1.34	0.11	0.19	0.02	0.05	1.02
22	Chemical and chemical products	−0.18	−0.05	0.05	0.87	−0.07	−0.07	0.54
23	Miscellaneous manufacturing	0.07	−0.46	0.02	0.98	–	0.05	0.65
24	Construction	−0.03	−0.07	−0.02	0.76	0.01	–	0.65
25	Air transportation and other utilities and transportation	−0.26	–	0.10	0.79	0.21	0.62	1.47
26	Railway transportation and telegraph	0.11	0.01	0.58	3.41	0.85	−0.02	4.95
27	Water transport	−0.23	0.11	−0.06	1.59	0.21	0.09	1.71
28	Motor transport	−0.39	−0.09	0.16	0.98	0.01	0.03	0.70
29	Urban and suburban transportation	−0.90	−0.20	−0.03	−0.62	−0.91	1.53	−1.13
30	Storage	0.19	0.04	0.12	1.10	−0.21	−0.05	1.19
31	Broadcasting	0.48	−0.28	0.03	2.65	−0.16	−0.36	2.37
32	Telephones	0.44	0.02	0.14	2.22	0.47	0.98	4.19
33	Electric power	0.13	−0.19	0.05	0.50	−0.07	0.09	0.52
34	Gas distribution	0.38	0.10	0.24	1.34	0.10	0.74	2.90
35	Trade	0.16	–	0.09	0.99	0.01	0.44	1.69
36	Finance, insurance, and real estate	−0.15	−0.04	0.03	0.05	−0.01	0.04	−0.07
37	Commercial services	0.08	−0.04	0.04	0.47	−0.16	−0.52	−0.14

Table 6-4. *Breakdown of the average of annual rates of growth of traditional MFP as an index of structural change, 1961–73*

		Coefficient						MFP rate
		Inter-mediate input	Imports	Govern-ment	Labour	CCA	Capital	
01	Agriculture and fishing	-0.30	-0.11	0.07	1.24	0.29	0.61	1.80
02	Forestry	-0.93	-0.15	–	2.26	-0.04	0.09	1.23
03	Mines, quarries, and oil wells	-0.32	-0.10	-0.05	1.29	-0.07	-0.06	0.69
04	Food and beverages	–	-0.02	0.02	0.55	-0.02	0.02	0.55
05	Tobacco products	0.87	-0.09	0.02	0.58	-0.03	0.37	1.71
06	Rubber and plastic products	0.83	-0.06	0.07	1.46	0.13	0.42	2.85
07	Leather	0.04	-0.41	–	0.94	-0.02	0.03	0.57
08	Textiles	0.42	0.14	0.04	1.53	0.17	0.30	2.60
09	Knitting mills	1.07	-0.56	0.06	1.58	0.10	0.23	2.49
10	Clothing	-0.49	-0.04	0.01	1.12	0.03	0.08	0.71
11	Woods	-0.65	-0.18	-0.03	0.78	-0.03	-0.05	-0.15
12	Furniture and fixtures	0.14	-0.15	0.02	1.27	0.03	0.02	1.33
13	Paper and allied industries	0.16	-0.07	0.03	0.79	-0.06	-0.05	0.81
14	Printing, publishing, and allied industries	-0.15	-0.09	0.05	1.10	–	0.04	0.96
15	Primary metals	-0.03	-0.13	0.02	0.64	0.03	0.10	0.64
16	Metal fabricating	0.22	-0.08	0.04	1.16	0.09	0.24	1.67
17	Machinery	-0.10	-0.63	0.05	1.18	0.05	0.39	0.94
18	Transportation equipment	0.80	-0.95	0.10	1.54	0.11	0.41	2.01

19	Electrical products	0.46	−0.11	0.05	1.44	0.04	0.35	2.22
20	Nonmetallic mineral products	0.12	0.11	0.06	1.17	0.08	0.25	1.78
21	Petroleum and coal products	0.38	0.05	0.03	0.35	0.06	0.12	0.99
22	Chemical and chemical products	0.30	−0.06	0.07	1.01	0.04	0.11	1.47
23	Miscellaneous manufacturing	0.08	−0.35	0.03	1.34	—	0.08	1.19
24	Construction	−0.12	−0.06	−0.04	0.90	0.03	0.08	0.79
25	Air transportation and other utilities and transportation	−0.07	−0.05	0.13	1.52	0.54	0.92	2.99
26	Railway transportation and telegraph	0.78	−0.04	0.01	4.21	1.09	0.03	6.08
27	Water transport	−0.86	−0.09	−0.11	2.55	0.30	0.12	1.91
28	Motor transport	−0.60	−0.19	0.17	1.19	0.03	0.14	0.76
29	Urban and suburban transportation	−0.74	−0.24	0.03	−0.01	−0.61	0.23	−1.33
30	Storage	0.50	0.09	0.03	0.55	−0.17	−0.11	0.89
31	Broadcasting	0.46	−0.59	−0.01	3.07	−0.19	−0.53	2.22
32	Telephones	0.46	0.02	0.10	1.88	0.24	0.65	3.34
33	Electric power	0.14	−0.18	0.09	0.66	0.13	0.28	1.12
34	Gas distribution	0.71	0.13	0.31	1.92	0.16	0.99	4.22
35	Trade	0.42	—	0.15	1.40	0.04	0.67	2.69
36	Finance, insurance, and real estate	−0.22	−0.05	0.02	−0.01	−0.01	0.05	−0.20
37	Commercial services	−0.09	−0.12	0.02	0.50	−0.12	−0.49	−0.29

Table 6-5. *Breakdown of the average of annual rates of growth of traditional MFP as an index of structural change, 1973–80*

		Coefficient						MFP rate
		Inter-mediate input	Imports	Govern-ment	Labour	CCA	Capital	
01	Agriculture and fishing	-0.17	-0.06	-0.02	0.27	-0.66	-0.13	-0.76
02	Forestry	-0.01	–	0.09	0.72	-0.19	-0.03	0.58
03	Mines, quarries, and oil wells	-3.78	-0.26	-0.09	-0.37	-0.62	-1.48	-6.60
04	Food and beverages	-0.06	0.06	0.01	0.33	0.02	-0.01	0.35
05	Tobacco products	1.07	-0.26	0.01	0.48	–	0.13	1.43
06	Rubber and plastic products	-0.59	0.04	0.01	0.42	-0.05	-0.15	-0.32
07	Leather	0.44	0.21	0.03	0.95	-0.01	–	1.63
08	Textiles	0.15	0.24	0.02	0.95	0.03	-0.05	1.34
09	Knitting mills	1.18	0.51	0.04	1.73	0.08	0.11	3.66
10	Clothing	0.38	0.31	0.02	1.06	–	0.14	1.63
11	Woods	0.66	-0.02	–	0.79	-0.07	-0.27	1.08
12	Furniture and fixtures	-0.15	-0.08	–	-0.02	-0.05	-0.20	-0.49
13	Paper and allied industries	-0.62	-0.22	0.03	0.23	0.02	-0.07	-0.62
14	Printing, publishing, and allied industries	0.18	-0.02	0.06	1.05	0.04	0.19	1.49
15	Primary metals	0.97	-0.42	-0.02	-0.09	-0.13	-0.04	0.28
16	Metal fabricating	0.69	-0.13	–	0.19	-0.04	-0.12	0.61
17	Machinery	0.90	-0.33	0.02	0.90	0.02	0.03	1.54
18	Transportation equipment	-0.14	0.19	–	0.11	-0.08	-0.21	-0.13

19	Electrical products	0.98	−0.50	0.02	0.86	−0.02	−0.09	1.16
20	Nonmetallic mineral products	−0.27	−0.22	−0.01	0.34	−0.23	−0.31	−0.70
21	Petroleum and coal products	−2.53	3.55	0.25	−0.08	−0.05	−0.07	1.07
22	Chemical and chemical products	−1.01	−0.03	0.01	0.64	−0.27	−0.38	−1.06
23	Miscellaneous manufacturing	0.04	−0.67	0.02	0.35	−0.01	0.01	−0.27
24	Construction	0.12	−0.08	0.02	0.51	−0.04	−0.13	0.40
25	Air transportation and other utilities and transportation	−0.58	0.09	0.04	−0.46	−0.35	0.11	−1.14
26	Railway transportation and telegraph	−1.03	0.11	1.56	2.05	0.44	−0.10	3.02
27	Water transport	0.86	0.44	0.03	−0.06	0.05	0.02	1.35
28	Motor transport	−0.03	0.07	0.14	0.61	−0.03	−0.15	0.60
29	Urban and suburban transportation	−1.18	−0.13	−0.13	−1.67	−1.42	3.75	−0.77
30	Storage	−0.32	−0.05	0.27	2.05	−0.29	0.06	1.71
31	Broadcasting	0.52	0.25	0.10	1.92	−0.11	−0.07	2.62
32	Telephones	0.42	0.02	0.22	2.80	0.86	1.34	5.65
33	Electric power	0.12	−0.20	−0.03	0.23	−0.41	−0.24	−0.53
34	Gas distribution	−0.17	0.05	0.11	0.34	—	0.31	0.63
35	Trade	−0.29	0.01	−0.02	0.27	−0.03	0.05	—
36	Finance, insurance, and real estate	−0.05	−0.03	0.04	0.16	−0.01	0.04	0.16
37	Commercial services	0.36	0.09	0.06	0.43	−0.24	−0.58	0.12

193

may be considered equal to the elasticities of output with respect to each factor input. Constant returns to scale also imply that the production function can be expressed in "per unit of labour input". Under these conditions, the rate of growth of labour productivity is equal to the sum of the rate of growth of traditional measures of MFP plus the weighted rate of growth of each input per unit of labour. Variations in output per hour worked, or labour productivity, can be decomposed into variations in the contribution of capital services per unit of labour, all other inputs per unit of labour, and the MFP rate. One can check to what extent variations in the rate of growth of labour productivity, in particular the post-1973 slowdown, are associated with changes in the capital–labour ratio or in the labour intensity of other inputs, rather than with changes in MFP.

From equation (4-8) one extracts the vector of labour input, and corresponding weight, from the primary input matrix E_p. The following result is obtained (see Appendix 6) using the traditional rate of growth of MFP:

$$
\begin{aligned}
\frac{d \ln l}{dt} = \text{diag}\bigg[& \hat{t}^* + \hat{p}^{-1}A'p\left(\frac{d \ln A}{dt} - \frac{d \ln L_a}{dt}\right) \\
& + \hat{p}^{-1}(E_c' \cdot W_c')\left(\frac{d \ln E_c}{dt} - \frac{d \ln L_c}{dt}\right) \\
& + \hat{p}^{-1}(E_p' \cdot W_p')\left(\frac{d \ln E_p}{dt} - \frac{d \ln L_p}{dt}\right)\bigg]
\end{aligned}
\tag{6-4}
$$

In terms of the new measures of the rate of MFP, however, the rate of growth of labour productivity is

$$
\begin{aligned}
\frac{d \ln l}{dt} = \text{diag}\bigg[& \hat{p}^{-1}A'\hat{p}\left(\frac{d \ln \hat{h}^{-1}A}{dt} - \frac{d \ln L_a}{dt}\right) \\
& + \hat{p}^{-1}(E_d' \cdot W_d')\left(\frac{d \ln \hat{h}^{-1}E_d}{dt} - \frac{d \ln L_d}{dt}\right) \\
& + \hat{p}^{-1}(E_k' \cdot W_k')\left(\frac{d \ln \hat{h}^{-1}E_k}{dt} - \frac{d \ln L_k}{dt}\right) \\
& + \hat{p}^{-1}(E_f' \cdot W_f')\left(\frac{d \ln \hat{h}^{-1}E_f}{dt} - \frac{d \ln L_f}{dt}\right) \\
& + \hat{p}^{-1}(E_r' \cdot W_r')\left(\frac{d \ln \hat{h}^{-1}E_r}{dt} - \frac{d \ln L_r}{dt}\right) \\
& + \hat{p}^{-1}(E_p' \cdot W_p')\left(\frac{d \ln E_p}{dt} - \frac{d \ln L_p}{dt}\right)\bigg]\hat{h}^*
\end{aligned}
\tag{6-5}
$$

where L_a, L_d, L_k, L_f, L_r, and L_p are matrices whose rows are all equal to the vector of labour input by industry and whose size is equal to that of the matrix from which they are subtracted. Putting all the $\hat{h}$'s together in (6-5) and substituting for the h^*'s in terms of the t^*'s, we write

$$
\frac{d \ln l}{dt} = \text{diag} \left[\hat{t}^* + \hat{p}^{-1} A' p \left(\frac{d \ln A}{dt} - \frac{d \ln L_a}{dt} \right) \right.
$$

$$
+ \hat{p}^{-1} (E_d' \cdot W_d') \left(\frac{d \ln E_d}{dt} - \frac{d \ln L_d}{dt} \right)
$$

$$
+ \hat{p}^{-1} (E_k' \cdot W_k') \left(\frac{d \ln E_k}{dt} - \frac{d \ln L_k}{dt} \right)
$$

$$
+ \hat{p}^{-1} (E_f' \cdot W_f') \left(\frac{d \ln E_f}{dt} - \frac{d \ln L_f}{dt} \right)
$$

$$
+ \hat{p}^{-1} (E_r' \cdot W_r') \left(\frac{d \ln E_r}{dt} - \frac{d \ln L_r}{dt} \right)
$$

$$
\left. + \hat{p}^{-1} (E_p' \cdot W_p') \left(\frac{d \ln E_p}{dt} - \frac{d \ln L_p}{dt} \right) \right] \qquad (6\text{-}6)
$$

Equation (6-6) can be further simplified and can, of course, be made equal to equation (6-4). Thus, the same rate of growth of labour productivity can be expressed in terms of *both* MFP rates. These formulae are equivalent to the more familiar ones that show the rate of growth of MFP plus the weighted rate of growth of other inputs per unit of labour. We have only made use of the I/O relations. The rate of growth of labour productivity is invariant with respect to the rate of growth of MFP. However, its breakdown between the contribution of inputs and of MFP is affected. When the new measures are used, the contribution of MFP is higher but all produced inputs taken together contribute just that much less. In this context, it is perhaps easier to see the difference between the two concepts of technical change. The difference concerns the interaction between technical change and produced inputs. The new concept embodies all technical change in the intermediate and capital outputs of the industries where it takes place. Thus, it provides a measure of the interconnectedness of technical change throughout industries, which is exactly what the decomposition of the labour productivity rate shows. The *same* rate of growth of labour productivity is associated with either a relatively lower traditional rate of MFP and a higher input intensity per unit of labour or a relatively higher rate of new MFP and lower rates of intensity per unit of labour for the primary inputs involved in the production of intermediate and capital inputs.

Tables 6-6 to 6-10 show the decomposition of the average annual rate of growth of labour productivity in relation to the average annual rate of growth of traditional MFP measures. The headings of the columns

Table 6-6. *Breakdown of the average of annual rates of growth of labour productivity in terms of traditional MFP, 1961–71*

		Q/L	=	Int/L	+	M/L	+	G/L	+	CCA/L	+	K/L	+	MFP rate
01	Agriculture and fishing	7.06		2.28		0.32		0.14		0.77		1.25		2.31
02	Forestry	5.23		2.62		0.37		0.15		0.41		0.25		1.42
03	Mines, quarries, and oil wells	4.72		1.99		0.32		0.15		0.73		1.83		−0.30
04	Food and beverages	3.49		2.31		0.19		–		0.09		0.27		0.63
05	Tobacco products	4.46		2.94		0.13		0.03		0.12		0.16		1.07
06	Rubber and plastic products	5.34		1.32		0.94		0.02		0.08		0.18		2.81
07	Leather	2.89		0.74		0.98		0.04		0.06		0.05		1.02
08	Textiles	6.39		2.38		1.10		0.05		0.11		0.17		2.57
09	Knitting mills	6.18		2.34		1.26		0.01		0.06		0.12		2.40
10	Clothing	3.22		2.07		0.45		0.02		0.01		0.07		0.61
11	Woods	3.26		2.17		0.31		0.10		0.14		0.24		0.30
12	Furniture and fixtures	3.44		1.54		0.47		0.05		0.04		0.33		1.01
13	Paper and allied industries	2.65		1.52		0.23		0.03		0.32		0.33		0.22
14	Printing, publishing, and allied industries	2.24		1.24		0.13		0.03		0.08		0.28		0.48
15	Primary metals	2.80		1.57		0.39		0.02		0.13		0.09		0.59
16	Metal fabricating	3.47		1.24		0.38		0.01		–		0.16		1.68
17	Machinery	3.73		1.62		1.08		0.01		0.04		0.17		0.81
18	Transportation equipment	7.52		2.42		3.02		−0.01		0.04		0.17		1.85
19	Electrical products	3.87		1.34		0.58		0.01		0.06		0.06		1.82
20	Nonmetallic mineral products	3.93		1.66		0.17		0.06		0.19		0.39		1.45
21	Petroleum and coal products	3.91		1.58		1.08		0.02		0.09		0.04		1.11
22	Chemical and chemical products	3.84		1.56		0.44		0.03		0.21		0.43		1.16

23	Miscellaneous manufacturing	3.99	1.55	0.82	0.06	0.12	0.33	1.10
24	Construction	3.22	1.77	0.24	0.24	0.01	0.08	0.88
25	Air transportation and other utilities and transportation	5.65	1.62	0.27	0.28	0.62	0.40	2.45
26	Railway transportation and telegraph	8.11	1.34	0.26	−0.34	0.38	0.04	6.44
27	Water transport	6.02	2.49	0.27	0.10	0.43	0.08	2.65
28	Motor transport	3.70	2.16	0.31	0.16	0.06	0.30	0.71
29	Urban and suburban transportation	−0.51	0.30	0.07	−0.09	0.68	−0.38	−1.09
30	Storage	1.97	−0.03	−0.01	0.20	0.25	0.63	0.94
31	Broadcasting	4.35	2.16	0.68	−2.10	0.46	1.11	2.04
32	Telephones	5.71	0.20	0.02	0.16	0.78	1.19	3.37
33	Electric power	1.94	0.30	0.36	0.03	0.50	0.68	0.07
34	Gas distribution	9.72	0.33	−0.05	0.27	0.85	3.64	4.69
35	Trade	2.90	0.37	0.06	−0.03	0.06	−0.16	2.61
36	Finance, insurance, and real estate	0.17	0.19	0.01	0.02	0.01	−0.03	−0.05
37	Commercial services	0.99	0.43	0.17	0.02	0.15	0.59	−0.38

Table 6-7. *Breakdown of the average of annual rates of growth of labour productivity in terms of traditional MFP, 1971–80*

		Q/L	= Int/L	+ M/L	+ G/L	+ CCA/L	+ K/L	+ MFP rate
01	Agriculture and fishing	2.58	1.66	0.25	0.03	1.06	0.33	−0.75
02	Forestry	3.66	2.57	0.19	0.12	0.28	−0.01	0.51
03	Mines, quarries, and oil wells	0.59	2.92	0.22	0.12	0.46	0.74	−3.88
04	Food and beverages	2.24	1.40	0.29	—	0.03	0.21	0.31
05	Tobacco products	2.95	−0.01	0.43	0.01	0.07	0.24	2.20
06	Rubber and plastic products	2.05	1.09	0.25	—	0.09	0.19	0.43
07	Leather	2.57	1.19	0.31	0.01	0.07	0.09	0.89
08	Textiles	3.50	1.04	0.59	0.02	0.06	0.15	1.65
09	Knitting mills	5.14	0.80	0.52	—	0.06	0.26	3.50
10	Clothing	3.46	1.03	0.49	—	0.01	0.39	1.53
11	Woods	2.25	1.26	0.22	0.02	0.12	0.32	0.31
12	Furniture and fixtures	1.00	0.43	0.19	−0.01	0.03	0.12	0.26
13	Paper and allied industries	1.87	1.11	0.28	−0.01	0.07	0.06	0.35
14	Printing, publishing, and allied industries	3.21	0.90	0.27	−0.02	0.03	0.13	1.90
15	Primary metals	0.77	−0.32	0.51	0.02	0.12	0.03	0.41
16	Metal fabricating	1.59	0.32	0.24	—	0.05	0.15	0.84
17	Machinery	3.20	0.34	1.16	—	0.01	0.12	1.55
18	Transportation equipment	1.23	0.13	0.40	0.01	0.05	0.13	0.53
19	Electrical products	3.88	0.52	1.05	—	0.08	0.38	1.58
20	Nonmetallic mineral products	2.06	0.90	0.32	0.01	0.24	0.35	0.22
21	Petroleum and coal products	0.78	2.16	−2.40	0.04	0.06	0.05	0.92
22	Chemical and chemical products	4.13	2.67	0.65	−0.01	0.42	0.50	−0.16

23	Miscellaneous manufacturing	1.73	0.57	0.90	—	0.03	0.07	0.16
24	Construction	1.07	0.27	0.17	0.03	0.06	0.15	0.39
25	Air transportation and other utilities and transportation	0.61	0.59	-0.05	-0.09	0.10	-0.32	0.37
26	Railway transportation and telegraph	4.66	2.34	0.05	-1.37	0.40	-0.05	3.31
27	Water transport	2.58	1.67	0.07	0.16	0.07	-0.03	0.65
28	Motor transport	1.56	0.37	0.05	—	0.09	0.36	0.69
29	Urban and suburban transportation	-0.82	1.33	0.32	0.06	0.98	-2.35	-1.17
30	Storage	3.39	0.99	0.03	-0.02	0.55	0.36	1.48
31	Broadcasting	4.33	1.52	0.35	-1.80	0.48	1.04	2.73
32	Telephones	6.80	0.35	0.06	0.19	0.52	0.58	5.11
33	Electric power	2.89	0.09	0.20	-0.01	0.87	0.72	1.01
34	Gas distribution	1.37	0.15	-0.02	-0.14	0.18	0.29	0.91
35	Trade	0.90	0.34	0.01	0.01	0.03	-0.17	0.68
36	Finance, insurance, and real estate	0.41	0.24	0.08	-0.01	0.06	0.13	-0.10
37	Commercial services	0.94	-0.09	-0.02	-0.04	0.26	0.70	0.12

Table 6-8. *Breakdown of the average of annual rates of growth of labour productivity in terms of traditional MFP, 1961–80*

		Q/L	=	Int/L	+	M/L	+	G/L	+	CCA/L	+	K/L	+	MFP rate
01	Agriculture and fishing	4.94		1.99		0.29		0.08		0.90		0.82		0.86
02	Forestry	4.49		2.60		0.29		0.13		0.35		0.13		0.99
03	Mines, quarries, and oil wells	2.76		2.43		0.28		0.14		0.60		1.31		-2.00
04	Food and beverages	2.90		1.88		0.24		—		0.06		0.24		0.48
05	Tobacco products	3.75		1.54		0.28		0.02		0.10		0.20		1.61
06	Rubber and plastic products	3.78		1.21		0.62		0.01		0.08		0.18		1.68
07	Leather	2.74		0.95		0.66		0.03		0.07		0.07		0.96
08	Textiles	5.02		1.74		0.86		0.04		0.09		0.16		2.14
09	Knitting mills	5.69		1.61		0.91		0.01		0.06		0.19		2.92
10	Clothing	3.33		1.58		0.47		0.01		0.01		0.22		1.05
11	Woods	2.78		1.74		0.26		0.06		0.13		0.28		0.30
12	Furniture and fixtures	2.29		1.01		0.34		0.02		0.03		0.23		0.66
13	Paper and allied industries	2.28		1.33		0.26		0.01		0.20		0.20		0.28
14	Printing, publishing, and allied industries	2.70		1.08		0.20		0.01		0.05		0.21		1.15
15	Primary metals	1.84		0.68		0.45		0.02		0.13		0.06		0.51
16	Metal fabricating	2.58		0.80		0.32		0.01		0.02		0.15		1.28
17	Machinery	3.48		1.01		1.12		0.01		0.03		0.15		1.16
18	Transportation equipment	4.54		1.33		1.80		-0.01		0.04		0.15		1.22
19	Electrical products	3.88		0.95		0.80		0.01		0.07		0.21		1.83
20	Nonmetallic mineral products	3.04		1.30		0.24		0.05		0.21		0.37		0.87
21	Petroleum and coal products	2.43		1.86		-0.57		—		0.07		0.04		1.02
22	Chemical and chemical products	3.98		2.09		0.54		0.04		0.31		0.46		0.54

23	Miscellaneous manufacturing	2.92	1.09	0.86	0.03	0.08	0.21	0.65
24	Construction	2.20	1.06	0.21	0.14	0.03	0.22	0.65
25	Air transportation and other utilities and transportation	3.26	1.13	0.12	0.10	0.37	0.06	1.47
26	Railway transportation and telegraph	6.48	1.81	0.16	−0.83	0.39	−0.01	4.95
27	Water transport	4.39	2.10	0.17	0.13	0.26	0.03	1.71
28	Motor transport	2.69	1.31	0.19	0.08	0.07	0.33	0.70
29	Urban and suburban transportation	−0.65	0.79	0.19	−0.02	0.82	−1.31	−1.13
30	Storage	2.64	0.45	0.01	0.10	0.39	0.50	1.19
31	Broadcasting	4.34	1.86	0.52	−1.96	0.47	1.08	2.37
32	Telephones	6.23	0.27	0.04	0.17	0.65	0.90	4.19
33	Electric power	2.39	0.20	0.29	0.01	0.68	0.70	0.52
34	Gas distribution	5.77	0.24	−0.04	0.08	0.53	2.05	2.90
35	Trade	1.95	0.36	0.04	−0.01	0.04	−0.17	1.69
36	Finance, insurance, and real estate	0.28	0.22	0.06	0.01	0.04	0.05	−0.07
37	Commercial services	0.96	0.19	0.08	−0.01	0.20	0.64	−0.14

Table 6-9. *Breakdown of the average of annual rates of growth of labour productivity in terms of traditional MFP, 1961–73*

		Q/L	= Int/L	+ M/L	+ G/L	+ CCA/L	+ K/L	+ MFP rate
01	Agriculture and fishing	6.70	2.61	0.37	0.13	0.84	0.95	1.80
02	Forestry	5.98	3.59	0.41	0.23	0.38	0.16	1.23
03	Mines, quarries, and oil wells	5.68	2.08	0.33	0.20	0.72	1.65	0.69
04	Food and beverages	3.36	2.15	0.29	–	0.08	0.27	0.55
05	Tobacco products	4.14	1.93	0.22	0.03	0.11	0.14	1.71
06	Rubber and plastic products	5.18	1.23	0.86	0.01	0.07	0.17	2.85
07	Leather	2.71	1.11	0.86	0.04	0.07	0.06	0.57
08	Textiles	5.93	2.03	1.06	0.04	0.07	0.13	2.60
09	Knitting mills	5.79	1.81	1.24	0.01	0.06	0.19	2.49
10	Clothing	3.44	2.00	0.59	0.01	–	0.13	0.71
11	Woods	2.78	2.24	0.31	0.07	0.11	0.19	-0.15
12	Furniture and fixtures	3.73	1.56	0.51	0.03	0.03	0.28	1.33
13	Paper and allied industries	3.14	1.49	0.24	0.03	0.29	0.28	0.81
14	Printing, publishing, and allied industries	2.70	1.20	0.20	0.02	0.07	0.25	0.96
15	Primary metals	3.18	1.78	0.51	0.02	0.14	0.08	0.64
16	Metal fabricating	3.74	1.51	0.40	0.01	0.01	0.14	1.67
17	Machinery	3.80	1.51	1.21	–	0.02	0.11	0.94
18	Transportation equipment	6.87	1.92	2.86	-0.02	0.01	0.08	2.01
19	Electrical products	4.56	1.45	0.71	0.01	0.06	0.11	2.22
20	Nonmetallic mineral products	4.13	1.60	0.20	0.06	0.16	0.31	1.78
21	Petroleum and coal products	4.88	2.10	1.62	0.01	0.11	0.05	0.99
22	Chemical and chemical products	4.46	1.79	0.58	0.03	0.20	0.39	1.47

23	Miscellaneous manufacturing	4.03	1.52	0.88	0.05	0.10	0.29	1.19
24	Construction	2.61	1.36	0.22	0.19	0.01	0.04	0.79
25	Air transportation and other utilities and transportation	6.15	1.81	0.29	0.24	0.54	0.29	2.99
26	Railway transportation and telegraph	7.96	1.45	0.24	-0.28	0.45	0.02	6.08
27	Water transport	7.02	3.86	0.53	0.21	0.46	0.05	1.91
28	Motor transport	3.41	1.75	0.31	0.16	0.07	0.36	0.76
29	Urban and suburban transportation	-0.03	0.75	0.24	-0.03	0.61	-0.25	-1.33
30	Storage	1.46	-0.13	-0.06	0.07	0.23	0.46	0.89
31	Broadcasting	4.91	2.32	0.84	-2.29	0.52	1.30	2.22
32	Telephones	5.45	0.18	0.03	0.16	0.70	1.03	3.34
33	Electric power	3.15	0.29	0.28	–	0.67	0.79	1.12
34	Gas distribution	8.29	0.17	-0.04	0.18	0.72	3.04	4.22
35	Trade	2.80	0.33	0.06	-0.04	0.04	-0.28	2.69
36	Finance, insurance, and real estate	-0.04	0.21	0.05	-0.03	–	-0.06	-0.20
37	Commercial services	1.02	0.37	0.16	0.01	0.15	0.62	-0.29

Table 6-10. *Breakdown of the average of annual rates of growth of labour productivity in terms of traditional MFP, 1973–80*

		Q/L	=	Int/L	+	M/L	+	G/L	+	CCA/L	+	K/L	+	MFP rate
01	Agriculture and fishing	1.92		0.92		0.15		0.01		1.02		0.58		-0.76
02	Forestry	1.92		0.90		0.08		-0.03		0.31		0.07		0.58
03	Mines, quarries, and oil wells	-2.24		3.04		0.18		0.03		0.39		0.73		-6.60
04	Food and beverages	2.10		1.41		0.14		—		0.01		0.18		0.35
05	Tobacco products	3.07		0.89		0.37		0.02		0.08		0.30		1.43
06	Rubber and plastic products	1.39		1.16		0.20		0.01		0.11		0.21		-0.32
07	Leather	2.80		0.68		0.32		0.01		0.07		0.09		1.63
08	Textiles	3.48		1.26		0.52		0.03		0.11		0.22		1.34
09	Knitting mills	5.50		1.26		0.33		0.01		0.06		0.18		3.66
10	Clothing	3.15		0.86		0.26		—		0.02		0.38		1.63
11	Woods	2.79		0.89		0.18		0.04		0.17		0.43		1.08
12	Furniture and fixtures	-0.20		0.07		0.04		—		0.05		0.15		-0.49
13	Paper and allied industries	0.81		1.05		0.28		-0.02		0.05		0.07		-0.62
14	Printing, publishing, and allied industries	2.71		0.87		0.19		—		0.03		0.13		1.49
15	Primary metals	-0.45		-1.22		0.34		0.01		0.11		0.03		0.28
16	Metal fabricating	0.60		-0.40		0.17		—		0.05		0.17		0.61
17	Machinery	2.94		0.17		0.96		0.01		0.04		0.22		1.54
18	Transportation equipment	0.54		0.33		-0.03		0.01		0.09		0.28		-0.13
19	Electrical products	2.71		0.10		0.96		0.01		0.09		0.39		1.16
20	Nonmetallic mineral products	1.18		0.78		0.31		0.04		0.30		0.46		-0.70
21	Petroleum and coal products	-1.78		1.45		-4.35		-0.02		0.01		0.04		1.07
22	Chemical and chemical products	3.16		2.60		0.47		0.05		0.50		0.59		-1.06

204

23	Miscellaneous manufacturing	1.01	0.35	0.81	—	0.04	0.08	-0.27
24	Construction	1.50	0.55	0.18	0.05	0.06	0.25	0.40
25	Air transportation and other utilities and transportation	-1.70	-4.02	-0.17	-0.13	0.09	-0.32	-1.14
26	Railway transportation and telegraph	3.93	2.43	0.01	-1.77	0.29	-0.06	3.02
27	Water transport	-0.10	-0.29	-0.44	-0.02	-0.07	-0.01	1.35
28	Motor transport	1.46	0.57	-0.02	-0.05	0.07	0.28	0.60
29	Urban and suburban transportation	-1.73	0.87	0.11	—	1.20	-3.13	-0.77
30	Storage	4.67	1.45	0.12	0.15	0.67	0.57	1.71
31	Broadcasting	3.36	1.06	-0.02	-1.39	0.38	0.71	2.62
32	Telephones	7.56	0.42	0.06	0.19	0.58	0.66	5.65
33	Electric power	1.10	0.06	0.29	0.04	0.69	0.53	-0.53
34	Gas distribution	1.43	0.36	-0.03	-0.11	0.21	0.37	0.63
35	Trade	0.50	0.40	—	0.03	0.04	0.02	—
36	Finance, insurance, and real estate	0.84	0.23	0.04	0.07	0.10	0.24	0.16
37	Commercial services	0.86	-0.12	-0.05	-0.04	0.28	0.68	0.12

reflect the fact that the rate of growth of output and inputs are now expressed per unit of labour. For instance, industry 01, agriculture and fishing, has an average rate of growth of labour productivity of 4.94 for the whole period 1961–80. This rate could be explained by increases in other inputs per unit of labour of 4.08, with the greatest contribution of 1.99 coming from increases in intermediate inputs per unit of labour (such as fertilizers and insecticides and herbicides), and the contribution of the rate of growth of MFP to the growth of labour productivity is relatively small at 0.86. By comparison, if we take industry 32, telephones, for the same period, opposite results appear. This industry has a very high average growth of labour productivity, 6.23, only 2.03 of which can be explained by increases in the rate of growth of inputs per unit of labour with the greatest contribution (0.90) coming from increases in the capital-labour ratio; the rest, 4.19, comes from increases in the rate of MFP.

Over the whole period, all industries experienced labour productivity increases, some substantial. The highest rate of growth of labour productivity belongs to railway transport and telegraph, with an annual average of 6.48 per year, followed by telephones, 6.23; gas distribution, 5.77; knitting mills, 5.69; textiles, 5.02; and agriculture and fishing, 4.94. All of these industries have also some of the highest rates of growth of traditional and new MFP.[3] In fact, this is the single most important contributor to the increasing labour productivity.

In general, the weighted rate of growth of inputs per unit of labour is positive for all industries. Increases in the ratio of intermediate goods (both imported and domestic) per unit of labour is the single most important contributor to increases in labour productivity after the MFP rate. Capital per unit of labour also increases over time.

For the period 1973–80, seven industries have a negative rate of growth of labour productivity, a definite deterioration compared to other periods. Yet it remains a better picture than that offered by the MFP rates. A negative average annual rate of growth of MFP in some industries was offset by increases in labour productivity and the intensity by which other inputs were being used with respect to the labour input. For some industries, the decline in MFP was offset by increases in labour productivity that were not matched by increases in other inputs per unit of labour. It is also interesting to see that standard measures of capital services per unit of labour input did not suffer any major declines, with the exception of

---

[3] Earlier we questioned the validity of the MFP rate for some industries, including the "Railways Transport and Telegraph". However, to the extent the output measures are satisfactory, the rate of growth of labour productivity is not affected, only the composition, which is affected by the questionable weights. For this reason, we do not discuss the decomposition for these industries.

one industry – air transport – even though the growth in capital per unit of labour slowed down over that period.

Tables 6-11 to 6-15 show the same rate of growth of labour productivity by industry, but the breakdown is in terms of the new measures of MFP. Take, for instance, the same two industries illustrated previously. For agriculture and fishing the contribution of inputs per unit of labour goes down to 2.90 from 4.08 and that of the MFP rate increases from 0.86 to 2.04. For telephones, the contribution of inputs decreases to 0.98 from 2.03, whereas the MFP rate increases to 5.25 from an already high 4.19; of course, only the domestically produced intermediate inputs are affected. Similar results are obtained for all other industries.

A comparison of Tables 6-6 to 6-10 and 6-11 to 6-15 for any given period makes clear that the contribution of the new rate of MFP to the rate of growth of labour productivity is substantially higher with very few exceptions; whereas the contribution of the domestically produced inputs are substantially lower. The adjusted capital per unit of labour has in many instances declined. That is, when all produced inputs are adjusted for their rate of technical change or the diminishing inputs that would go into producing them under current technologies, one measures a decline in the capital–labour ratio and a less significant one in the intermediate inputs–labour ratio.

Table 6-11. *Breakdown of the average of annual rates of growth of labour productivity in terms of new MFP and "adjusted" produced domestic inputs, 1961-71*

		Q/L	= Int/L	+ M/L	+ G/L	+ CCA/L	+ K/L	+ MFP rate
01	Agriculture and fishing	7.06	1.26	0.32	0.14	0.48	0.70	4.16
02	Forestry	5.23	1.55	0.37	0.15	0.31	0.15	2.70
03	Mines, quarries, and oil wells	4.72	1.39	0.32	0.15	0.51	1.21	1.14
04	Food and beverages	3.49	0.06	0.19	–	0.06	0.08	3.10
05	Tobacco products	4.46	0.62	0.13	0.03	0.09	-0.18	3.77
06	Rubber and plastic products	5.34	0.10	0.94	0.02	0.02	-0.07	4.33
07	Leather	2.89	-0.50	0.98	0.04	0.04	-0.02	2.35
08	Textiles	6.39	0.93	1.10	0.05	0.05	-0.01	4.25
09	Knitting mills	6.18	0.46	1.26	0.01	0.01	-0.06	4.49
10	Clothing	3.22	0.49	0.45	0.02	-0.01	-0.06	2.33
11	Woods	3.26	0.64	0.31	0.10	0.09	0.14	1.98
12	Furniture and fixtures	3.44	0.22	0.47	0.05	0.01	0.17	2.52
13	Paper and allied industries	2.65	0.22	0.23	0.03	0.21	0.15	1.81
14	Printing, publishing, and allied industries	2.24	0.42	0.13	0.03	0.04	0.11	1.51
15	Primary metals	2.80	0.50	0.39	0.02	0.05	-0.02	1.86
16	Metal fabricating	3.47	0.07	0.38	0.01	-0.04	-0.04	3.09
17	Machinery	3.73	0.67	1.08	0.01	0.01	-0.11	2.07
18	Transportation equipment	7.52	1.23	3.06	-0.01	–	0.03	3.21
19	Electrical products	3.87	0.20	0.58	0.01	0.03	-0.16	3.21
20	Nonmetallic mineral products	3.93	0.51	0.17	0.06	0.10	0.14	2.95
21	Petroleum and coal products	3.91	0.66	1.08	0.02	0.02	-0.07	2.20
22	Chemical and chemical products	3.84	0.37	0.44	0.03	0.12	0.19	2.69

23	Miscellaneous manufacturing	3.99	0.53	0.82	0.06	0.08	0.15	2.35
24	Construction	3.22	0.43	0.24	0.24	-0.02	0.02	2.31
25	Air transportation and other utilities and transportation	5.65	0.93	0.27	0.28	0.27	-0.04	3.94
26	Railway transportation and telegraph	8.11	0.50	0.26	-0.34	-0.02	0.02	7.69
27	Water transport	6.02	0.98	0.27	0.10	0.22	–	4.45
28	Motor transport	3.70	1.18	0.31	0.16	–	0.03	2.02
29	Urban and suburban transportation	-0.51	-0.09	0.07	-0.09	0.37	-0.25	-0.52
30	Storage	1.97	-0.70	-0.01	0.20	0.14	0.15	2.19
31	Broadcasting	4.35	0.94	0.68	-2.10	0.36	0.84	3.58
32	Telephones	5.71	-0.12	0.02	0.16	0.43	0.56	4.66
33	Electric power	1.94	0.02	0.36	0.03	-0.04	-0.04	1.61
34	Gas distribution	9.72	0.07	-0.05	0.27	0.63	2.60	6.20
35	Trade	2.90	-0.31	0.06	-0.03	–	-0.46	3.64
36	Finance, insurance, and real estate	0.17	-0.23	0.01	0.02	-0.19	-0.72	1.28
37	Commercial services	0.99	-0.33	0.17	0.02	0.09	0.35	0.69

Table 6-12. *Breakdown of the average of annual rates of growth of labour productivity in terms of new MFP and "adjusted" produced domestic inputs, 1971–80*

		Q/L	=	Int/L	+	M/L	+	G/L	+	CCA/L	+	K/L	+	MFP rate
01	Agriculture and fishing	2.58		1.46		0.25		0.03		0.95		0.20		−0.31
02	Forestry	3.66		2.14		0.19		0.12		0.24		−0.04		1.01
03	Mines, quarries, and oil wells	0.59		2.77		0.22		0.12		0.37		0.59		−3.48
04	Food and beverages	2.24		1.16		0.29		—		0.02		0.14		0.63
05	Tobacco products	2.95		−0.89		0.43		0.01		0.06		—		3.34
06	Rubber and plastic products	2.05		0.76		0.25		—		0.06		0.13		0.85
07	Leather	2.57		0.74		0.31		0.01		0.06		0.07		1.38
08	Textiles	3.50		0.38		0.59		0.02		0.03		0.08		2.40
09	Knitting mills	5.14		−0.14		0.52		—		0.04		0.14		4.58
10	Clothing	3.46		0.10		0.49		—		0.01		0.27		2.59
11	Woods	2.25		0.70		0.22		0.02		0.10		0.28		0.93
12	Furniture and fixtures	1.00		−0.07		0.19		−0.01		0.02		0.05		0.82
13	Paper and allied industries	1.87		0.62		0.28		−0.01		0.02		0.04		0.92
14	Printing, publishing, and allied industries	3.21		0.42		0.27		−0.02		0.01		0.04		2.49
15	Primary metals	0.77		0.28		0.51		0.02		0.08		—		−0.12
16	Metal fabricating	1.59		0.05		0.24		—		0.03		0.08		1.19
17	Machinery	3.20		−0.04		1.16		0.01		—		0.04		2.03
18	Transportation equipment	1.23		−0.20		0.40		—		0.04		0.06		0.93
19	Electrical products	3.88		0.06		1.05		0.01		0.06		0.25		2.45
20	Nonmetallic mineral products	2.06		0.78		0.32		0.04		0.20		0.25		0.47
21	Petroleum and coal products	0.78		3.50		−2.40		−0.01		0.03		0.05		−0.39
22	Chemical and chemical products	4.13		2.40		0.65		0.05		0.38		0.45		0.20

23	Miscellaneous manufacturing	1.73	0.22	0.90	—	0.01	0.02	0.58
24	Construction	1.07	-0.07	0.17	0.03	0.05	0.12	0.77
25	Air transportation and other utilities and transportation	0.61	0.40	-0.05	-0.09	-0.04	-0.43	0.82
26	Railway transportation and telegraph	4.66	1.96	0.05	-1.37	0.26	-0.04	3.80
27	Water transport	2.58	1.24	0.07	0.16	—	-0.02	1.13
28	Motor transport	1.56	-0.05	0.05	—	0.08	0.28	1.20
29	Urban and suburban transportation	-0.82	1.13	0.32	0.06	0.90	-2.07	-1.16
30	Storage	3.39	0.70	0.03	-0.02	0.51	0.25	1.92
31	Broadcasting	4.33	0.71	0.35	-1.80	0.42	0.89	3.76
32	Telephones	6.80	0.15	0.06	0.19	0.27	0.24	5.89
33	Electric power	2.89	0.10	0.20	-0.01	0.64	0.50	1.46
34	Gas distribution	1.37	0.02	-0.02	-0.14	0.08	-0.05	1.48
35	Trade	0.90	0.05	0.01	0.01	0.01	-0.28	1.10
36	Finance, insurance, and real estate	0.41	0.02	0.08	-0.01	-0.01	-0.09	0.42
37	Commercial services	0.94	-0.38	-0.02	-0.04	0.24	0.63	0.51

Table 6-13. *Breakdown of the average of annual rates of growth of labour productivity in terms of new MFP and "adjusted" produced domestic inputs, 1961–80*

		Q/L	= Int/L	+ M/L	+ G/L	+ CCA/L	+ K/L	+ MFP rate
01	Agriculture and fishing	4.94	1.36	0.29	0.08	0.70	0.47	2.04
02	Forestry	4.49	1.83	0.29	0.13	0.28	0.06	1.90
03	Mines, quarries, and oil wells	2.76	2.04	0.28	0.14	0.45	0.90	-1.05
04	Food and beverages	2.90	0.58	0.24	–	0.04	0.11	1.93
05	Tobacco products	3.75	-0.09	0.28	0.02	0.07	-0.10	3.57
06	Rubber and plastic products	3.78	0.41	0.62	0.01	0.04	0.02	2.68
07	Leather	2.74	0.09	0.66	0.03	0.05	0.02	1.89
08	Textiles	5.02	0.67	0.86	0.04	0.04	0.04	3.37
09	Knitting mills	5.69	0.17	0.91	0.01	0.03	0.04	4.53
10	Clothing	3.33	0.30	0.47	0.01	–	0.10	2.45
11	Woods	2.78	0.67	0.26	0.06	0.09	0.22	1.48
12	Furniture and fixtures	2.29	0.08	0.34	0.02	0.02	0.12	1.71
13	Paper and allied industries	2.28	0.41	0.26	0.01	0.12	0.09	1.39
14	Printing, publishing, and allied industries	2.70	0.42	0.20	0.01	0.02	0.07	1.98
15	Primary metals	1.84	0.40	0.45	0.02	0.06	-0.01	0.92
16	Metal fabricating	2.58	0.06	0.32	0.01	-0.01	0.01	2.19
17	Machinery	3.48	0.33	1.12	0.01	–	-0.03	2.05
18	Transportation equipment	4.54	0.55	1.80	-0.01	0.02	0.05	2.13
19	Electrical products	3.88	0.13	0.80	0.01	0.04	0.05	2.85
20	Nonmetallic mineral products	3.04	0.64	0.24	0.05	0.14	0.19	1.78
21	Petroleum and coal products	2.43	2.00	-0.57	–	0.03	-0.01	0.98
22	Chemical and chemical products	3.98	1.33	0.54	0.04	0.25	0.31	1.51

23	Miscellaneous manufacturing	2.92	0.38	0.86	0.03	0.05	0.08	1.52
24	Construction	2.20	0.20	0.21	0.14	0.01	0.06	1.58
25	Air transportation and other utilities and transportation	3.26	0.68	0.12	0.10	0.13	−0.23	2.46
26	Railway transportation and telegraph	6.48	1.19	0.16	−0.83	0.12	−0.01	5.85
27	Water transport	4.39	1.10	0.17	0.13	0.12	−0.01	2.88
28	Motor transport	2.69	0.60	0.19	0.08	0.04	0.15	1.63
29	Urban and suburban transportation	−0.65	0.49	0.19	−0.02	0.62	−1.11	−0.82
30	Storage	2.64	−0.04	0.01	0.10	0.31	0.20	2.06
31	Broadcasting	4.34	0.83	0.52	−1.96	0.39	0.90	3.66
32	Telephones	6.23	0.01	0.04	0.17	0.36	0.40	5.25
33	Electric power	2.39	0.06	0.29	0.01	0.28	0.21	1.54
34	Gas distribution	5.77	0.05	−0.04	0.08	0.37	1.35	3.96
35	Trade	1.95	−0.14	0.04	−0.01	0.01	−0.39	2.44
36	Finance, insurance, and real estate	0.28	−0.11	0.05	0.01	−0.10	−0.45	0.88
37	Commercial services	0.96	−0.36	0.08	−0.01	0.16	0.48	0.61

Table 6-14. *Breakdown of the average of annual rates of growth of labour productivity in terms of new MFP and "adjusted" produced domestic inputs, 1961–73*

		Q/L	=	Int/L	+	M/L	+	G/L	+	CCA/L	+	K/L	+	MFP rate
01	Agriculture and fishing	6.70		1.58		0.37		0.13		0.54		0.55		3.67
02	Forestry	5.98		2.53		0.41		0.23		0.27		0.06		2.49
03	Mines, quarries, and oil wells	5.68		1.38		0.33		0.20		0.50		0.69		2.24
04	Food and beverages	3.36		0.02		0.29		–		0.05		0.16		2.91
05	Tobacco products	4.14		–0.49		0.22		0.03		0.08		0.16		4.56
06	Rubber and plastic products	5.18		–0.08		0.86		0.01		–		0.23		4.47
07	Leather	2.71		–0.12		0.86		0.04		0.04		–0.47		1.88
08	Textiles	5.93		0.52		1.06		0.04		–		0.2		4.35
09	Knitting mills	5.79		–0.10		1.24		0.01		0.01		0.09		4.63
10	Clothing	3.44		0.38		0.59		0.01		–0.01		0.28		2.47
11	Woods	2.78		0.81		0.31		0.07		0.06		0.41		1.44
12	Furniture and fixtures	3.73		0.21		0.51		0.03		–		0.15		2.88
13	Paper and allied industries	3.14		0.07		0.24		0.03		0.18		0.06		2.51
14	Printing, publishing, and allied industries	2.70		0.20		0.20		0.02		0.03		0.09		2.19
15	Primary metals	3.18		0.37		0.51		0.02		0.05		0.03		2.26
16	Metal fabricating	3.74		0.22		0.40		0.01		–0.04		0.17		3.22
17	Machinery	3.80		0.47		1.21		–		–0.01		0.19		2.28
18	Transportation equipment	6.87		0.69		2.86		–0.02		–0.02		0.27		3.43
19	Electrical products	4.56		0.19		0.71		0.01		0.02		0.34		3.77
20	Nonmetallic mineral products	4.13		0.30		0.20		0.06		0.06		0.45		3.47
21	Petroleum and coal products	4.88		0.77		1.62		0.01		0.04		0.04		2.47
22	Chemical and chemical products	4.46		0.43		0.58		0.03		0.11		0.6		3.16

23	Miscellaneous manufacturing	4.03	0.41	0.88	0.05	0.06	0.07	2.54
24	Construction	2.61	-0.04	0.22	0.19	-0.02	0.23	2.29
25	Air transportation and other utilities and transportation	6.15	1.01	0.29	0.24	0.18	-0.36	4.58
26	Railway transportation and telegraph	7.96	0.60	0.24	-0.28	0.05	-0.03	7.34
27	Water transport	7.02	2.52	0.53	0.21	0.23	–	3.52
28	Motor transport	3.41	0.73	0.31	0.16	0.02	0.27	2.12
29	Urban and suburban transportation	-0.03	0.30	0.24	-0.03	0.28	-2.93	-0.76
30	Storage	1.46	-0.79	-0.06	0.07	0.11	0.52	2.13
31	Broadcasting	4.91	1.05	0.84	-2.29	0.41	0.61	3.85
32	Telephones	5.45	-0.15	0.03	0.16	0.32	0.47	4.72
33	Electric power	3.15	-0.04	0.28	–	0.11	0.46	2.72
34	Gas distribution	8.29	-0.10	-0.04	0.18	0.49	0.21	5.75
35	Trade	2.80	-0.36	0.06	-0.04	-0.01	-0.02	3.75
36	Finance, insurance, and real estate	-0.04	-0.23	0.05	-0.03	-0.20	0.21	1.13
37	Commercial services	1.02	-0.41	0.16	0.01	0.10	0.64	0.79

215

Table 6-15. *Breakdown of the average of annual rates of growth of labour productivity in terms of new MFP and "adjusted" produced domestic inputs, 1973–80*

		Q/L	= Int/L	+ M/L	+ G/L	+ CCA/L	+ K/L	+ MFP rate
01	Agriculture and fishing	1.92	0.97	0.15	0.01	0.98	0.41	-0.74
02	Forestry	1.92	0.63	0.08	-0.03	0.30	0.05	0.88
03	Mines, quarries, and oil wells	-2.24	3.18	0.18	0.03	0.36	1.03	-6.68
04	Food and beverages	2.10	1.54	0.14	–	0.01	0.09	0.25
05	Tobacco products	3.07	0.59	0.37	0.02	0.07	-0.26	1.86
06	Rubber and plastic products	1.39	1.25	0.20	0.01	0.10	-0.08	-0.40
07	Leather	2.80	0.43	0.32	0.01	0.06	0.01	1.91
08	Textiles	3.48	0.93	0.52	0.03	0.10	-0.04	1.70
09	Knitting mills	5.50	0.64	0.33	0.01	0.06	–	4.37
10	Clothing	3.15	0.17	0.26	–	0.02	–	2.42
11	Woods	2.79	0.44	0.18	0.04	0.16	0.09	1.56
12	Furniture and fixtures	-0.20	-0.14	0.04	–	0.04	0.1	-0.29
13	Paper and allied industries	0.81	1.00	0.28	-0.02	0.02	0.11	-0.53
14	Printing, publishing, and allied industries	2.71	0.80	0.19	–	0.02	0.06	1.61
15	Primary metals	-0.45	0.45	0.34	0.01	0.09	-0.03	-1.37
16	Metal fabricating	0.60	-0.22	0.17	–	0.04	-0.07	0.44
17	Machinery	2.94	0.10	0.96	0.01	0.03	-0.15	1.65
18	Transportation equipment	0.54	0.32	-0.03	0.01	0.08	-0.07	-0.11
19	Electrical products	2.71	0.04	0.96	0.01	0.08	-0.14	1.28
20	Nonmetallic mineral products	1.18	1.22	0.31	0.04	0.28	0.04	-1.12
21	Petroleum and coal products	-1.78	4.12	-4.33	-0.02	–	-0.03	-1.59
22	Chemical and chemical products	3.16	2.87	0.47	0.05	0.48	0.15	-1.31

23	Miscellaneous manufacturing	1.01	0.34	0.81	—	0.03	0.09	-0.24
24	Construction	1.50	0.61	0.18	0.05	0.06	-0.03	0.37
25	Air transportation and other utilities and transportation	-1.70	0.10	-0.17	-0.13	0.03	-0.15	-1.17
26	Railway transportation and telegraph	3.93	2.20	0.01	-1.77	0.23	0.01	3.29
27	Water transport	-0.10	-1.33	-0.44	-0.02	-0.09	0.01	1.78
28	Motor transport	1.46	0.38	-0.02	-0.05	0.08	0.07	0.80
29	Urban and suburban transportation	-1.73	0.82	0.11	—	1.20	-0.06	-0.93
30	Storage	4.67	1.26	0.12	0.15	0.66	—	1.96
31	Broadcasting	3.36	0.47	-0.02	-1.39	0.35	1.05	3.34
32	Telephones	7.56	0.28	0.06	0.19	0.41	0.37	6.15
33	Electric power	1.10	0.22	0.29	0.04	0.58	0.08	-0.49
34	Gas distribution	1.43	0.31	-0.03	-0.11	0.15	2.01	0.90
35	Trade	0.50	0.25	—	0.03	0.04	-0.6	0.20
36	Finance, insurance, and real estate	0.84	0.09	0.04	0.07	0.06	-0.76	0.45
37	Commercial services	0.86	-0.27	-0.05	-0.04	0.28	0.37	0.30

CHAPTER 7

Measures of multifactor productivity for the aggregate economy

There are two methods to derive measures of MFP for the aggregate private business economy. They can be based on the equality, as contained in the I/O tables, between the value of aggregate final demand and aggregate gross domestic product. Alternatively, the industry measures can be aggregated, using a suitable set of weights, to yield the economy's measure.

In this section we explore two issues. If method 1 is used, what is the *implicit* set of industry weights? To this end we derive the economy's measure starting from the accounting identity for the economy as a whole for the traditional and new measures of MFP. If method 2 is used, what explicit weights should be used to aggregate over the industry measures? Should the weights be the same for both the traditional and new measures? With these issues resolved, we present and discuss the values of the rates of MFP for the economy for the periods under consideration.

Equations (7-1) show all the basic I/O relationships; the first set [(7-1a)] is technical in nature, the second [(7-1b)] is the associated dual-price equation, and the third [(7-1c)] is the accounting identity for the economy as a whole:

$$f = (I - A)g$$
$$y_d = E_d g$$
$$y_k = E_k g$$
$$y_f = E_f g \tag{7-1a}$$
$$y_r = E_r g$$
$$y_p = E_p g$$

$$p' = p'A + i'(W_d \cdot E_d) + i'(W_k \cdot E_k) + i'(W_f \cdot E_f) + i'(W_r \cdot E_r) + i'(W_p \cdot E_p) \tag{7-1b}$$

$$p'(I - A)g = i'(W_c \cdot E_c)g + i'(W_p \cdot E_p)g \tag{7-1c}$$

Applying the definition of MFP to equation (7-1c), we get the rate of traditional MFP for the economy as a whole, which we call T^*:

$$T^* = -(p'f)^{-1}g'\left[\frac{dA'}{dt}p + \left(W_c' \cdot \frac{dE_c'}{dt}\right)i + \left(W_p' \cdot \frac{dE_p'}{dt}\right)i\right] \quad (7\text{-}2)$$

Alternatively, the same measure can be obtained by aggregating the industry measures using as weights the ratio of the value of gross industry output to the total value of final demand. To prove this, we apply these weights to equation (4-9), the set of industry MFP rates, and obtain

$$T^* = -(p'f)^{-1}p'\hat{g}\left[\hat{p}^{-1}\frac{dA'}{dt}p + \hat{p}^{-1}\left(\frac{dE_c'}{dt} \cdot W_c'\right)i + \hat{p}^{-1}\left(\frac{dE_p'}{dt} \cdot W_p'\right)i\right]$$

$$= -(p'f)^{-1}g'\left[\frac{dA'}{dt}p + \left(\frac{dE_c'}{dt} \cdot W_c'\right)i + \left(\frac{dE_p'}{dt} \cdot W_p'\right)i\right] \quad (7\text{-}3)$$

which is the same as equation (7-2). Hence, we have established that the implicit set of industry weights proceeding from the accounting identity to the MFP rate for the entire economy are the ratios of gross outputs to final demand. These weights are favoured in the literature because they do not ignore the contribution of industries producing mainly or only intermediate inputs, as final demand weights would. Hulten[1] showed that the rate of MFP for the entire economy, defined as the Divisia index of final demand minus the Divisia index of primary inputs, is equal to the one obtained by using Domar's[2] aggregation rule over industry MFP rates. Our result is the same as Hulten's, but it is derived from an I/O model without making explicit use of equilibrium conditions.

Turning to the new industry measures, one wonders whether a similar type of result is possible, that is, to derive the economy's new measure from the final demand accounting identity and then to show the relationship between this and the industry rates of new measures of MFP. To this end, it will be desirable to obtain the economy's measure first from the national product accounting identity. Hence, we write equation (7-1c) as

$$p'(I-A)g = i'(W_d \cdot E_d)g + i'(W_k \cdot E_k)g + i'(W_f \cdot E_f)g$$
$$+ i'(W_r \cdot E_r)g + i'(W_p \cdot E_p)g \quad (7\text{-}4)$$

Note that it will be inconsistent to introduce the new MFP adjustment to both sides of equation (7-4). As we have seen, intermediate inputs and their prices are adjusted for the rate of MFP of the industry where they originate. However, such an adjustment cannot apply to the net output equation. That is, to express (7-4) as

[1] C. Hulten, "Growth Accounting with Intermediate Inputs", *Review of Economic Studies,* XLV, October 1978, 511–18.

[2] E. D. Domar, "On the Measurement of Technological Change", *Economic Journal,* LXXI, December 1961, 709–29.

$$p'\hat{h}\hat{h}^{-1}(I-A)g = i'[(\hat{h}W_d)\cdot(\hat{h}^{-1}E_d)]g$$
$$+i'[(\hat{h}W_k)\cdot(\hat{h}^{-1}E_k)]g$$
$$+i'[(\hat{h}W_f)\cdot(\hat{h}^{-1}E_f)]g$$
$$+i'[(\hat{h}W_r)\cdot(\hat{h}^{-1}E_r)]g$$
$$+i'(W_p\cdot E_p)g$$

is incorrect because it adjusts net output, the left-hand side of the equation for technical change, whereas only inputs should undergo such an adjustment. We can, however, make use of Hulten's result and our own and not adjust intermediate inputs. As we have seen, their contribution to the economy's rate of MFP is fully accounted in the traditional aggregate measure through the weights used, without any intermediate input adjustment. We rewrite (7-4) as

$$p'(I-A)g = i'[(\hat{h}W_d)\cdot(\hat{h}^{-1}E_d)]g$$
$$+i'[(\hat{h}W_k)\cdot(\hat{h}^{-1}E_k)]g$$
$$+i'[(\hat{h}W_f)\cdot(\hat{h}^{-1}E_f)]g$$
$$+i'[(\hat{h}W_r)\cdot(\hat{h}^{-1}E_r)]g$$
$$+i'(W_p\cdot E_p)g \tag{7-5}$$

Applying the definition of MFP to this equation, we obtain H^*, the new rate of MFP for the economy:

$$H^* = -(p'f)^{-1}g'\left[\frac{dA'}{dt}p+\left(\frac{dE_c'}{dt}\cdot W_c'\right)i+\left(\frac{dE_p'}{dt}\cdot W_p'\right)i\right]$$
$$+(p'f)^{-1}g'[(W_d'\cdot E_d')+(W_k'\cdot E_k')+(W_f'\cdot E_f')+(W_r'\cdot E_r')]h^* \tag{7-6}$$

The first line is, of course, the economy's traditional rate of MFP [see equation (7-2)]; hence, the productivity effect arising from more and better intermediate inputs is acknowledged. The second line is a weighted sum of the rate of growth of the new MFP of industries, where the weights are the sum of the shares of all domestically produced inputs (other than intermediate) in final demand. The first effect is then the direct effect plus the indirect effects coming from gains in productivity through the intermediate inputs used. It could be called the total MFP rate based on inputs produced in the current period. The second one is the MFP rate prevailing if all domestically produced inputs produced in previous periods were to be produced with the technology of the present period, that is, if they were to benefit from productivity gains in their producing industries – their lower and/or better input content in terms of current-period technology.

We may further explore the relationship between the two rates by substituting for the traditional rate in (7-6),

$$H^* = T^* + (p'f)^{-1}g'[(W'_d \cdot E'_d) + (W'_k \cdot E'_k) + (W'_f \cdot E'_f) + (W'_r \cdot E'_r)]h^*$$

Expressed in terms of industry rates,

$$\begin{aligned}
T^* &= (p'f)^{-1}(p'\hat{g})t^* \\
&= (p'f)^{-1}(p'\hat{g})(I-S)h^* \\
&= (p'f)^{-1}g'(W'_p \cdot E'_p)h^*
\end{aligned}$$

Substituting for T^* in H^*, we get

$$\begin{aligned}
H^* &= (p'f)^{-1}g'[(W'_d \cdot E'_d) + (W'_k \cdot E'_k) + (W'_f \cdot E'_f) \\
&\quad + (W'_r \cdot E'_r) + (W'_p \cdot E'_p)]h^* \\
&= (p'f)^{-1}p'\hat{f}h^*
\end{aligned} \tag{7-7}$$

This proves that the new rate of MFP for the entire economy is the weighted sum of the new industry measures, where the weights are final demand weights, that is, the share of each industry's final demand in the total value of final demand. Hence, a similar result prevails for the new measure as for its traditional counterpart. The former can be derived from the (adjusted) National Accounting identity, and the same measure can be obtained by a weighted sum of new industry measures where the weights are final demand shares. This result is not surprising, for gross output weights will be too large when the contribution of industries is already channelled through other industries rather than accounted for at the final stage of the economy level.

We can compare the economy's traditional MFP to its new counterpart by expressing the former in terms of new industry rates. From equation (7-7) we have

$$\begin{aligned}
T^* &= (p'f)^{-1}g'(W'_p \cdot E'_p)h^* \\
H^* &= (p'f)^{-1}p'\hat{f}h^*
\end{aligned} \tag{7-8}$$

The economy's traditional rate, T^*, weights each industry's new measure by its share of primary inputs in total final demand,[3] and H^* weights each by its share of final demand in total final demand. Obviously, the former weights are smaller, so that given a positive rate of MFP,

$$\begin{aligned}
T^* &< H^* \quad \text{if } h_i^* \geq 0, \forall i \\
H^* - T^* &= (p'f)^{-1}g'(W'_c \cdot E_c)h^*
\end{aligned} \tag{7-9}$$

Here H^* is greater than T^* by the sum of industry shares of domestically produced inputs (other than intermediate) in final demand times the new industry measures. One more manipulation may clarify the meaning

---

[3] Note that these weights do not add up to 1; they are less than 1.

further. If we write the traditional and new economywide rates in terms of only the traditional measures in equation (7-8), we get

$$H^* = (p'f)^{-1}p'\hat{f}(I-S)^{-1}t^*$$

$$T^* = (p'f)^{-1}p'\hat{g}t^* \tag{7-10}$$

Under the assumption that the only produced inputs in the economy are intermediate inputs, all other being primary inputs, S will equal the transpose of matrix of intermediate input coefficients in current-dollar (or value) terms. Hence

$$H^* = (p'f)^{-1}p'\hat{f}(I-\hat{p}^{-1}A'p)^{-1}t^*$$

and substituting for $p'\hat{g}$ in T^*, we get

$$T^* = (p'f)^{-1}p'\hat{f}(I-\hat{p}^{-1}A'p)^{-1}t^*$$

and $H^* = T^*$. Thus, we have shown that the economy's traditional and new rate of MFP are the same if equation (7-1c) reduces to

$$p'(I-A)g = i'(W_p \cdot E_p)g$$

In this case, the application of Domar's aggregation rule to both the traditional industry rates and the new industry rates will yield the same economy rate. Domar's rule weights an industry's MFP by the ratio of the final output to the industry to the final output to the sector. Hulten has shown that when the sector is the whole economy, Domar's rule is equivalent to the ratio of an industry gross output to the total of final demand. Domar's rule can be applied without corrections to the new rate under the preceding assumption. When capital goods are used in the economy, of course, there is no possible equality between the two rates, although it is clear from the preceding that one rate can always be obtained from the other by using the proper weights. We now present the empirical results.

Table 7-1 gives the annual percentage rate of growth of the traditional and new measures of MFP for the economy as a whole; the numbers in parentheses next to each column show the rankings. Overall, a steady decline in the rate of growth of MFP has accomplished its cyclical movements. The post-1973 slowdown extends over the rest of the period; the rate of growth of productivity is the lowest (it is, in fact, the greatest negative) for the years 1974–5 for the period under analysis.

The empirical findings for the economy's rate parallel those obtained for industries. The year 1973 is a clear turning point in the series; the MFP growth rates for years prior to 1973 are positive in all but two of the twelve years, and the higher rankings also belong to the 1961–73 period; for the period 1973–80 negative growth rates in five of the seven years surround a rather strong, short-lived recovery in 1975.

Table 7-1. *The economy's rate of growth of MFP*

	Traditional	New
1961–2	5.10 (1)	6.86 (1)
1962–3	2.20 (6)	2.77 (6)
1963–4	2.41 (5)	3.29 (4)
1964–5	1.76 (8)	2.29 (8)
1965–6	1.63 (10)	2.00 (10)
1966–7	−0.62 (17)	−0.29 (16)
1967–8	3.16 (2)	4.24 (2)
1968–9	1.65 (9)	2.25 (9)
1969–70	−0.18 (15)	−0.16 (14)
1970–1	1.46 (11)	1.83 (11)
1971–2	1.99 (7)	2.48 (7)
1972–3	2.72 (3)	3.62 (3)
1973–4	−1.36 (18)	−1.55 (18)
1974–5	−1.85 (19)	−1.71 (19)
1975–6	2.55 (4)	2.92 (5)
1976–7	−0.07 (14)	−0.13 (13)
1977–8	−0.07 (13)	−0.30 (17)
1978–8	1.06 (12)	1.33 (12)
1979–80	−0.55 (16)	−0.21 (15)

A comparison between the two rates shows that the new rate exceeds the traditional one every year that this is positive, as proved in equation (7-9). However, for three of the seven years with negative traditional rates – 1973, 1976, and 1977 – the new rate is smaller. This is the result of negative MFP growth in industries that supply others with capital inputs and therefore receive larger weights under the new measure [see again equation (7-9)]. The ranks are almost the same for the two rates. At the economy level, the new adjustment has no significant effect on the rankings.

Averaged over the years, as in Table 7-2, we see that the Canadian economy has registered gains in efficiency in every period except the last despite negative growth in some years. Just as the annual rates revealed, the 1960s were most productive. The breakdown 1961–73 and 1973–80 also makes clear the extent to which the slowdown is a post-1973 phenomenon. The economy's rate of MFP for the post-1973 period is very close to zero for both concepts. The last column in Table 7-2 measures the second equation in (7-9), which accounts for the contribution to the economy's new rate of MFP from changes in the rate of MFP of capital-goods-producing industries relating to the existing stocks of capital goods

Table 7-2. *The economy's average of annual rates of growth of MFP by periods*

	Traditional	New	Difference
1961–71	1.86	2.51	0.65
1971–80	0.49	0.72	0.23
1961–80	1.21	1.66	0.45
1961–73	1.94	2.60	0.66
1973–80	−0.04	0.05	0.09

used in the economy coming from those industries rather than to the year's output. The traditional rate does not attempt to measure this term as it treats capital inputs as primary inputs.

The decomposition of the average rate of growth of MFP is shown in Table 7-3 for the traditional measure and in Table 7-4 for the new one. For each period, the rate of growth of MFP, be it traditional or new, is obtained as the difference between the rate of growth of output and the weighted rate of growth of each input class used to produce that output.

In Table 7-3 the rate of growth of output minus the weighted rate of growth of intermediate inputs is shown to equal the rate of growth of value added, the third row in the table, which for the economy equals the growth rate of final demand. Subtracting the growth rates of all other inputs from that of value added, we obtain the traditional MFP rate. It achieves its biggest growth rate when output growth is also at its peak value. In fact, the ranks of value-added growth rates and MFP rates coincide. There is a strong positive correlation between the two.

The weighted labour input grew at a relatively larger pace than other inputs in every period except the last. By contrast, the weighted average annual rate of growth of capital was close to being constant regardless of output growth. This confirms that it was certainly not a shortage of capital or of labour that caused the slowdown[4] and that these inputs do not adjust quickly to declines in the rate of growth of output.

A look at the results obtained for the complementary periods 1961–71 and 1971–80 show that the annual average rate of growth of value added fell from 5.50 in the first period to 4.02 in the second, whereas the weighted rates of growth of labour, CCA, and capital inputs are higher

[4] This result could be different if the capital input had been adjusted for changes in the capital utilization rate, but then one would have to reckon with the meaning of a possible decline in the rate of growth of the capital stock in the presence of widespread under-utilization of capital in some years.

Table 7-3. *Breakdown of the economy's average of annual rates of growth of traditional MFP*

	1961–71	1971–80	1961–80	1961–73	1973–80
Output	8.84	6.43	7.70	9.28	4.99
Intermediate inputs	−3.34	−2.41	−2.90	−3.42	−2.01
Value added	5.50	4.02	4.80	5.86	2.98
Intermediate imports	−0.91	−0.52	−0.72	−1.00	−0.24
Government inputs	−0.29	−0.21	−0.25	−0.30	−0.17
Labour	−1.02	−1.26	−1.14	−1.20	−1.03
CCA	−0.42	−0.52	−0.47	−0.43	−0.52
Capital	−1.01	−1.02	−1.02	−0.99	−1.06
MFP rate	1.86	0.49	1.21	1.94	−0.04

Percentage of contribution of primary input and MFP to value-added growth

	1961–71	1971–80	1961–80	1961–73	1973–80
Intermediate imports	16.47	12.85	15.03	17.05	8.23
Government inputs	5.19	5.15	5.17	5.05	5.58
Labour	18.57	31.48	23.70	20.49	34.55
CCA	7.60	12.88	9.70	7.37	17.57
Capital	18.39	25.45	21.19	16.96	35.50
MFP rate	33.77	12.19	25.20	33.09	−1.44

for the second period. Comparing the two periods 1961–73 and 1973–80, the annual percentage of the average growth rate of output is 5.86 for the first period and down to 2.98 for the second; yet the weighted rates for CCA and capital are again higher in the second period, whereas labour's rate falls from 1.20 to 1.03. These inputs seem to adjust only slowly and with difficulties to output changes. It must then be the (annual percentage of the average) rate of growth of MFP that adjusts, if only because of the residual nature of its measurement. This is in fact what we observe, a rate of MFP that is relatively more volatile than that of inputs and outputs and follows the movements in the output rate.

The bottom of Table 7-3 shows the percentage contribution of each input category and of MFP to the growth of output. Note that the contribution of government input is constant over the whole period. The same is true, to a lesser degree, for intermediate imports. Labour and capital, however, increase their percentage contribution as the rate of MFP slows down, but this is just another way of describing the observations made in the preceding paragraph. Thus, there seem to be negative correlations between these two inputs and MFP, as if increases in output when MFP is low were possible only through relatively greater increases

Table 7-4. *Breakdown of the economy's average of annual rates of growth of new MFP*

	1961–71	1971–80	1961–80	1961–73	1973–80
Output	5.36	3.99	4.71	5.62	3.15
Intermediate inputs	−0.95	−1.15	−1.04	−0.92	−1.24
Intermediate imports	−0.57	−0.33	−0.46	−0.63	−0.16
Government inputs	−0.20	−0.15	−0.18	−0.21	−0.13
Labour	−0.69	−0.85	−0.77	−0.81	−0.68
CCA	−0.14	−0.25	−0.19	−0.14	−0.28
Capital	−0.31	−0.54	−0.42	−0.30	−0.61
MFP rate	2.51	0.72	1.66	2.60	0.05

Percentage of contribution of inputs and MFP to final output growth

Intermediate inputs	17.68	28.76	22.13	16.45	39.55
Intermediate imports	10.63	8.27	9.68	11.22	4.95
Government inputs	3.77	3.75	3.76	3.69	3.98
Labour	12.80	21.40	16.25	14.46	21.73
CCA	2.54	6.38	4.08	2.54	8.81
Capital	5.72	13.48	8.84	5.39	19.39
MFP rate	46.86	17.96	35.25	46.24	1.59

in labour and capital. However, our knowledge of the causes of the post-1973 slowdown suggests that the poor productivity performance of the economy is the result (rather than the cause) of output declines and input misalignment in the face of the relative price changes produced by the exogenous oil price shock.

An equivalent set of results is presented in Table 7-4 for the new measures. The annual average rate of growth of new MFP is decomposed into the average annual rate of growth of output minus the weighted average annual rate of growth of each input class. For this rate, the contribution of MFP to the economy's output growth is quite substantial, except for the post-1973 period. With respect to government input and imports, the same constancy is observed as for the traditional measures. However, the contribution of produced inputs and of MFP becomes much more volatile. The negative correlation between the growth of the new rate and of the produced inputs and labour is exaggerated. Thus, with a high growth rate of new MFP, the contribution of intermediate inputs and capital and labour are lower and vice-versa.

A comparison of Tables 7-3 and 7-4 shows that no single cell in a table is equal to the same cell in the other, compared to industry tables where the growth rates for output and nonproduced inputs are always equal. At the economy level this is so because of the different weights used to aggregate over industries in order to get to the economy's rate. In this study we used the second equation in (7-10) to derive the traditional rate and the second equation in (7-8) to obtain the new counterpart. However, regardless of the equation used, it is clear from the algebra that one obtains the same value for the rate of MFP whether new or traditional but that the decomposition of each measure is different, for each equation used.

CHAPTER 8

Summary and conclusion

To improve the estimates of MFP further, development of a data base is required. With the resources available at Statistics Canada, we made progress in putting together a comprehensive data base. Yet the empirical results obtained point out the need for further work, particularly in the following areas: consistent industry classification and aggregation between output and inputs and a change in the measures of capital stocks and labour input to reflect the different vintages of capital and their rates of return and the characteristics of different groups of workers. Indirect taxes and subsidies should be treated differently in order to arrive at purchasers' prices on the input side and producers' prices on the output side.

At the theoretical level we have defined two concepts of MFP and called them traditional and new. The difference between these two is in their treatment of produced inputs. The traditional measures account only for changes in the quantities used, whereas the new account for both the changes in quantities and the lower input content necessary to replace all produced inputs under improved technology. Under conditions of advances in technology, the amount of such required inputs is declining over time. Therefore, the resulting new MFP rate should be greater than the traditional measure. We observed this to be the case for most industries in most years. However, there are exceptions, notably in the post-1973 period, when many industries suffered widespread declines in productivity or in the efficiency with which inputs are used to produce outputs.

Under conditions of declining productivity, the new measures could be lower than the traditional counterparts, as we have seen. It is not clear, however, what is the sense of correcting produced inputs for negative changes in productivity. It may be that these are purely cyclical in nature and reflect temporary maladjustments; for in theory, technical change is either positive or zero. The meaning of MFP measures is unclear under conditions of widespread unemployment of resources as a result of insufficient aggregate demand, price shocks, government deficits, and the like. More theoretical work and empirical research need to be done in this area, a problem common in economics.

228

The traditional measures may be thought of as answering the question: Given the percentage increases in inputs, labour, and capital goods, what is the percentage increase in output that could be produced with the technology of the current period as compared to that of the previous? The newer question, by contrast, is: What is the additional percentage increase in output that could be produced with the technology of the current relative to the previous period, given the percentage increase in primary inputs, if all produced inputs were to be produced with the technology of the current period? To many students, both questions would seem legitimate, and the answers to them may be used for different purposes. We now give a few examples of their relevance.

1. If one wanted to know the MFP of an industry coming only from the use of its own inputs, disregarding how these are being produced, the measures to use are the traditional ones alone or corrected perhaps for an industry's use of its own output as intermediate input. Note that if it was the case that an industry used only its own input as intermediate inputs, then the traditional and new rates would coincide if the traditional measures used unduplicated output concepts.

2. If one wanted to know the MFP of an industry coming from the use of its own inputs and from the productivity changes in the industries supplying it with intermediate inputs, then one would use a "partial" new measure where only intermediate inputs would be adjusted for changes in the MFP rate of their industry of origin. This measure will be aggregated to the aggregate economy level using final demand weights. There is no traditional counterpart to this. However, the traditional industry measures could be aggregated to produce the new economy rate by using as weights the industry gross output to the economy's final demand. The traditional and the new measures coincide, at the economy level, when intermediate inputs are the only produced inputs.

3. If one wanted to know the MFP of the industry in case 2 but wanted to include as well the efficiency changes coming from industries producing the capital used up in the industry in question, then one would have another "partial new measure" where both intermediate inputs and CCA would be adjusted for changes in MFP rate in their producing industries. There is no traditional counterpart to this measure.

4. By adjusting all domestically produced inputs for their changes in MFP, one finally arrives at the "full-fledged" new measure. Enough has been said about it in this study.

In the text, we have defined other concepts such as the output effect, the input effect, and the total contribution of an industry to MFP. The possibilities of carrying out interindustry productivity analysis in the new framework are many. Those discussed here are some of the possibilities that the new measures of multifactor productivity offer.

Appendices

Appendix 1 Aggregation parameters from I/O industries to MFP industries

	MFP industries	I/O industries[a]
01	Agriculture and fishing	1, 3
02	Forestry	2
03	Mines, quarries, and oil wells	4–15
04	Food and beverages	16–32
05	Tobacco products	33, 34
06	Rubber and plastic products	35–38
07	Leather	39–42
08	Textiles	43–55
09	Knitting mills	56, 57
10	Clothing	58
11	Woods	59–64
12	Furniture and fixtures	65–68
13	Paper and allied industries	69–72
14	Printing, publishing, and allied industries	73, 74
15	Primary metals	75–82
16	Metal fabricating	83–91
17	Machinery	92–95
18	Transportation equipment	96–102
19	Electrical products	103–110
20	Nonmetallic mineral products	111–120
21	Petroleum and coal products	121, 122
22	Chemical and chemical products	123–130
23	Miscellaneous manufacturing	131–137
24	Construction	138–146
25	Air transportation and other utilities and transportation	147, 155, 156
26	Railway transportation and telegraph	150
27	Water transport	149
28	Motor transport	148, 151, 152
29	Urban and suburban transportation	153
30	Storage	157
31	Broadcasting	158
32	Telephones	159

231

(cont.)

MFP industries	I/O industries[a]
33 Electric power	161
34 Gas distribution	162
35 Trade	164, 165
36 Finance, insurance, and real estate	166–170
37 Commercial services	171–183

[a] The numbers correspond to those given in Statistics Canada, 15-201, *The Input Output Structure of the Canadian Economy* (Ottawa: Statistics Canada, 1984), 49–50.

Appendix 2   Aggregation parameters from capital stock industries to MFP industries

MFP industries	Capital stock industries[a]
01 Agriculture and fishing	24, 26
02 Forestry	25
03 Mines, quarries, and oil wells	27
04 Food and beverages	3
05 Tobacco products	4
06 Rubber and plastic products	5
07 Leather	6
08 Textiles	7
09 Knitting mills	8
10 Clothing	9
11 Woods	10
12 Furniture and fixtures	11
13 Paper and allied industries	12
14 Printing, publishing, and allied industries	13
15 Primary metals	14
16 Metal fabricating	15
17 Machinery	16
18 Transportation equipment	17
19 Electrical products	18
20 Nonmetallic mineral products	19
21 Petroleum and coal products	20
22 Chemical and chemical products	21
23 Miscellaneous manufacturing	22
24 Construction	28
25 Air transportation and other utilities and transportation	29, 34, (35–warehousing), 40
26 Railway transportation and telegraph	30

(cont.)

	MFP industries	Capital stock industries[a]
27	Water transport	31
28	Motor transport	32
29	Urban and suburban transportation	33
30	Storage	36 (plus unpublished data for warehousing)
31	Broadcasting	37
32	Telephones	38
33	Electric power	39
34	Gas distribution	Unpublished data for gas distribution
35	Trade	41
36	Finance, insurance, and real estate	42 plus housing stock
37	Commercial services	48 plus private schools and private hospitals

[a] The numbers correspond to those given in Statistics Canada, 13-568, *Fixed Capital Flows and Stocks* (Ottawa: Statistics Canada, 1978), XV.

Appendix 3 Partition of the matrix of primary inputs for the new measures of MFP

We start with the I/O matrices of primary inputs Y and the associated matrix of coefficients E that are 9×37 in current dollars and 7×37 in constant dollars. The rows of these matrices are as follows:

Item no.	Current dollars	Constant dollars
1	Noncompeting imports	Same
2	Unallocated imports and exports	Same
3	Competing imports	Same
4	Indirect taxes	Same
5	Subsidies	Same
6	Government-produced goods and services	Same
7	Wages and salaries	This is just one item in the constant
8	Net income unincorporated business	dollar matrix called GDP at factor cost, obtained by the method of
9	Operating surplus	double deflation.

Item 8 is allocated to items 7 and 9 according to their relative proportions; that is, the resulting new row 7 is equal to the old 7 plus (item $8 \times [7/(7+9)]$) and similarly for item 9. The new row 7 is called "total wages and salaries" and the new 9 is "gross operating surplus", while item 8 is now empty.

We obtained data by industry on capital consumption allowances (CCAs) in machinery and equipment (M&E) and construction from Statistics Canada, Science, Technology and Capital Stock Division. The sum total of these two items was subtracted from item 9, gross operating surplus, in order to arrive at net operating surplus.

From the vector CCA in M&E we subtracted the amount of "imported CCA", or depreciation of imported capital goods. This amount was calculated using the year's proportion of imported capital goods from the investment matrix in final demand; for example, if 25 percent of investment goods in, say, 1971, was imported, it was assumed that 25 percent of depreciation in 1971 was on imported capital goods. The difference is "domestic CCA".

This vector of domestic CCA was given the breakdown of the investment (I) matrix in final demand in each year, and in this manner the industry of production of CCA in M&E was assumed to be known.[1] Hence

$$Y_d = (\text{norm } I) \cdot (\text{diagonal matrix of domestic CCA in M\&E})$$

where Y_d is the resulting matrix of domestic CCA (both M&E and construction) and I is the matrix of domestic investment goods in M&E, and it is normalized over the purchasing industries.

All construction is produced domestically by the construction industry; there is no imported component, and only one construction industry is specified in our industry classification (this industry is an aggregation over all construction industries). Therefore, the vector of CCA in construction by industry is left untouched, and it becomes row 24 of the Y_d matrix. This row is empty when only CCA in the M&E is included because the construction industry does not produce any M&E.

For the capital stock in M&E we follow the same procedure as for CCA in M&E. First, we subtract imported capital goods from the total and then we derive the composition of the domestic capital goods. Hence

$$Y_k = (\text{norm } I) \cdot (\text{diagonal matrix of domestic capital stock in M\&E})$$

Again, the capital stock in construction becomes row 24 of the Y_k matrix.

---

[1] Note that the (industry) composition of investment in any one year does not have to represent the composition of the existing capital stock. Only in the case where all components of the capital stock exhibit the same constant rate of growth will the composition of investment in the year coincide with that of the capital stock. It may be more realistic to obtain a moving average of investment matrices over a period of years to get the composition of the capital stock in any one year.

The matrix of inventories of finished goods and goods in process, Y_f, consists of the inventories of the own output of industries. Hence, the Y_f matrix is diagonal; yf_{ii} is the output of the ith industry held as inventory by the ith industry and yf_{ij} is zero.

There is a final component of capital stock, the inventories of raw materials. It was assumed that industries store inputs in the proportion in which they use them. Hence, raw material inventories in any year were assumed to have an imported component equal to the proportion of intermediate inputs that are imported in that year. The balance, the domestic component, was given a breakdown according to the year's intermediate input matrix. Hence, the matrix Y_r is defined as

$$Y_r = (\text{norm } G) \cdot (\text{diagonal matrix of domestic raw material inventories})$$

where G is the matrix of intermediate inputs normalized over input space. To summarize, the resulting matrices of "primary" inputs are:

Current dollars	Matrices	Constant dollars	Size
$W_d \cdot Y_d$	CCA	Y_d	37×37
$W_k \cdot Y_k$	Capital stock	Y_k	37×37
$W_f \cdot Y_f$	Finished goods inventories	Y_f	37×37
$W_r \cdot Y_r$	Raw material inventories	Y_r	37×37
$W_p \cdot Y_p$	Primary proper	Y_p	9×37

For the current-dollar matrices, the row sum over $W_k \cdot Y_k$, $W_f \cdot Y_f$, and $W_r \cdot Y_r$ results in net operating surplus because the rate of return on the current-dollar value of the capital stock is calculated residually by industry. So for the ith industry, we have

$$r_i = \frac{(\text{net operating surplus})_i}{\text{sum (current dollars capital stocks and inventories)}_i}$$

so that all capital in one industry is assumed to be earning the same rate of return. For example, the matrix of "prices" W_k is defined as

$$W_k = P_k \hat{r}$$

where P_k is the matrix of price indexes of capital goods by industry and r is a diagonal matrix with the industry-specific rates of return in its diagonal and zero elsewhere. The matrices W_f and W_r are similarly defined.

Finally, the rows of the Y_p matrices consist of the followings:

> Noncompeting imports,
> Unallocated imports and exports,

Competing exports,
Indirect taxes,
Subsidies,
Government-produced goods and services,
Hours of work,
"Imported" CCA in M&E,
"Imported" capital stock in M&E,
"Imported" raw material inventory.

Appendix 4   Derivation of traditional MFP measures for industries

The identity between the value of total inputs and total outputs for the ith industry, using equation (4-8), is

$$p_i g_i = \sum_j p_j g_{ji} + \sum_l wc_{li} yc_{li} + \sum_p wp_{pi} yp_{pi} \tag{1}$$

or in vector notation,

$$p_i g_i = p' \bar{g}_i + wc_i' yc_i + wp_i' yp_i \tag{2}$$

where $\bar{g}$, the ith column of the matrix of the values of intermediate inputs, has a bar on top to distinguish it from g_i, the total output of the ith industry. Taking derivatives with respect to time, for any x,

$$dx = \begin{cases} \hat{x} \, d \ln x & \text{if } x \text{ is a vector} \\ x \, d \ln x & \text{if } x \text{ is a scalar} \end{cases}$$

$$
\begin{aligned}
p_i \frac{d \ln p_i}{dt} g_i + p_i g_i \frac{d \ln g_i}{dt} &= \frac{d \ln p'}{dt} \hat{p} \bar{g}_i + p' \hat{\bar{g}}_i \frac{d \ln \bar{g}_i}{dt} \\
&\quad + \frac{d \ln wc_i'}{dt} \widehat{wc}_i yc_i + wc_i' \widehat{yc}_i \frac{d \ln yc_i}{dt} \\
&\quad + \frac{d \ln wp_i'}{dt} \widehat{wp}_i yp_i + wp_i' \widehat{yp}_i \frac{d \ln yp_i}{dt}
\end{aligned}
\tag{3}
$$

Dividing through by $p_i g_i$ and separating price and quantity changes, we have

$$
\begin{aligned}
\frac{d \ln g_i}{dt} - (p_i g_i)^{-1} & \left[p' \hat{\bar{g}}_i \frac{d \ln \bar{g}_i}{dt} + wc_i' \widehat{yc}_i \frac{d \ln yc_i}{dt} + wp_i' \widehat{yp}_i \frac{d \ln yp_i}{dt} \right] \\
&= (p_i g_i)^{-1} \left[\frac{d \ln p'}{dt} \hat{p} \bar{g}_i + \frac{d \ln wc_i'}{dt} \widehat{wc}_i yc_i + \frac{d \ln wp_i'}{dt} \widehat{wp}_i yp_i \right] - \frac{d \ln p_i}{dt} \\
&= t_i^*
\end{aligned}
\tag{4}
$$

Dropping the price side of the equation and making use of the I/O technology relations on the quantity side, we have

$$\bar{g}_i = a_i g_i \qquad \frac{d \ln \bar{g}_i}{dt} = \frac{d \ln a_i}{dt} + i' \frac{d \ln g_i}{dt}$$

$$yc_i = ec_i g_i \qquad \frac{d \ln yc_i}{dt} = \frac{d \ln ec_i}{dt} + i' \frac{d \ln g_i}{dt} \tag{5}$$

$$yp_i = ep_i g_i \qquad \frac{d \ln yp_i}{dt} = \frac{d \ln ep_i}{dt} + i' \frac{d \ln g_i}{dt}$$

where i is a 37×1 unit vector. Substituting for (5) in (4),

$$t_i^* = \frac{d \ln g_i}{dt} - \left[(p_i g_i)^{-1} (p' \hat{\bar{g}}_i + wc_i' \widehat{yc}_i + wp' \widehat{yp}_i) i \frac{d \ln g_i}{dt} \right.$$

$$- (p_i g_i)^{-1} p' \bar{g}_i \frac{d \ln a_i}{dt}$$

$$- (p_i g_i)^{-1} wc_i' \widehat{yc}_i \frac{d \ln ec_i}{dt}$$

$$\left. - (p_i g_i)^{-1} wp_i' \widehat{yp}_i \frac{d \ln ep_i}{dt} \right] \tag{6}$$

and since $(p_i g_i)^{-1} (p' \hat{\bar{g}}_i + wc_i' \widehat{yc}_i + wp_i' \widehat{yp}_i) i = 1$, we get

$$t_i^* = - (p_i g_i)^{-1} \left[p' \hat{\bar{g}}_i \frac{d \ln a_i}{dt} + wc' \widehat{yc}_i \frac{d \ln ec_i}{dt} + wp_i' \widehat{yp}_i \frac{d \ln ep_i}{dt} \right] \tag{7}$$

and finally, cancelling the g_i's and again using the I/O relations, we have

$$t_i^* = - p_i^{-1} \left[p' \hat{a}_i \frac{d \ln a_i}{dt} + wc_i' \widehat{ec}_i \frac{d \ln ec_i}{dt} + wp_i' \widehat{ep}_i \frac{d \ln ep_i}{dt} \right]$$

$$= - p_i^{-1} \left[p' \frac{d(a_i)}{dt} + wc_i' \frac{d(ec_i)}{dt} + wp_i' \frac{d(ep_i)}{dt} \right] \tag{8}$$

and therefore the vector t^*, containing all the t_i^*'s for $i = 1, \ldots, 37$ is, in matrix notation

$$t^* = - \text{diag} \left[\hat{p}^{-1} A' \hat{p} \frac{d \ln A}{dt} + \hat{p}^{-1} (E_c \cdot W_c)' \frac{d \ln E_c}{dt} \right.$$

$$\left. + \hat{p}^{-1} (E_p \cdot W_p)' \frac{d \ln E_p}{dt} \right]$$

$$= - \left[\hat{p}^{-1} \frac{dA'}{dt} p + \hat{p}^{-1} \left(\frac{dE_c'}{dt} \cdot W_c' \right) i + \hat{p}^{-1} \left(\frac{dE_p'}{dt} \cdot W_p' \right) i \right] \tag{9}$$

Appendix 5   Derivation of the new MFP rate for industries

For the ith industry the identity between the value of total inputs with the new adjustment is

$$
p_i g_i = \sum_j p_j h_j h_j^{-1} g_{ji} + \sum_j wd_{ji} h_j h_j^{-1} yd_{ji} + \sum_j wk_{ji} h_j h^{-1} yk_{ji}
$$
$$
+ wf_{ii} h_i h_i^{-1} yf_{ii} + \sum_j wr_{ji} h_j h_j^{-1} yr_{ji} + \sum_p wp_{pi} yp_{pi} \qquad (10)
$$

or in vector form and letting $h = [h_j]$,

$$
p_i g_i = p' \hat{h} \hat{h}^{-1} \bar{g}_i + wd_i' \hat{h} \hat{h}^{-1} yd_i + wk_i' \hat{h} \hat{h}^{-1} yk_i
$$
$$
+ wf_i' \hat{h} \hat{h}^{-1} yf_i + wr_i' \hat{h} \hat{h}^{-1} yr_i + wp_i' yp_i \qquad (11)
$$

Repeating for (11) all the manipulations that were done to (2), we get

$$
\frac{d \ln h_i}{dt} = h_i^* = \frac{d \ln g_i}{dt} - (p_i g_i) \left[p\hat{h}\hat{h}^{-1} g_i \frac{d \ln(\hat{h}^{-1} g_i)}{dt} \right.
$$
$$
+ wd_i' \hat{h}\hat{h}^{-1} yd_i \frac{d \ln(\hat{h}^{-1} yd_i)}{dt}
$$
$$
+ wk_i' \hat{h}\hat{h}^{-1} yk_i \frac{d \ln(\hat{h}^{-1} yk_i)}{dt}
$$
$$
+ wf_i' \hat{h}\hat{h}^{-1} yf_i \frac{d \ln(\hat{h}^{-1} yf_i)}{dt}
$$
$$
+ wr_i' \hat{h}\hat{h}^{-1} yr_i \frac{d \ln(\hat{h}^{-1} yr_i)}{dt}
$$
$$
\left. + wp_i' \widehat{yp}_i \frac{d \ln yp_i}{dt} \right] \qquad (12)
$$

substituting for the I/O relations as before, cancelling the g_i's, and separating logarithms, we have

$$
h_i^* = -(p_i g_i)^{-1} \left[p' \bar{g}_i \frac{d \ln \hat{h}^{-1} a_i}{dt} + wd_i' \widehat{yd}_i \frac{d \ln \hat{h}^{-1} ed_i}{dt} \right.
$$
$$
+ wk_i' \widehat{yk}_i \frac{d \ln \hat{h}^{-1} ek_i}{dt} + wf_i' \widehat{yf}_i \frac{d \ln \hat{h}^{-1} ef_i}{dt}
$$
$$
\left. + wr_i' \widehat{yr}_i \frac{d \ln \hat{h}^{-1} er_i}{dt} + wp_i' \widehat{yp}_i \frac{d \ln ep_i}{dt} \right]
$$
$$
= -p_i^{-1} \left[-p' \hat{a}_i \frac{d \ln h}{dt} - wd_i' \widehat{ed}_i \frac{d \ln h}{dt} - wk_i' \widehat{ek}_i \frac{d \ln h}{dt} \right.
$$
$$
\left. - wf_i' \widehat{ef}_i \frac{d \ln h}{dt} - wr_i' \widehat{er}_i \frac{d \ln h}{dt} \right]
$$

$$-p_i^{-1}\left[p'\frac{d(a_i)}{dt}+wd_i'\frac{d(ed_i)}{dt}+wk_i'\frac{d(ek_i)}{dt}\right.$$

$$\left.+wf_i'\frac{d(ef_i)}{dt}+wr_i'\frac{d(er_i)}{dt}\right]+wp_i'\frac{d(ep_i)}{dt} \tag{13}$$

and since this last line is equal to t_i^*, the traditional measure,

$$h_i^*=t_i^*+p_i^{-1}(p'\hat{a}_i+wd_i'\widehat{ed}_i+wk_i'\widehat{ek}_i+wf_i'\widehat{ef}_i+wr_i\widehat{er}_i)h^*$$

$$=t_i^*+S_ih^* \tag{14}$$

where

$$S_i=p_i^{-1}(p'\hat{a}_i+wd_i'\widehat{ed}_i+wk_i'\widehat{ek}_i+wf_i'\widehat{ef}_i+wr_i'\widehat{er}_i)$$

and hence the set of all new MFP rates $[h_i^*]=h^*$ is, in matrix notation,

$$h^*=-\mathrm{diag}\left[\hat{p}^{-1}A'\hat{p}\frac{d\ln(\hat{h}^{-1}A)}{dt}+\hat{p}^{-1}(E_d'\cdot W_d')\frac{d\ln(\hat{h}^{-1}E_d)}{dt}\right.$$

$$+\hat{p}^{-1}(E_k'\cdot W_k')\frac{d\ln(\hat{h}^{-1}E_k)}{dt}+\hat{p}^{-1}(E_f'\cdot W_f')\frac{d\ln(\hat{h}^{-1}E_f)}{dt}$$

$$\left.+\hat{p}_i(E_r'\cdot W_r')\frac{d\ln(\hat{h}^{-1}E_r)}{dt}+p^{-1}(E_p'\cdot W_p')\frac{d\ln(E_p)}{dt}\right]$$

$$=t^*+[\hat{p}^{-1}A'\hat{p}+\hat{p}^{-1}(E_d'\cdot W_d')+\hat{p}^{-1}(E_k'\cdot W_k')+\hat{p}^{-1}(E_f'\cdot W_f')$$

$$+\hat{p}^{-1}[E_r'\cdot W_r')]h^*$$

$$=t^*+Sh^*$$

$$=(I-S)^{-1}t^*$$

Appendix 6 Derivation of the rate of growth of labour productivity

From equation (8) in Appendix 4, the traditional rate of growth of MFP for the ith industry is

$$t_i^*=-p^{-1}\left(p'\hat{a}_i\frac{d\ln a_i}{dt}+wc_i'\widehat{ec}_i\frac{d\ln ec_i}{dt}+wp_i'\widehat{ep}_i\frac{d\ln ep_i}{dt}\right)$$

$$=-p_i^{-1}\sum_j p_j a_{ij}\frac{d\ln a_{ij}}{dt}+\sum_l wc_{li}ec_{li}\frac{d\ln ec_{li}}{dt}$$

$$+\sum_p wp_{pi}ep_{pi}\frac{d\ln ep_{pi}}{dt} \tag{15}$$

Leaving the coefficient of labour input, say, ep_{hi}, in the left and transferring the rest to the right, we get

$$t^* + p_i^{-1}\left[\sum_j p_j a_{ij}\frac{d\ln a_{ij}}{dt} + \sum_l wc_{li}\,ec_{li}\frac{d\ln ec_{li}}{dt}\right.$$

$$\left. + \sum_{p\neq h} wp_{pi}\,ep_{pi}\frac{d\ln ep_{pi}}{dt}\right]$$

$$= -p_i^{-1}wp_{hi}\,ep_{hi}\frac{d\ln ep_{hi}}{dt} \tag{16}$$

because of price relations:

$$-p_i^{-1}wp_{hi}\,ep_{hi} = -p_i^{-1}\left(p_i - \sum_j p_j a_{ji} - \sum_l wc_{li}\,ec_{li} - \sum_{p\neq h} wp_{pi}\,ep_{pi}\right)$$

$$= -1 + p_i^{-1}\sum_j p_j a_{ji} + p_i^{-1}\sum_l wc_{li}\,ec_{li}$$

$$+ p_i^{-1}\sum_{p\neq h} wp_{pi}\,ep_{pi} \tag{17}$$

Substituting for (17) in (16), we get

$$t_i^* + p_i^{-1}\left[\sum_j p_j a_{ji}\left(\frac{d\ln a_{ji}}{dt} - \frac{d\ln ep_{hi}}{dt}\right)\right]$$

$$+ p_i^{-1}\left[\sum wc_{li}\,ec_{li}\left(\frac{d\ln ec_{li}}{dt} - \frac{d\ln ep_{hi}}{dt}\right)\right]$$

$$+ p_i^{-1}\left[\sum wp_{pi}\,ep_{pi}\left(\frac{d\ln ep_{pi}}{dt} - \frac{d\ln ep_{hi}}{dt}\right)\right]$$

$$= \frac{d\ln ep_{hi}}{dt}$$

Using the I/O relations,

$$\frac{-d\ln ep_{hi}}{dt} = \frac{-d\ln(yp_{hi}/g_i)}{dt}$$

$$= \frac{d\ln g_i}{dt} - \frac{d\ln yp_{hi}}{dt}$$

$$= \frac{d\ln l_i}{dt}$$

where yp_{hi} is total hours worked in the ith industry, and hence, $d\ln l_i/dt$ is the rate of growth of labour productivity in the ith industry. For all industries, using matrix notation, we write

$$\frac{d \ln l}{dt} = \operatorname{diag}\left[\hat{t}^* + \hat{p}^{-1}A'\hat{p}\left(\frac{d \ln A}{dt} - \frac{d \ln L_a}{dt}\right)\right.$$

$$+ \hat{p}^{-1}(E'_p \cdot W'_p)\left(\frac{d \ln E_c}{dt} - \frac{d \ln L_c}{dt}\right)$$

$$\left. + \hat{p}^{-1}(E'_p \cdot W'_p)\left(\frac{d \ln E_p}{dt} - \frac{d \ln L_p}{dt}\right)\right]$$

which proves the results, and a similar but mechanically more complex derivation applies to equation (7-2), the aggregate decomposition of labour productivity for the new version of multifactor productivity.

Bibliography

Arrow, K. J. and Starrett, D. A. (1973), "Cost- and Demand-Theoretical Approaches to the Theory of Price Discrimination", eds. J. R. Hicks and W. Weber, *Carl Menger and the Austrian School of Economics* (Oxford: Clarendon Press).

Baumol, W. J. (1984), "On Productivity in the Long Run", *Atlantic Economic Journal,* XII, 5–11.

Baumol, W. J. and Wolff, E. N. (1983), "Feedback from Productivity Growth to R&D", *Scandinavian Journal of Economics,* XXXV, 147–57.

(1984), "On Interindustry Differences in Absolute Productivity", *Journal of Political Economy,* XCII, 1017–34.

Belancourt, R. B. and Clague, C. K. (1981), *Capital Utilization: A Theoretical and Empirical Analysis* (Cambridge: Cambridge University Press).

Blackorby, C., Lovell, C. A. K. and Thursby, M. C. (1976), "Extended Hicks Neutral Technical Change", *Economic Journal,* LXXXVI, December, 845–52.

Blaug, M. (1974), *The Cambridge Revolution: Success or Failure* (London: Institute for Economic Analysis).

Bliss, C. (1975), *Capital Theory and the Distribution of Income* (Amsterdam: North-Holland).

Brown, M. (1980), "The Measurement of Capital Aggregates: A Post Reswitching Problem", ed. D. Usher, *The Measurement of Capital* (Chicago: University of Chicago Press for the NBER).

Bruno, M. (1978), "Duality, Intermediate Inputs and Value-Added", eds. M. Fuss and D. McFadden, *Production Economics: A Dual Approach to Theory and Applications,* Vol. II (Amsterdam: North-Holland).

(1984), "Raw Materials, Profits, and the Productivity Slowdown", *Quarterly Journal of Economics,* XCIX, February, 1–29.

Burmeister, E. (1980), *Capital Theory and Dynamics* (Cambridge: Cambridge University Press).

Cas, A., Diewert, W. E. and Ostensoe, L. A. (1988), "Productivity Growth and Changes in the Terms of Trade in Canada", ed. R. C. Feenstra, *Empirical Methods for International Trade* (Cambridge, Mass.: Massachusetts Institute of Technology Press).

Caves, D. W., Christensen, L. R. and Diewert, W. E. (1982), "The Economic Theory of Index Numbers and the Measurement of Input–Output and Productivity", *Economic Journal,* L, 1393–1413.

243

244   Bibliography

Chambers, R. G. (1983), "Scale and Productivity Measurement under Risk", *American Economic Review*, LXXIII, 804-5.
  (1988), *Applied Production Analysis: A Dual Approach* (Cambridge: Cambridge University Press).
Chan, M. W. L. and Mountain, D. C. (1983), "Economies of Scale and the Törnquist Discrete Measure of Productivity Growth", *Review of Economics and Statistics*, LXV, 663-7.
Christensen, L. R., Jorgenson, D. W. and Lau, L. J. (1973), "Transcendental Logarithmic Production Functions", *Review of Economics and Statistics*, LXV, 28-45.
Cocks, D. L. (1981), "Company Total Factor Productivity: Refinements, Production Functions, and Certain Effects of Regulation", *Business Economics*, V, 5-14.
Creamer, D. (1972), "Measuring Capital Input for Total Factor Productivity Analysis: Comments by a Sometime Estimator", *Review of Income and Wealth*, XVIII, 55-78.
Denison, E. (1972), "Some Major Issues in Productivity Analysis: An Examination of Estimates by Jorgenson and Griliches", *Survey of Current Business*, LII, May, 37-63.
Denison, E. F. (1957), "Theoretical Aspects of Quality Change, Capital Consumption and Net Capital Formation", *Problems of Capital Formation: Concepts, Measurement and Controlling Factors* (Princeton: Princeton University Press for the NBER).
  (1972), "Issues in Growth Accounting", *Survey of Current Business*, LII, May, 65-94.
  (1989), *Estimates of Productivity Change by Industry. An Evaluation and an Alternative* (Washington, D.C.: The Brookings Institution).
Denny, M. and Fuss, M. (1983), "A General Approach to Intertemporal and Interspatial Productivity Comparisons", *Journal of Econometrics*, XXIII, 315-30.
Denny, M., Fuss, M. and Waverman, L. (1979), "The Measurement and Interpretation of Total Factor Productivity in Regulated Industries, with an Application to Canadian Telecommunications", *Working Paper Series*, No. 7911, University of Toronto.
Denny, M. and May, J. D. (1978), "Homotheticity and Real Value-Added in Canadian Manufacturing", eds. M. Fuss and D. McFadden, *Production Economics: A Dual Approach to Theory and Applications*, Vol. II (Amsterdam: North-Holland), 53-70.
Diewert, W. E. (1976), "Exact and Superlative Index Numbers", *Journal of Econometrics*, IV, 114-45.
  (1978a), "An Application of the Shephard Duality Theorem: A Generalized Leontief Production Function", *Journal of Political Economy*, LXX, 481-507.
  (1978b), "Hicks Aggregation Theorem and the Existence of Real Value-Added Function", eds. M. Fuss and D. McFadden, *Production Economics: A Dual Approach to Theory and Applications*, Vol. II (Amsterdam: North-Holland).

(1980), "Aggregation Problems in the Measurement of Capital", ed. D. Usher, *The Measurement of Capital,* Studies in Income and Wealth, Vol. 45 (Chicago: National Bureau of Economic Research, University of Chicago Press).

Diewert, W. E. and Montmarquette, C. (1983), *Price Level Measurement* (Ottawa: Supply and Services, Government of Canada).

Diewert, W. E. and Morrison, C. J. (1986), "Adjusting Output and Productivity Indexes for Changes in the Terms of Trade", *Economic Journal,* XCVI, 659–79.

Domar, E. D. (1961), "On the Measurement of Technological Change", *Economic Journal,* LXXI, 709–29.

Dougherty, C. (1980), *Interest and Profit* (London: Metheun).

Fraumeni, B. M. and Jorgenson, D. W. (1981), "Capital Formation and U.S. Productivity Growth, 1948–1976", ed. A. Dogramaci, *Productivity Analysis: A Range of Perspectives* (Boston: Martinus Nijhoff Publishing).

Griliches, Z. (1979), "Issues in Assessing the Contribution of Research and Development to Productivity Growth", *Bell Journal of Economics,* X, 92–116.

Griliches, Z. and Lichtenberg, F. (1984), "Interindustry Technology Flows and Productivity Growth: A Reexamination", *Review of Economics and Statistics,* LXVI, 324–9.

Hahn, F. (1984), "The Neo-Ricardians", *Cambridge Journal of Economics,* VI, December 1982, reprinted in his *Equibrium and Macroeconomics* (Oxford: Blackwell).

Haltmaier, J. (1984), "Measuring Technical Change", *Economic Journal,* XCIV, 924–30.

Harcourt, G. (1972), *Some Cambridge Controversies in the Theory of Capital* (Cambridge: Cambridge University Press).

Harrod, R. (1948), *Towards a Dynamic Economics* (London: Macmillan).

Harrod, R. F. (1937), "Keynes and Traditional Theory", in his *Economic Essays* (London: Macmillan).

(1961), "The Neutrality of Improvements", *Economic Journal,* LXXI, June, 300–4.

(1969), *Money* (London: Macmillan).

Helliwell, J. F. (1983), "Stagflation and Productivity Decline in Canada, 1974–1982", The 1983 W. A. Mackintosh Lecture, Discussion Paper 521, Queen's University, Kingston.

Hicks, J. R. (1971), *The Social Framework: An Introduction to Economics,* 4th ed. (Oxford: Clarendon Press).

Hicks, Sir John (1963), *The Theory of Wages,* 2nd ed. (London: Macmillan).

Hill, T. P. (1971), *The Measurement of Real Product* (Paris: OECD).

Hulten, C. K. (1979), "On the Importance of Productivity Change", *American Economic Review,* LXIX, March, 126–36.

Hulten, C. R. (1973), "Divisia Index Numbers", *Econometrica,* XLI, 1017–25.

(1975), "Technical Change and the Reproducibility of Capital", *American Economic Review,* LXV, 956–65.

(1978), "Growth Accounting with Intermediate Inputs", *Review of Economic Studies,* XLV, 511–19.

Hulten, C. R. and Nishimizu, M. (1980), "The Importance of Productivity Change in the Economic Growth of Nine Industrialized Countries", eds. S. Maital and N. Meltz, *Lagging Productivity Growth* (Cambridge: Ballinger).

Hulten, C. R. and Wykoll, F. C. (1981), "The Measurement of Economic Depreciation", ed. C. R. Hulten, *Depreciation, Inflation and the Taxation of Income from Capital* (Washington, D.C.: The Urban Institute).

Jones, R. W. (1965), "Neutral Technological Change", *American Economic Review,* LV, September, 848–55.

Jorgenson, D. (1966), "The Embodiment Hypothesis", *Journal of Political Economy,* LXXIV, February, 1–17.

Jorgenson, D. W. (1980), "Accounting for Capital", ed. G. M. von Furstenberg, *Capital, Efficiency and Growth* (Cambridge, Mass.: Ballinger Publishing).

(1981), "Taxation and Technical Change", *Technology in Society,* III, Nos. 1–2, 151–171.

Jorgenson, D. W. and Gollop, F. M. (1980), "U.S. Productivity Growth by Industry 1947–73", eds. J. W. Kendrick and B. N. Vaccara, *New Developments in Productivity Measurement and Analysis* (Chicago: University of Chicago Press).

Jorgenson, D. W., Gollop, F. M. and Fraumeni, B. (1987), *Productivity and U.S. Economic Growth* (Cambridge, Mass.: Harvard University Press).

Jorgenson, D. W. and Griliches, Z. (1967), "The Explanation of Productivity Change", *Review of Economic Studies,* XXXIV, 249–83.

(1972), "Final Reply", *Survey of Current Business,* LII, May, 111.

(1973), "Issues in Growth Accounting: A Reply to Edward F. Denison", *Survey of Current Business,* LII, May, 65–94.

Jorgenson, D. W. and Landau, R., eds. (1989), *Technology and Capital Formation* (Cambridge, MA: MIT Press).

Keynes, J. M. (1973), *The General Theory of Employment, Interest and Money* (London: Macmillan for the Royal Economic Society).

Kim, M. (1988), "The Structure of Technology with Endogenous Capital Utilization", *International Economic Review,* XXIX, February, 111–30.

Leontief, W. (1953), *Studies in the Structure of the American Economy* (Oxford: Oxford University Press).

Mark, J. A. and Waldorf, W. H. (1983), "Multifactor Productivity: A New BLS Measure", *Monthly Labour Review,* VI, 3–15.

Marshall, A. (1961), *Principles of Economics,* Guillebaud ed. (London: Macmillan).

May, J. D. and Denny, M. (1979), "Post-war Productivity in Canadian Manufacturing", *Canadian Journal of Economics,* XII, 29–41.

Merrilees, W. J. (1971), "Notes and Memoranda: The Case Against Divisia Index Numbers as a Basis in a Social Accounting System", *Review of Income and Wealth,* XVII, 81–5.

Mohr, M. F. (1986), "The Theory and Measurement of the Rental Prices of Capital in Industry Specific Productivity Analysis: A Vantage Rental Price of Capital Model", ed. A. Dogramaci, *Measurement Issues and Productivity Variables* (Boston: Kluer Mijhoff).

Nadiri, M. I. (1970), "Some Approaches to the Theory and Measurement of Total Factor Productivity: A Survey", *Journal of Economic Literature,* VIII, 1137–77.

(1972), "Internal Studies of Factor Inputs and Total Factor Productivity: A Brief Survey", *Review of Income and Wealth,* XIX, 129–54.

(1980), "Contribution and Determinants of Research and Development Expenditures in the U.S. Manufacturing Industries", ed. G. M. von Furstenberg, *Capital, Efficiency and Growth* (Cambridge, Mass.: Ballinger Publishing).

Nelson, R. R. (1973), "Recent Exercises in Growth Accounting: New Understanding or Dead End", *American Economic Review,* LXIII, 462–8.

(1981), "Research on Productivity Growth and Productivity Differences: Dead Ends and New Departures", *Journal of Economic Literature,* XIX, 1029–64.

Nishimizu, M. and Page, J. M., Jr. (1982), "Total Factor Productivity Growth, Technological Progress and Technical Efficiency Change: Dimensions of Productivity Change in Yugoslavia 1965–78", *Economic Journal,* XCII, 920–36.

Norsworthy, J. R. and Malmquist, D. H. (1983), "Input Measurement and Productivity Growth in Japanese and U.S. Manufacturing", *American Economic Review,* LXXIII, 947–67.

Nuti, D. M. (1976), "On the Rates of Return on Investment", eds. M. Brown et al., *Essays in Modern Capital Theory* (Amsterdam: North-Holland).

Pasinetti, L. (1980), *Essays in the Theory of Joint Production* (New York: Columbia University Press).

(1981), *Structural Change and Economic Growth* (Cambridge: Cambridge University Press).

Peterson, W. (1979), "Total Factor Productivity in the U.K.: A Disaggregated Analysis", eds. K. D. Patterson and K. Schott, *The Measurement of Capital: Theory and Practice* (London: Macmillan).

Postner, H. H. and Wesa, L. (1983), *Canadian Productivity Growth: An Alternative (Input–Output) Analysis* (Ottawa: Economic Council of Canada).

Rao, P. S. and Preston, R. S. (1984), "Inter-Factor Substitution, Economies of Scale and Technical Change: Evidence from Canadian Industries", *Empirical Economics,* IX, 87–111.

Read, L. M. (1961), "The Measurement of Total Factor Productivity" (Ottawa: Dominion Bureau of Statistics, mimeo).

(1968), "The Measure of Total Factor Productivity Appropriate to Wage–Price Guidelines", *Canadian Journal of Economics,* I, May, 349–58.

Robinson, J. (1962), *Essays in the Theory of Economic Growth* (London: Macmillan.

(1969), *The Accumulation of Capital,* 3rd ed. (London: Macmillan).

(1975), *Collected Economic Papers,* Vol. III (Oxford: Blackwell).

Rymes, T. K. (1968), "Professor Read and the Measurement of Total Factor Productivity", *Canadian Journal of Economics,* I, May, 359–67.

(1971), *On Concepts of Capital and Technical Change* (Cambridge: Cambridge University Press).

(1972), "The Measurement of Capital and Total Factor Productivity in the Context of the Cambridge Theory of Capital", *Review of Income and Wealth,* XVIII, March, 79–108.

(1983), "More on the Measurement of Total Factor Productivity", *Review of Income and Wealth,* XXXIX, September, 297–316.

(1986), "The Measurement of Multifactor Productivity in an Input–Output Framework: New Canadian Estimates", eds. A. Franz and N. Rainer, *Problems of Computation of Input–Output Tables* (Wien: Orac-Verlag).

(1989), "Technical Progress, Research and Development", ed. G. Feiwel, *Joan Robinson and Modern Economic Theory* (London: Macmillan).

Sato, K. (1976), "The Meaning and Measurement of the Real Value-added Index", *Review of Economics and Statistics,* LVIII, 434–42.

Scherer, F. M. (1982), "Inter-Industry Technology Flows and Productivity Growth", *Review of Economics and Statistics,* LXIV, 627–31.

Sen, A. K. (1974), "On Some Debates in Capital Theory", *Economica,* XLI, February, 328–35.

Snooks, G. D. (1976), "A Note on the Use of Alternative Total Factor Productivity Indexes", *Economic Record,* 372–7.

Solow, R. M. (1957a), "The Explanation of Productivity Change", *Review of Economics and Statistics,* XXXIX, 249–83.

(1957b), "Technological Change and the Aggregate Production Function", *Review of Economics and Statistics,* XXXIX, August, 312–20.

(1983), "Modern Capital Theory", eds. E. C. Braun and R. M. Solow, *Paul Samuelson and Modern Economic Theory* (New York: McGraw-Hill).

Star, S. and Hall, R. E. (1976), "An Approximate Divisia Index of Total Factor Productivity", *Econometrics,* XLIV, 257–63.

Steedman, I. (1983), "On the Measurement and Aggregation of Productivity Increase", *Metroeconomica,* XXXV, October, 223–33.

(1985), "On the Impossibility of Hicks-Neutral Technical Change", *Economic Journal,* XCV, September, 746–58.

Stone, R. (1980), "Whittling Away at the Residual: Some Thoughts on Denison's Growth Accounting. A Review Article", *Journal of Economic Literature,* XVIII, 1539–43.

Sudit, E. F. and Finger, N. (1981), "Methodological Issues in Aggregate Productivity Analysis", eds. A. Dogramaci and N. R. Adam, *Aggregate and Industry-Level Productivity Analysis* (Amsterdam: Martinus Nijhoff).

Sveikauskas, L. (1981), "Technological Inputs and Multifactor Productivity Growth", *Review of Economics and Statistics,* LXIII, 275–82.

Triplett, J. (1983), "Concepts of Quality in Input and Output Price Measures: A Resolution of the User-Value Resource–Cost Debate", ed. M. F. Foss, *The U.S. National Income and Product Accounts: Selected Topics* (Chicago: University of Chicago press for the NBER).

Triplett, J. E. (1988), "Price Index Research and Its Influence on Data: A Historical Review", paper presented at the Conference on Research in Income and Wealth, NBER.

Uri, N. D. (1984), "The Impact of Technical Change on the Aggregate Production Function", *Applied Economics,* XVI, 555–67.

Usher, D. (1974), "The Suitability of the Divisia Index for the Measurement of Economic Aggregates", *Review of Income and Wealth,* XX, 273–88.

(1980), *The Measurement of Economic Growth* (New York: Columbia University Press).

Watanabe, T. (1971), "A Note on Measuring Sectoral Input Productivity", *Review of Income and Wealth,* XVII, 335–9.

Yeager, L. B. (1979), "Capital Paradoxes and the Concept of Waiting", ed. M. J. Rizzo, *Time, Uncertainty and Disequilibrium: Exposition of Austrian Themes* (Lexington, Mass.: D. C. Heath).

Yu, E. S. H. (1981), "On Factor Market Distributions and Economic Growth", *Southern Economic Journal,* XLVIII, 172–8.

Name index

Acheson, Keith, 83 n.15
Arrow, Kenneth, 9 n.7

Bauer, P. W., 32 n.23
Betancourt, R. R., 82 n.12
Blackburn, Keith, xv
Blackorby, C., 48 n.1
Blaug, Mark, 7 n.2
Bliss, Christopher, 8 n.3, 87 n.19, 88 n.20
Brown, E. Cary, 7 n.2
Brown, Murray, 7 n.2
Bruno, M., 65 n.11
Burmeister, E., 7 n.2

Carter, Michael, xv, 71 n.16
Chambers, R. G., 72 n.17
Clague, C. K., 82 n.12
Cornes, Richard, xv

Dean, Edward, xv
Denison, Edward, xv, 41 n.35, 61 n.6,
    78 n.8, 78 n.9, 91 n.24, 97, 97 n.6,
    146 n.3
Diewert, W. Erwin, xv, 26 n.19, 76 n.4,
    96 n.1, 123 n.1
Domar, Evsey D., 33 n.28, 50, 65 n.10, 66,
    76 n.3, 92, 93, 96, 96 n.2, 97,
    118 n.11, 219, 219 n.2, 222
Dougherty, Christopher, 7 n.2
Durand, Rene, xv

Feiwel, George, 71 n.15
Ferris, Steve, 83 n.156

Gigantes, Terry, xv
Gruen, Fred, xv, 71 n.16

Hahn, Frank, 7 n.2
Harcourt, Geoffrey, 7 n.2, 89 n.22
Harrod, Sir Roy, 1, 1 n.3, 2, 11 n.8, 12,
    12 n.9, 48, 49, 53, 57, 58, 61, 63, 64

Hatta, T., 7 n.2
Hennings, K. H., 9 n.7
Hicks, Sir John, 2, 2 n.4, 3 n.6, 48 n.1,
    48, 49, 50, 58
Hill, Peter, 33 n.26
Hulten, Charles H., 9 n.6, 14 n.14, 33
    n.28, 50, 65 n.10, 66, 76 n.3, 92, 93,
    97, 97 n.5, 219, 219 n.1, 220

Johnson, James, xv
Jones, Ronald W., 58 n.4
Jorgenson, Dale, 31 n.22, 77 n.5, 147 n.4

Keynes, John Maynard, 61, 81, 82, 82 n.12,
    86 n.17, 87 n.19
Kim, M., 82 n.12
Kurz, H. D., 7 n.2

Lal, Kishori, xv
Landau, R., 62 n.7
Leontief, W., 96, 96 n.3, 118, 118 n.11, 181
    n.1, 182, 182 n.2
Lovell, C. A. K., 48 n.1

Marshall, Alfred, 9 n.7
McBride, Gwen, xv
McCormick, Basil, xv
Mohr, M. F., 87 n.19

Nuti, D., 87 n.19

Ostensoe, L. A., 76 n.4

Pasinetti, Luigi L., 7 n.2, 67, 67 n.12,
    71 n.15, 83 n.14, 91 n.24, 92, 93,
    98
Patterson, K. D., 9 n.6
Peterson, William, 9 n.6
Postner, Harry, xv, 9 n.6, 76 n.3, 119
    n.12, 149 n.7
Preston, R. S., 65 n.11

This index includes all names in the text except those found in the bibliography.

Subject index

253